SUMO.

LORD K2

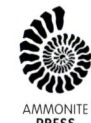

AMMONITE PRESS

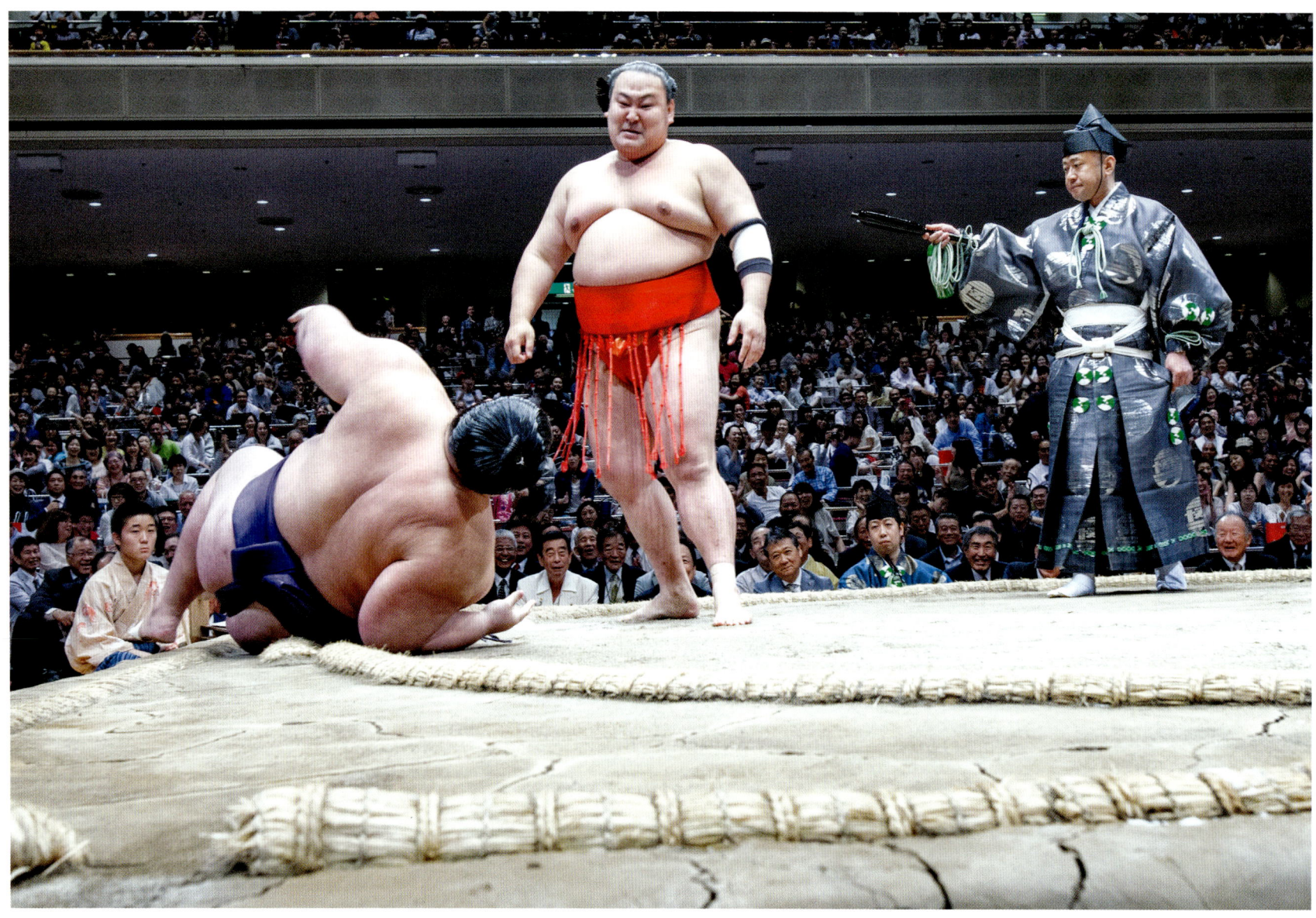

INTRODUCTION

In the epicentre of the world's largest city lies a grand stadium draped in ancient symbolism and brimming with anticipation as crowds pour in, settling onto their cushions as the *dohyō* is swept to perfection, as it has been for two millennia. Spectators chatter eagerly as warm sake is poured into small cups. The chatter grows to a clamour as, from the corner of the arena, giants emerge. Immense 150kg (330lb) men, wrapped in loincloths and sporting stern faces, waddle into the ring, their bodies rippling. They toss salt high into the air over the *dohyō*, ritually cleansing the stage, as applause ripples across the auditorium.

The sport is one of the oldest in the world. Within the Japanese establishment exists a great sense of pride that during the last millennium very little about the sport has changed. As Japan has surged forward into modernity, this corner of culture has remained anchored to ancient tradition. Sumo is an entity in which history, culture, pride and athleticism combine.

Sumo can trace its origins back through deeply religious roots to the Shinto temples of the third century AD. Originally fights were arranged as a spectacle for the entertainment of the gods. Sumo developed into its own as a professional sport during the Edo period circa 1603 AD. Wrestlers from across the land were invited to battle in front of the imperial courts as grand entertainment events for the nobility. Many wrestlers were samurai working part time for extra income. Fights were brutal and blood was frequently drawn.

The sport, however, was a far cry from today's well-scripted art form. Fighters usually found themselves in the ring to settle scores, often on behalf of their masters. It was as much of a blood sport as it was a duel of wits and cunning, not dissimilar to Roman gladiators. The first professional sumo tournament didn't take place until 1684 at the Tomioka Hachiman Shrine in Tokyo. The event became biannual and is considered to be the birth of today's sumo. The sport became more regulated by the late eighteenth century, culminating in the formation of the Dai Nihon Ozumo Kyokai (All-Japan Grand Sumo Association) in the 1920s. Today, the organization is known as the Nihon Sumo Kyokai (Japan Sumo Association).

前書き

世界最大の都市の中心に、2000年以上前より続く日本古来の伝統競技が観戦できる大競技場がある。日本の象徴とも言える桜の紋章が入った幕、天上から吊るされた古典的な屋根、所狭しと並べられた座布団、土俵は完璧なまでに掃きあげられ、その魅了させられる空間には、人々の期待と熱気で溢れている。熱燗を呑みながら、待ちきれない様子で興奮しておしゃべりをする観衆たち。その話し声は、会場の隅から巨体の男たちが現れるとともに熱狂的な叫び声へと変化していく。褌を締めた巨大な150キロの男たちが身体を波打たせながら、険しい顔をして土俵へ向かって歩いていく。その舞台を清める儀式として、男たちが土俵の上で塩を高く撒くと、拍手が競技場全体に響き渡っていく。

このスポーツは、世界で最も古い競技種目の一つである。約1000年前に現在見られている競技形態に落ち着いた。日本人の大きな誇りとともに、このスポーツは今日まで1000年もの間、ほぼ形態を保ったまま、変わらぬ姿で受け継がれてきた。日本が急速に近代化していく中で、この文化は古えからの伝統がしっかりと守られ続けているのである。相撲は、歴史・文化・誇り、そして精神的・肉体的な運動の要素が組み合わさった存在である。

相撲は、その起源をたどると、紀元前3世紀の神道が色濃い時代まで遡る。もともとは、力くらべとして興行されていたと神話に記述があり、その後、江戸時代の1603年頃にプロ力士というスポーツの職業が生まれるに至るまでの発展を遂げた。たくさんの力士たちが各地から召集され、将軍の観戦のもとで興行された。力士の多くは、副収入を得るために働く侍たちであり、その闘いは激しく、残忍で血を見ることも頻繁にあった。

しかしこのスポーツは、今日の芸術としての相撲の在り方とは一線を画すものであった。試合は基本的に、力士たちが主人の代わりに競技場で得点獲得のために競い合い、知恵とずる賢さとともに行われた。古代ローマにおける剣闘士の戦いとも似通うほどの流血を伴う決闘だったのである。1685年に東京の富岡八幡宮で初めてプロの相撲トーナメントが開催され、そのイベントは年に2回開催されるようになり、これが今日の相撲の誕生であると考えられている。18世紀後半には規制が収束され、1920年代には大日本大相撲

The rules of sumo are relatively simple. The winner of a bout is either the first wrestler to force his opponent out of the *dohyō*, or the first wrestler to force his opponent to touch the ground with any part of his body other than the bottom of his feet.

Despite its centuries spent metamorphosing, today those in the upper echelons in the sport are deeply dogmatic about reformation, preferring to maintain sumo as a fascinating antiquity. However, at the turn of this millennium its popularity and relevance in contemporary Japanese culture was beginning to wane.

Crowd numbers thinned to just the elderly and tourists, and fights ceased to be broadcast on national television. There were fears of its eventual demise. However, recent years have seen something of a resurgence, perhaps in part due to PR campaigns, perhaps as a push back against increasingly postmodern lifestyles. Tickets now regularly sell out during tournaments and stadiums are filling up again with spectators eager to hark back to a different time, a different Japan. One steeped in tradition, mysticism, respect and honour.

Wrestlers are highly revered by their fans, not just for their sporting prowess, but also for the nobility and dedication with which they live their lives.

Back at the stables where wrestlers live and train, drills for new recruits start at 5am, while the seniors roll out of bed by 7am. The stable master sits and observes the training, occasionally barking instruction and advice to the wrestlers. The wrestlers begin with a series of stretches, followed by clashing into one another in the *dohyō* to build their endurance and hone their technical skills. They lift weights and work on their individual physique. The senior wrestlers typically groom the lower ranked wrestlers either by hazing or offering technical advice, before training winds down with a stretching routine.

By 9am, the new recruits leave to begin preparing breakfast. The wrestlers then plough into a mammoth, high-calorie meal followed by sake and beer before taking a nap in order to effectively process the food into fat.

協会が設立された。現在では「日本相撲協会」として知られている。

相撲のルールは比較的シンプルで、どちらか一方が対戦相手を土俵から押し出すか、対戦相手の足の裏以外のどこでも体の一部が地面に着いた時点で勝者が決まる。

何世紀にもわたって変容を遂げながらも、今日のこの業界における上流層の人々は、新たな改革を深く論じており、相撲を古代からの魅力的な伝統文化として維持することを望んでいる。しかし、今世紀の変わり目には、現代の日本文化におけるその人気と可能性は衰退し始めていたのである。

観戦者たちは高齢者や観光客だけで僅少になり、試合の様子は一時期は国営放送ですら放送されなくなった。消滅危機の不安もあったが、近年では復活の兆しがみられるようになった。宣伝会社のお陰や、ポストモダンなライフスタイルへの反発のせいかもしれない。観戦チケットは、今やトーナメント中売切れが続き、競技場はかつての日本、かつての時代を思い起こさせるようである。伝統、神秘性、尊厳と誇りに満ちみちた空間が、たくさんの観客で埋め尽くされている。

力士はスポーツ選手としての才能だけではなく、人生を相撲に捧げたひたむきな生き方、気高さの面からも、ファンから高い評価を得ている。

力士たちが住み込みで稽古を重ねる相撲部屋では、朝5時から新弟子たちの厳しい訓練が始まり、先輩力士たちは7時までには起きてくる。稽古中は、親方が目の前に座って観ながら、指図やアドバイスを大声で叫んでいる。力士たちは一連のストレッチを行った後に、土俵の中で互いにぶつかりあって、耐久性を高めると共に、技に磨きをかけていく。一般的に稽古は、先輩力士たちが階級下の後輩たちの面倒を見る。先輩力士は後輩力士を厳しく指導したり、技術的なアドバイスをしたりするのが一般的で、稽古はストレッチで締めくくられる。

9時になると、新弟子たちは朝食の用意を始める。そして力士たちはとてつもなく高カロリーな食事を摂るのである。食べたものを効率よく脂肪へ変えていくために、食事後は酒やビールを飲んでから昼寝へと移っていく。

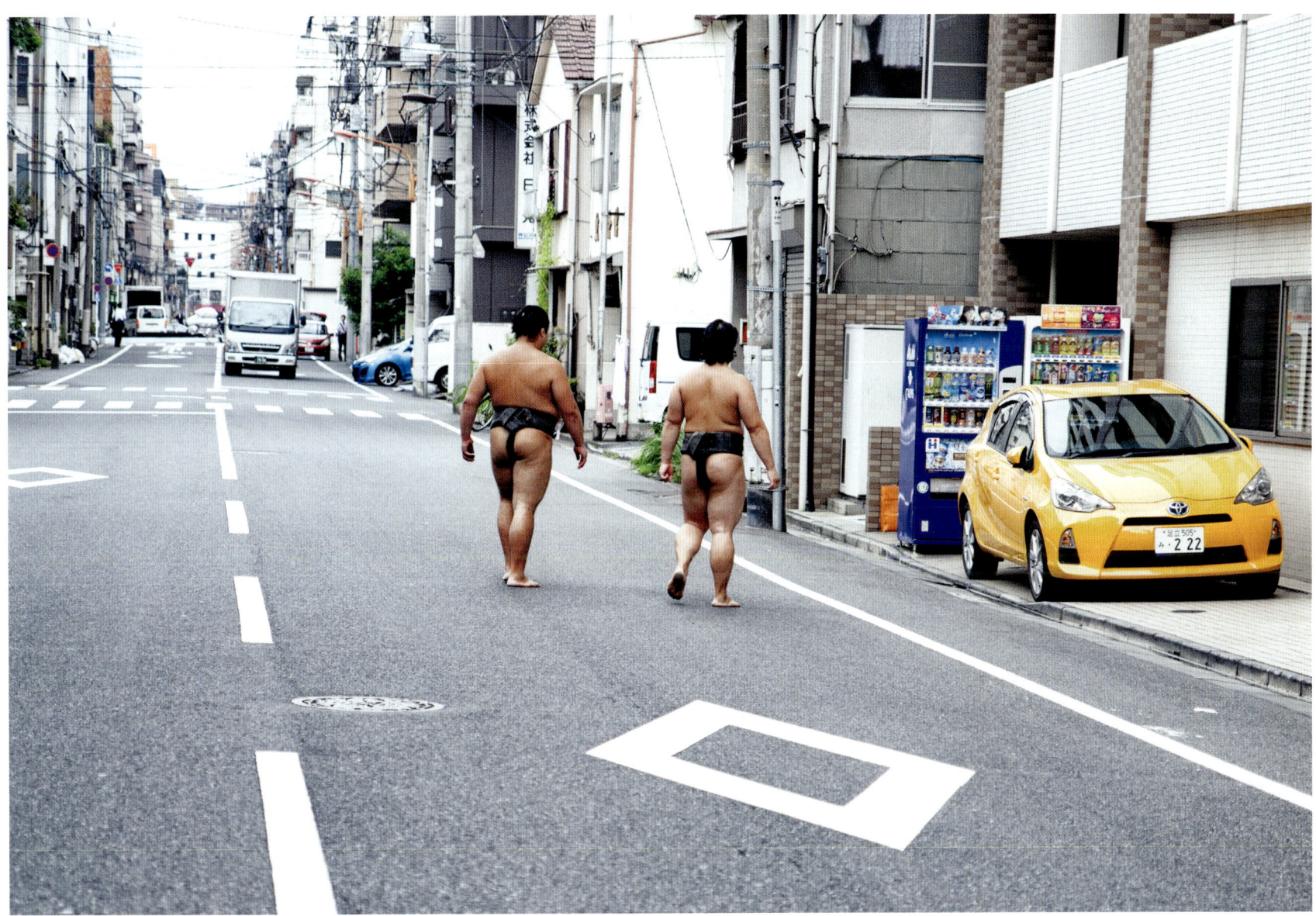

相撲　7

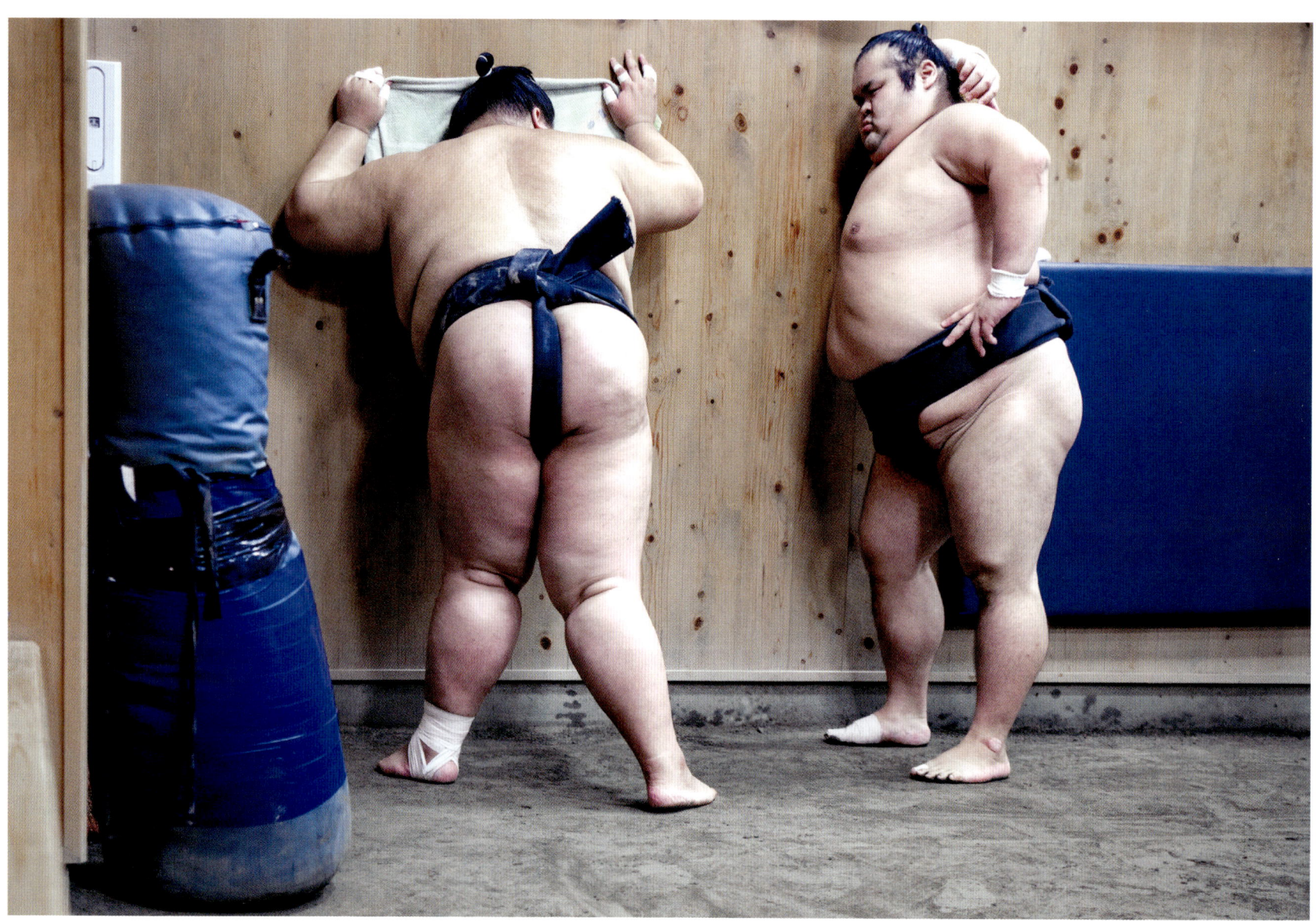

Inside the stables there exists a strict hierarchy. The higher ranked wrestlers enjoy all the perks while the novices spend much of their time taking care of the stable and serving seniors. The stables also house the referees, ushers and hairdressers. There are 43 stables in Japan housing several hundred active sumo wrestlers.

Competitive wrestlers live by an extremely strict code of conduct both in and outside of the stable. They can be spotted riding local trains or cycling around Tokyo in traditional kimonos, as they're forbidden from driving cars or wearing contemporary clothes. Even their public demeanour is tightly governed. Rules dictate that in public wrestlers must be softly spoken and self-effacing at all times. Even after fights the victor is not permitted to show any signs of vitriol or schadenfreude. This, along with the stringent dietary and training requirements, necessitates enormous dedication.

The life expectancy of a sumo wrestler is between 60 and 65 years, 10 years less than the average Japanese male. Due to high levels of fat, wrestlers are prone to high blood pressure, cholesterol and heart attacks.

Committing to the sport requires complete dedication from a young age. In today's age of advanced technology, abundance and convenience, it's becoming increasingly difficult to attract young boys to the sport. While the will to find new recruits is strong, Japan is a land where football and baseball reign supreme, and the more laid-back training methods and the potential of a glamorous lifestyle offer more appeal to children.

Today's Japanese youth are not attracted to the regimented life of sleeping in dormitories, rising at dawn, and living in servitude towards their seniors. Training is gruelling and involves brutal hazing, deemed necessary to filter out those who lack the spirit to be a true sumo warrior. Another barrier is parental consent, as most parents would rather see their offspring go on to higher education, knowing that few succeed in sumo.

It is only natural that the Japanese sumo community and fans alike would like to see their own wrestlers succeed, yet the sport has attracted numerous foreign wrestlers,

相撲部屋は厳しい階級制度のもとに成り立っている。上位の力士たちはその特権を楽しみ、一方で、新参者たちは生活のほとんどの時間を相撲部屋の管理か先輩たちの身の回りの世話に捧げる事になる。相撲部屋には審判（行司）・案内係（出方）・美容師（床山）たちも共に生活している。

競争力のある力士たちは、相撲部屋の内外を問わず、非常に厳格な行動規範を守っている。彼らは車の運転や、洋服を着ることは禁じられているので、伝統的な着物を羽織り、地下鉄に乗っている姿や、東京の街を自転車で移動する姿を見ることがある。公共の場における作法ですら管理されているのだ。公共の場では、力士は常に穏やかに話し、控えめでなければならない。たとえ試合に勝ったとしても、相手に対して皮肉った発言をしたり、他人の不幸を喜ぶような態度は許されない。食事と稽古における厳格な要件と併せて、このことも多大な努力を必要とする。

相撲力士の平均寿命は６０歳から６５歳の間で、平均的な日本人男性より１０歳短い。力士は高い脂肪率により、高血圧・高コレステロール血症や心臓発作を起こしやすいためである。

このスポーツは、若い頃から相撲に打ち込むことが求められている。超・新資本主義の、何でも便利な日本において、相撲界に新弟子を迎えることは、ますます困難となっている。新弟子を見つけることに意欲は高いものの、少年たちをプロの道へといざなうのは容易いことではない。日本では、華やかなライフスタイルや、トレーニング内容に、よりゆとりのあるサッカーや野球が人気を博するのである。

現代の日本の若者は、寮生活で、明け方に起床し、先輩たちに仕えるというような暮らしには惹かれないのだ。稽古は過酷で、厳しくしごかれ、真の相撲取りとしての精神性に欠けるものたちはふるいに掛けられ、排除されていく。そして、もう一つの障壁は、ほとんどの親が相撲で成功するのは稀であるということを知っており、子どもたちには高等教育を受けさせることを望んでいることである。

日本の相撲界やファンが自国の力士の活躍を望むのは当然だが、東欧を中

especially from Eastern Europe as well as Hawaii, Brazil and Egypt. However, the past decade has seen Mongolian fighters dominate the sport. Mongolian wrestlers are considered to hold a true fighter's spirit as well as a winning appetite, in part as they tend to come from poor rural regions. Unlike Japanese wrestlers, they also have the responsibility of supporting their families back home, furthering the incentive to rise to greatness. However, Japanese wrestlers have made a comeback in recent years, winning half of all the major tournaments.

Behind the scenes the sport is shrouded in secrets and mystery. Foreigners, particularly Westerners, are discouraged from sticking their noses in or interfering with its ancient traditions anyway. It's considered a sport invented by Japanese, for Japanese. Sumo stables are not tourist attractions; only a few stables can be visited, and only as long as the list of behavioural restrictions is strictly adhered to.

Those who dedicate themselves to the sport give not only their body but their lives. They give themselves as a relic, an offering to the past masters and gods. *Rikishi* are not just wrestlers, they are the antiquated, traditional Japanese gentlemen. A century after the last samurai, their cousins live on. The depth of honour and esteem rewarded for such commitment is beyond the comprehension of most foreigners.

The Japan Sumo Association views itself as more of a cultural institution than a sporting authority; one that guards the soul of traditional Japanese culture. Today, sumo exists as a living, breathing showcase of ancient Japan.

心に、ハワイ、ブラジル、エジプトなど多くの外国人力士が活躍しており、しかしこの10年はモンゴル人力士が圧倒的な強さを見せている。モンゴル人力士は貧しい農村部の出身であることが多く、強い闘争心や勝利への貪欲さを持ちあわせていると言われている。日本の力士とは異なり故郷の家族を経済的に支える責任感から、その意欲も一層高まるのだ。近年になって日本人力士が復活し、大相撲の優勝回数が半数を占めるようになった。

このスポーツ界の舞台裏は多くの秘密と謎に包まれている。外国人、特に西洋人は、どんな形であれ、古代から受け継がれるこの伝統に口を出したり、首を突っ込むようなことはオススメしない。このスポーツは、日本人が生み出した、日本人のための競技であると見なされている。相撲部屋は観光名所ではないため、訪れることが許されているのは、厳しく制限されたごく一部の部屋のみである。

このスポーツに献身的な人々は、体だけでなく、全人生を相撲に懸けている。彼らは自分自身を、過去の巨匠たちや神々への捧げ物として奉納しているのである。相撲力士は単なる戦士ではなく、伝統を守り続ける日本の紳士であり、最後の侍の時代から1世紀を経た今でも、生き続けているのだ。外国人にとって理解するのは難しいかもしれないが、この献身に値する名誉と尊厳の深さは、相撲界の外の人間の理解を超えたものなのである。

相撲協会は、その存在をスポーツの権威ではなく、より文化的な機関として考えている。日本の伝統文化の魂を守るもの。今日の相撲は、生き続ける古の日本の魂そのものである。

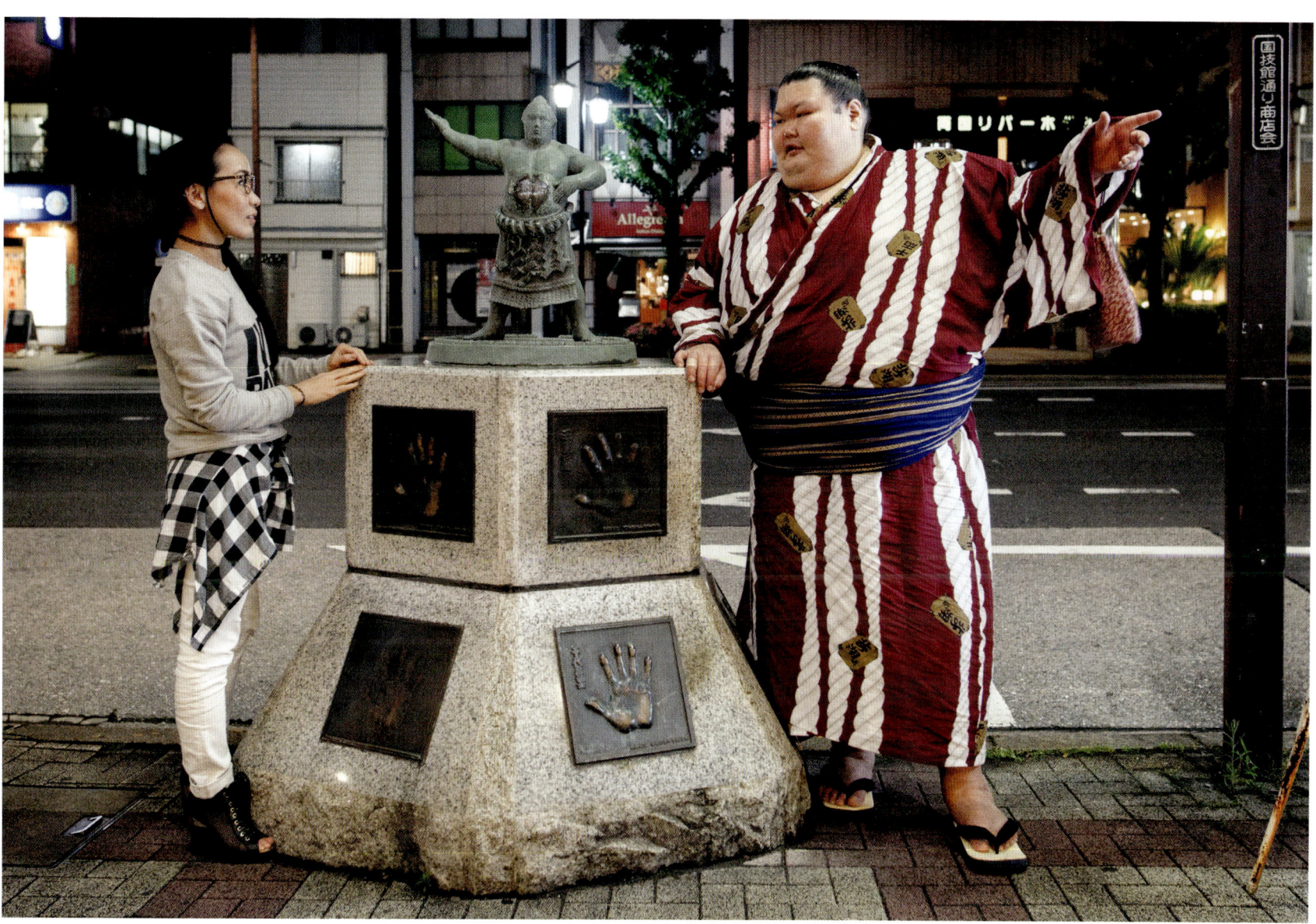

相撲　11

野心
AMBITION

A YOUNG BOY MAY HAVE THE AMBITION TO TURN PROFESSIONAL, YET HE WILL NOT KNOW UNTIL OVER A DECADE LATER IF HIS HEIGHT AND WEIGHT WILL SUFFICE.

この少年はプロになるという志を持つかもしれない。しかし、身長と体重が十分な要件を満たすかどうかを知るのは10年以上も先のことである。

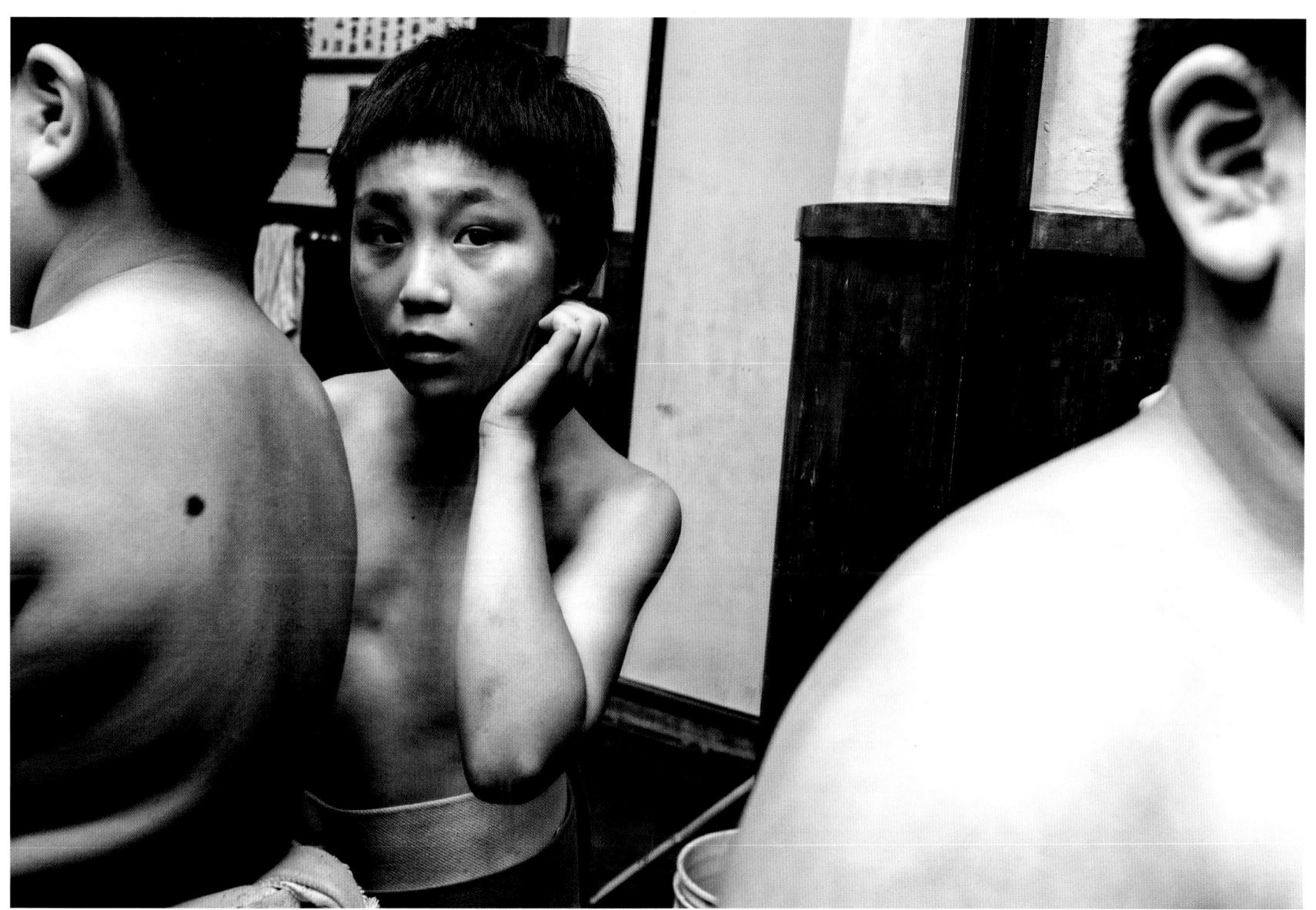

相撲　13

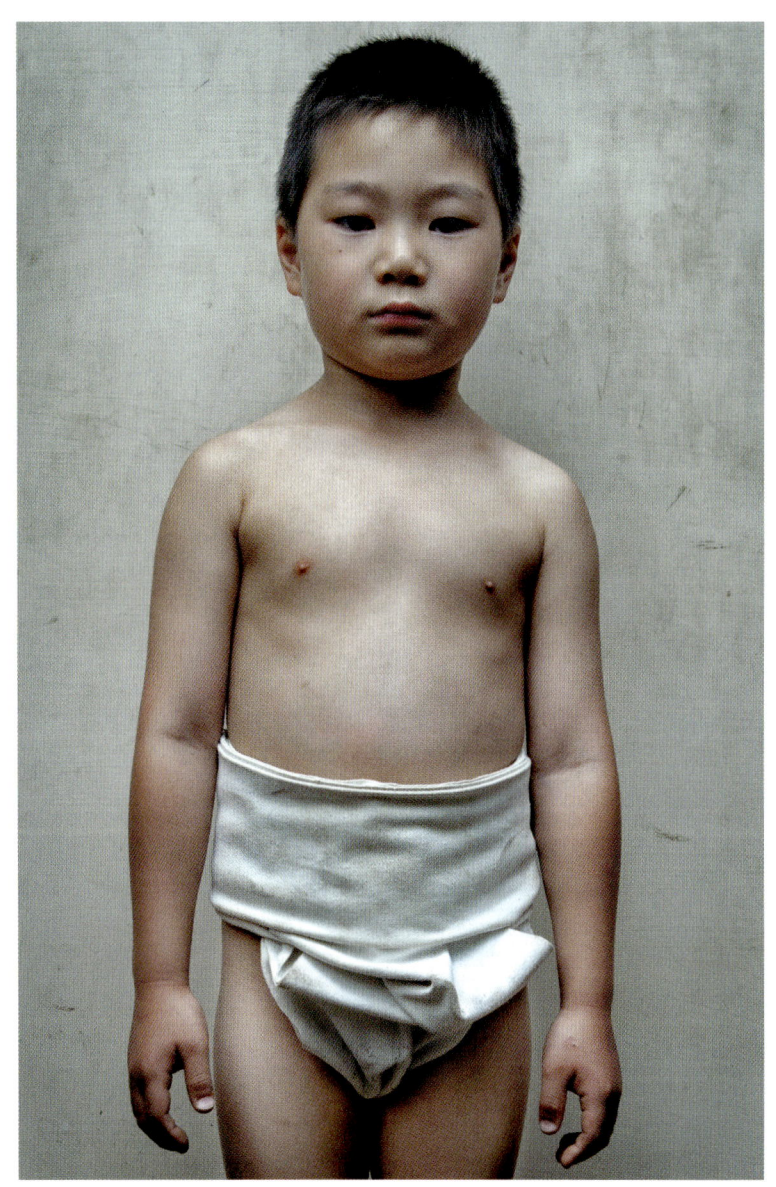

14 SUMO

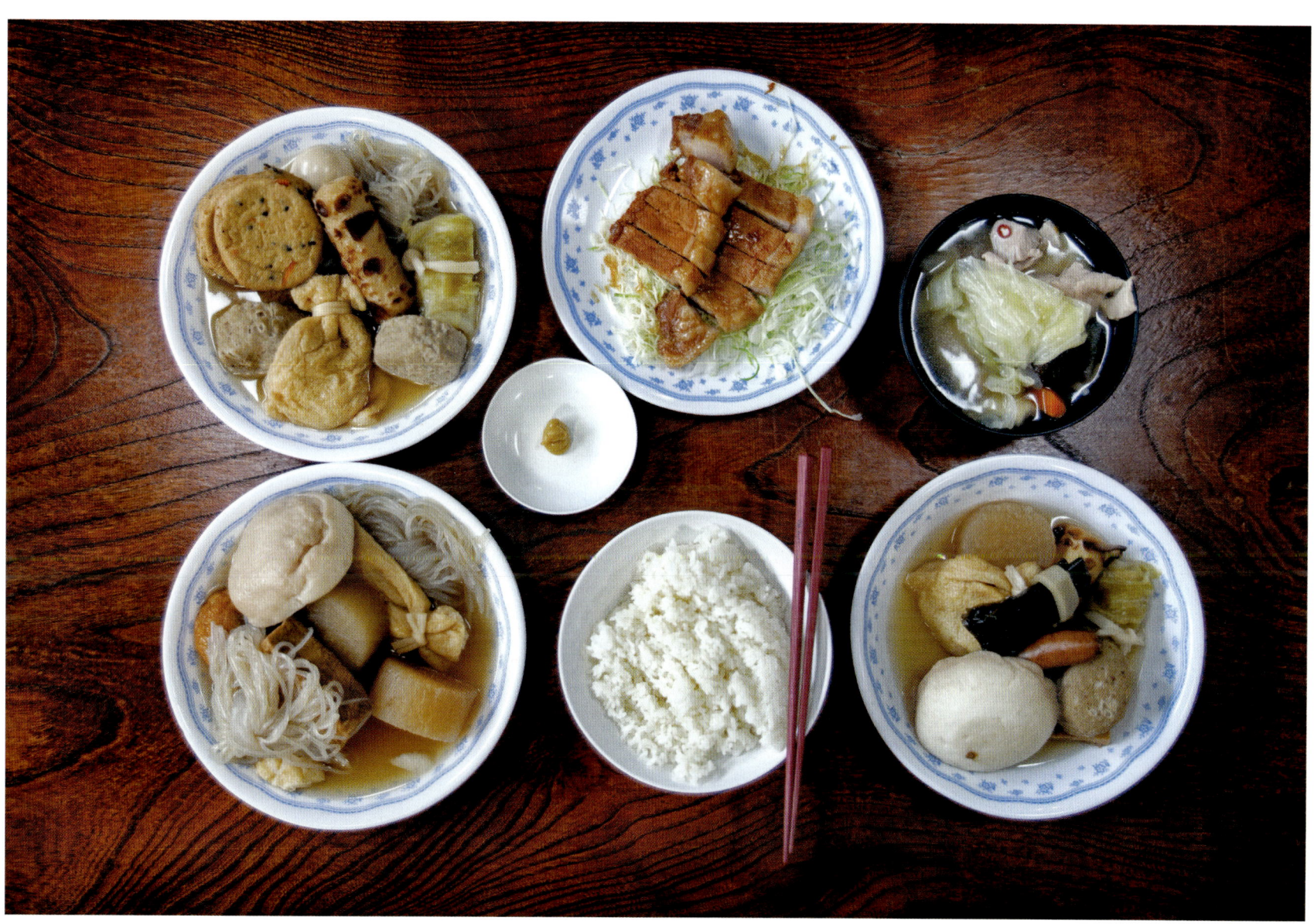

相撲 15

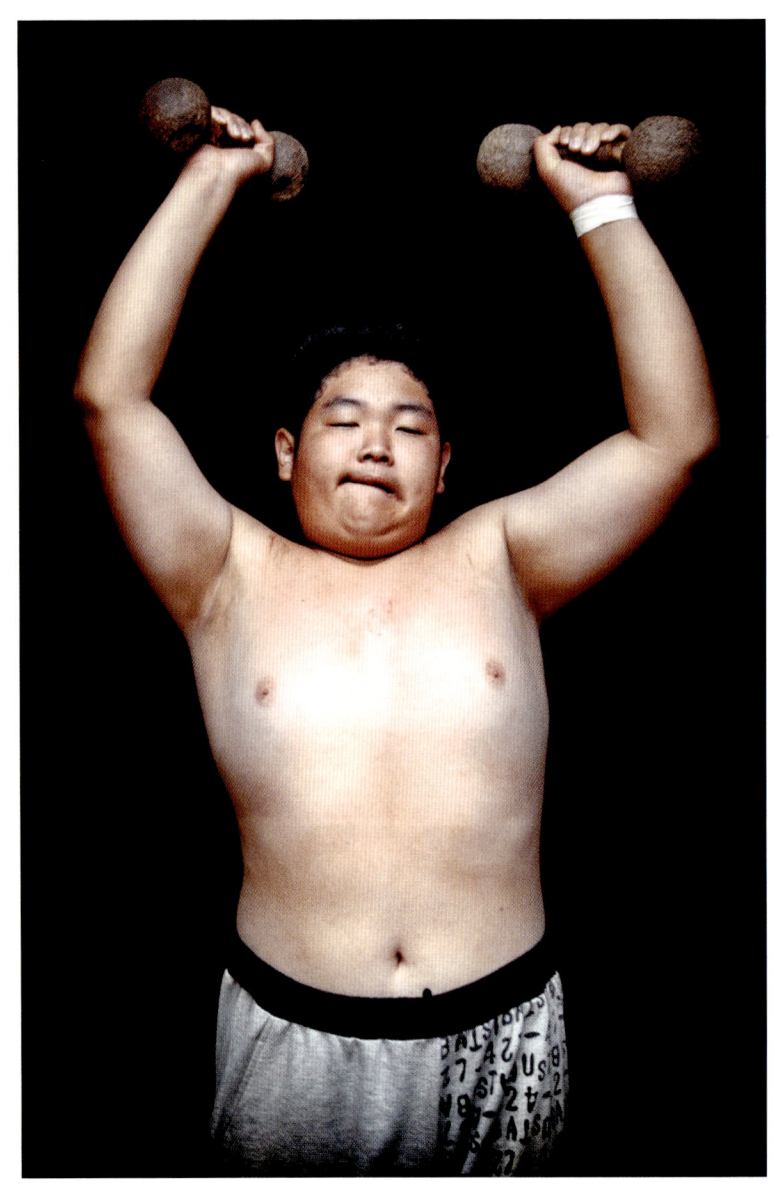

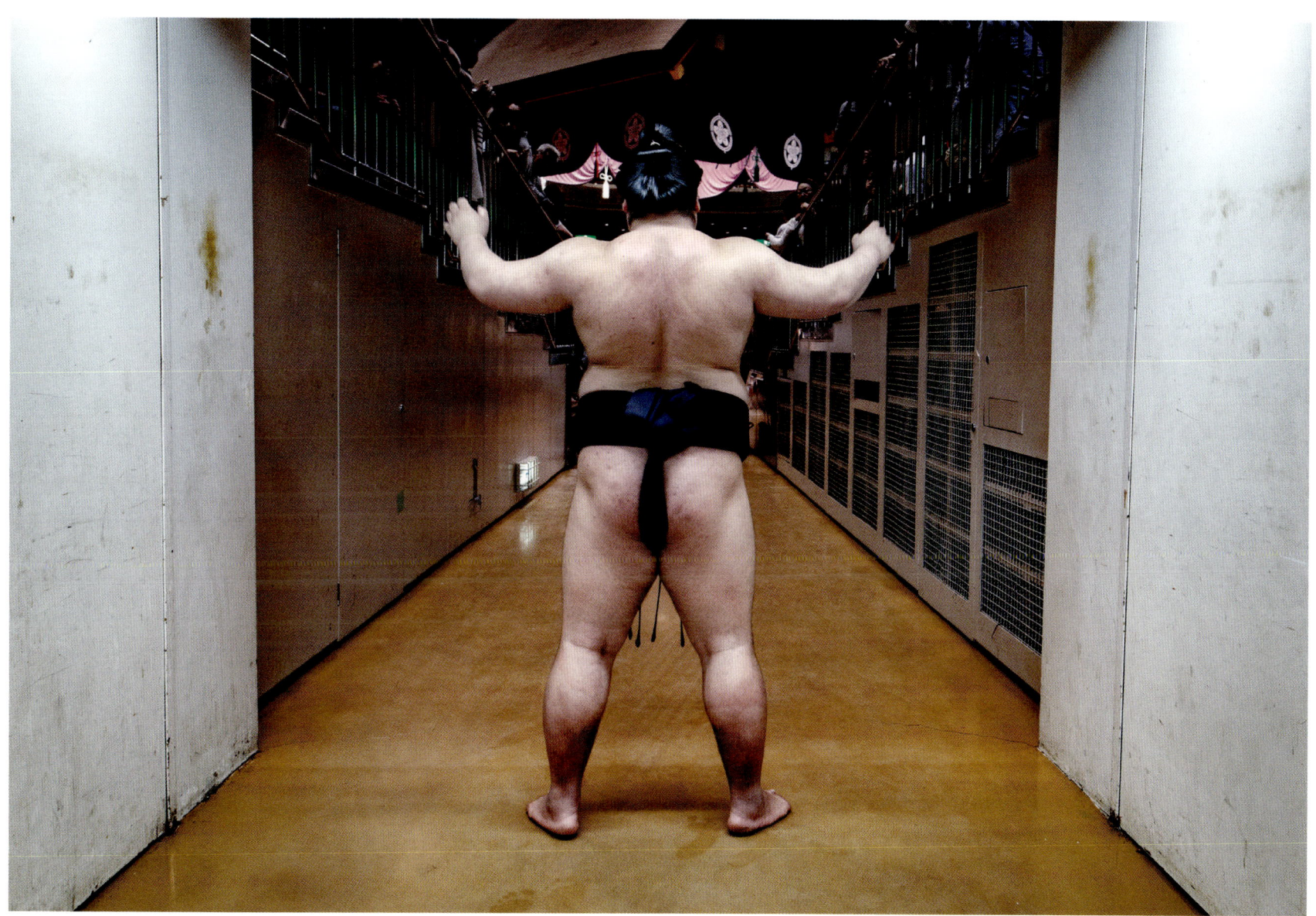

相撲 17

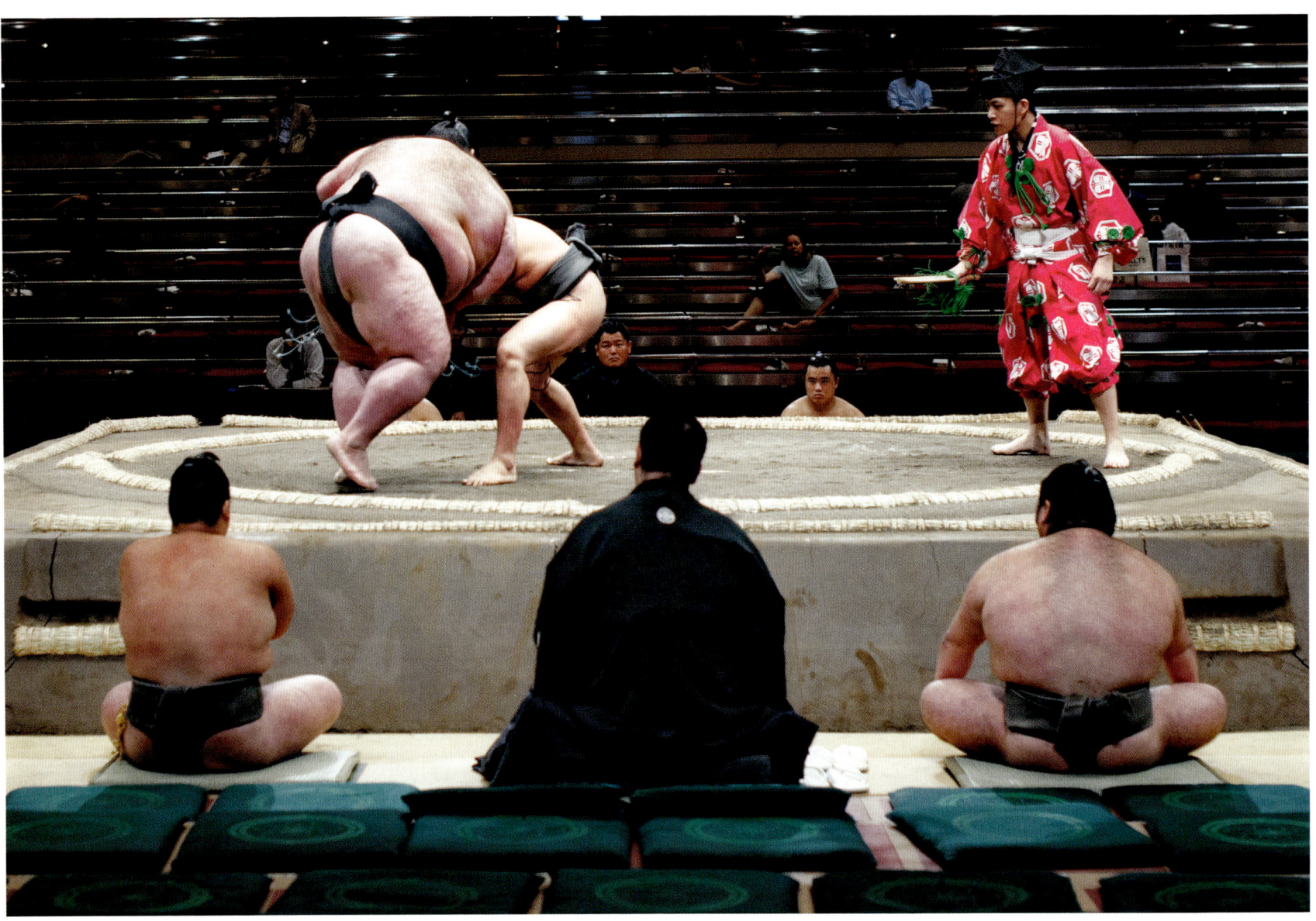

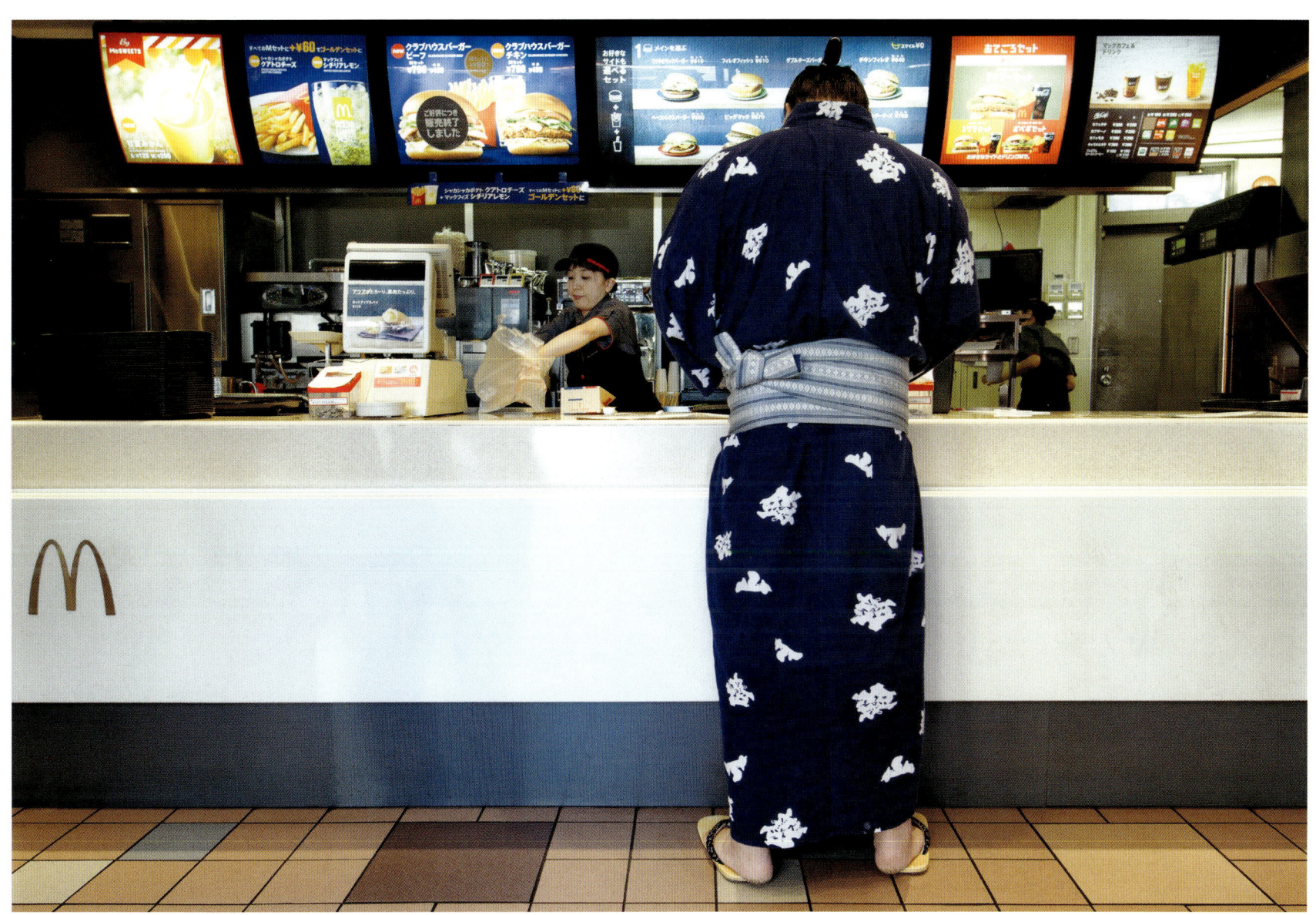

相撲 19

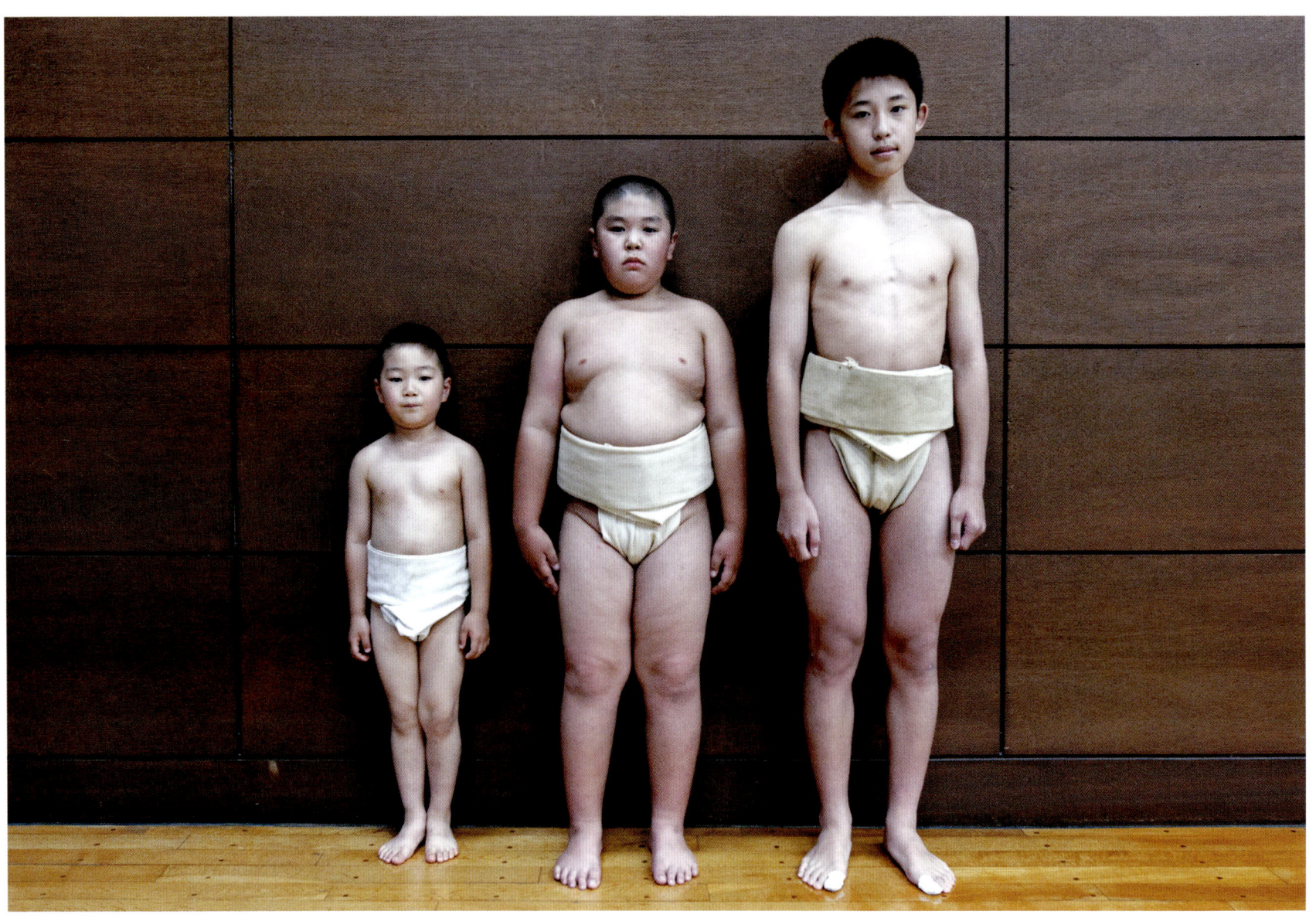

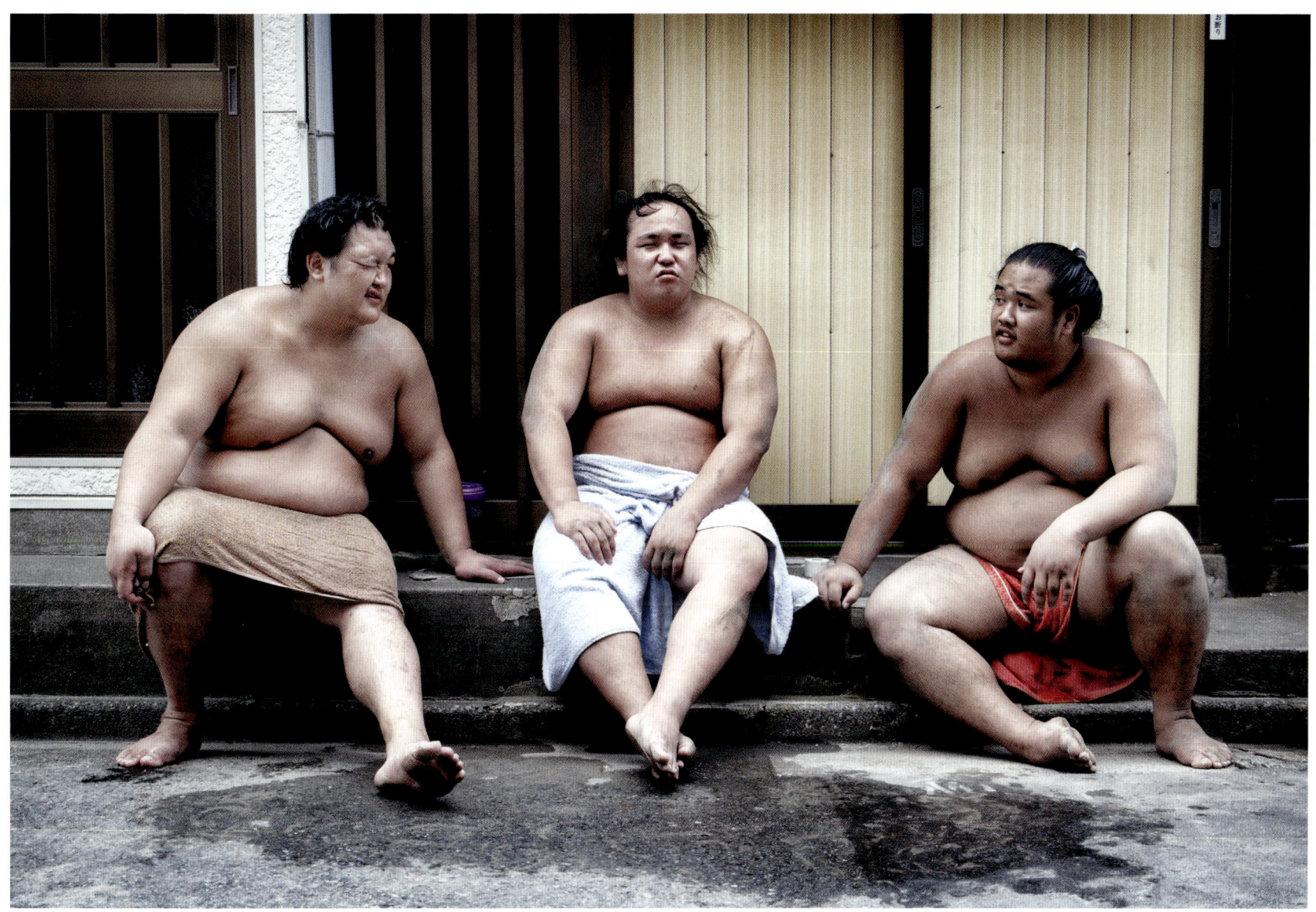

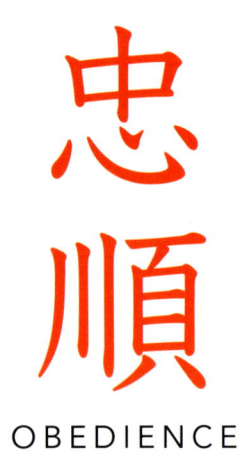

OBEDIENCE

NEW RECRUITS HAVE TO ENDURE A LIFE OF DISCIPLINE, OBEDIENCE AND HARDSHIPS IN ORDER TO PROGRESS AND GAIN THE ACCEPTANCE OF THEIR SENIORS.

新弟子たちは先輩力士からの信頼を獲得するために、規律・従順さと共に困難に耐えなくてはならない。

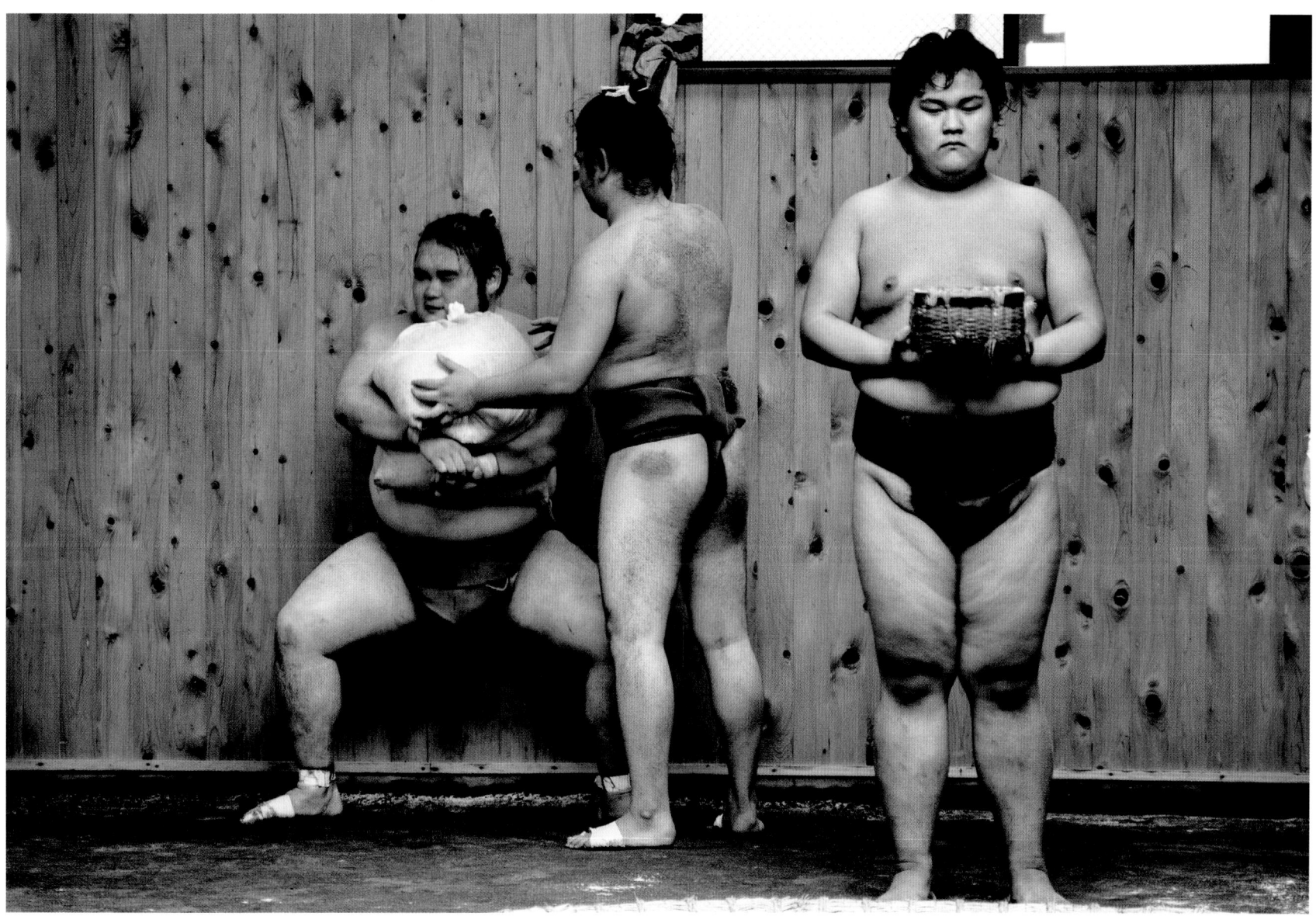

相撲　23

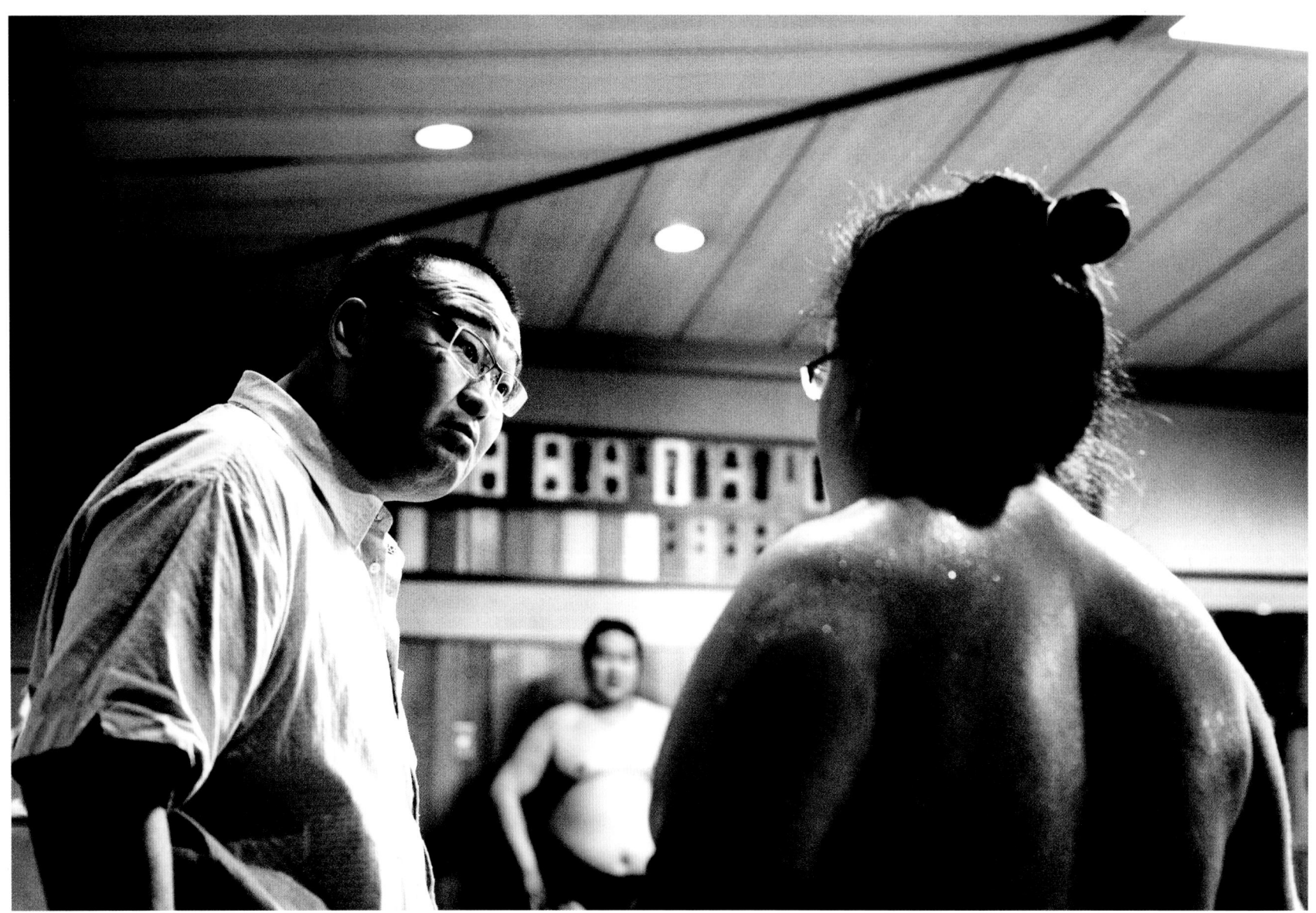

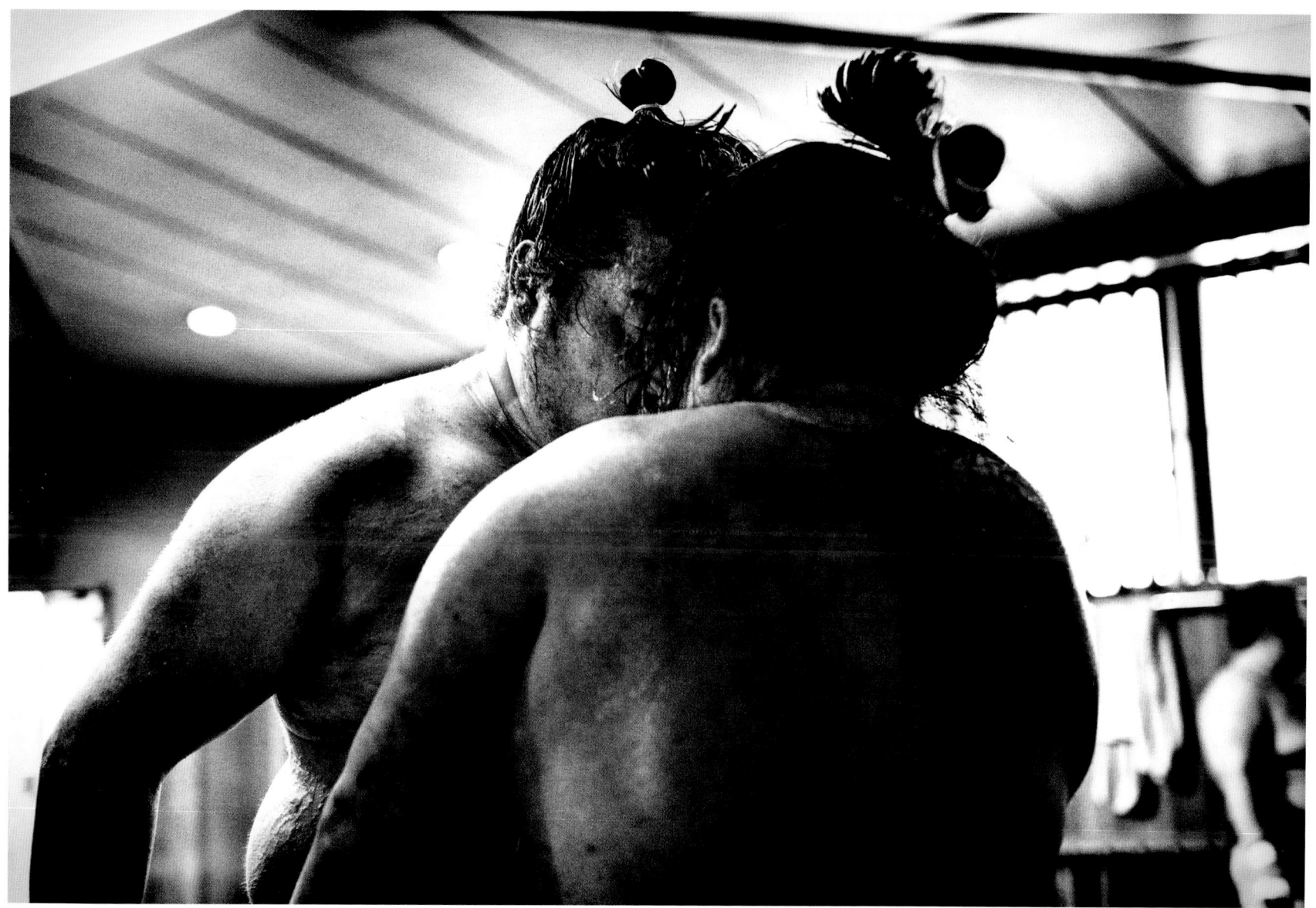

相撲 25

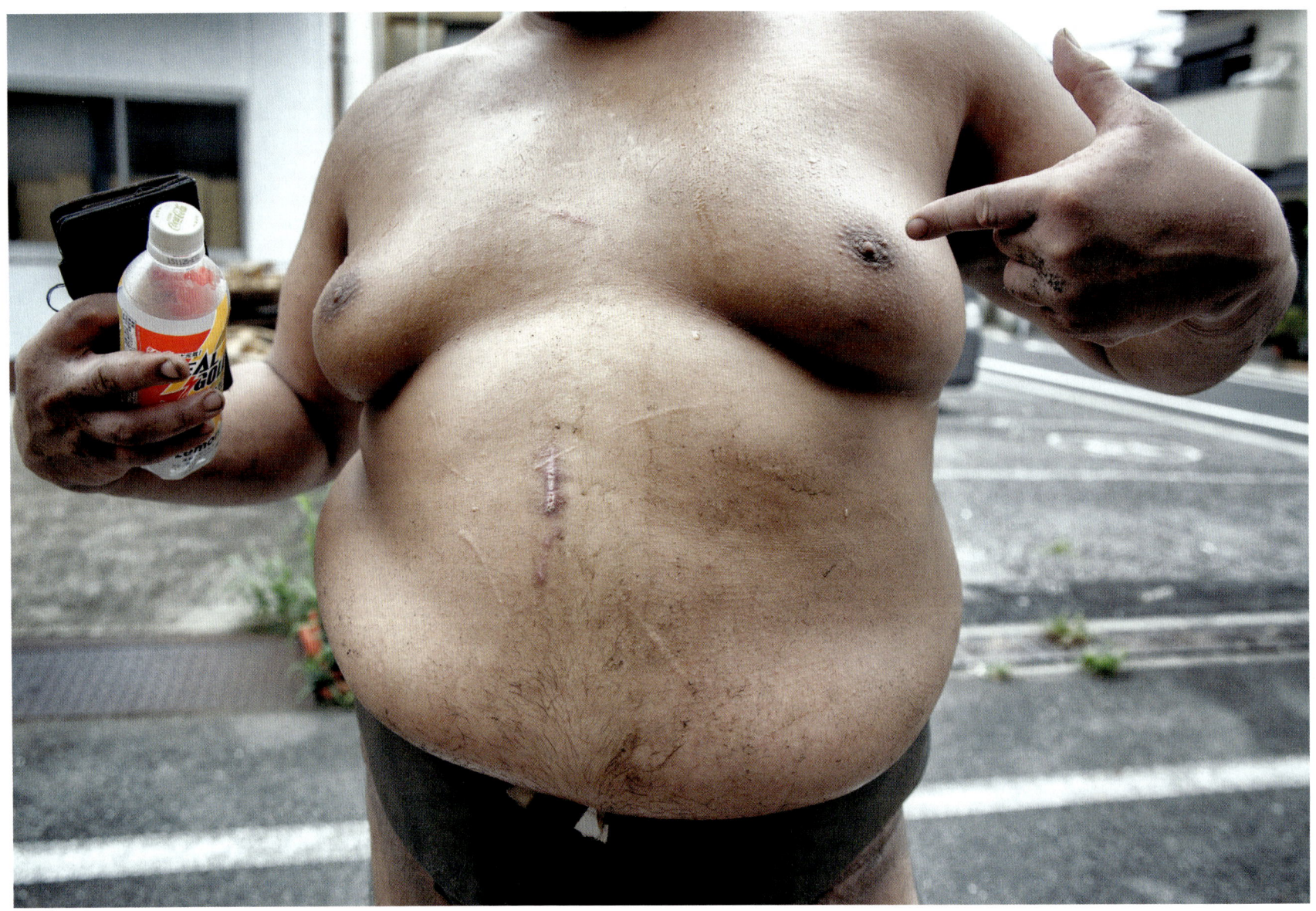

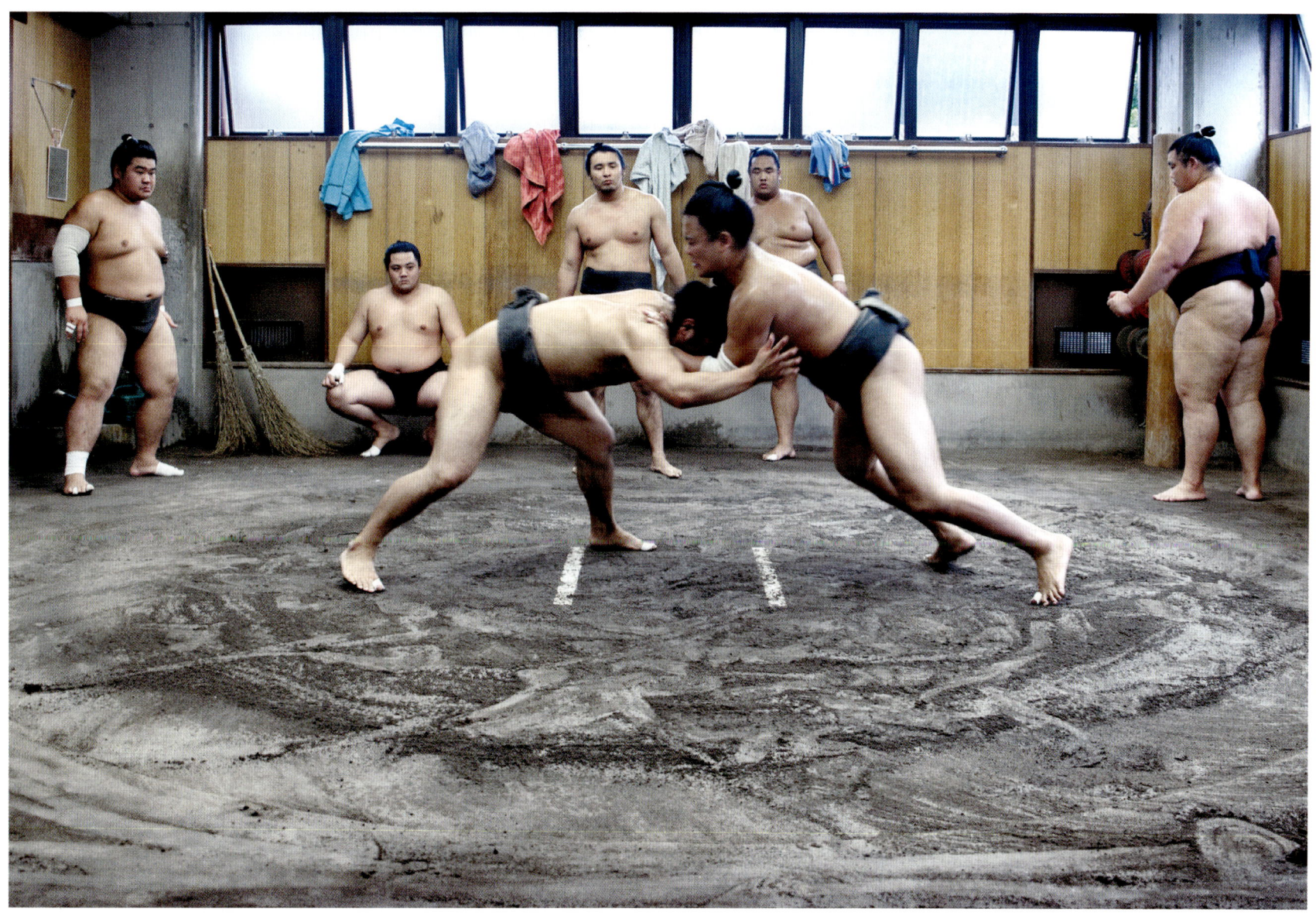

相撲　27

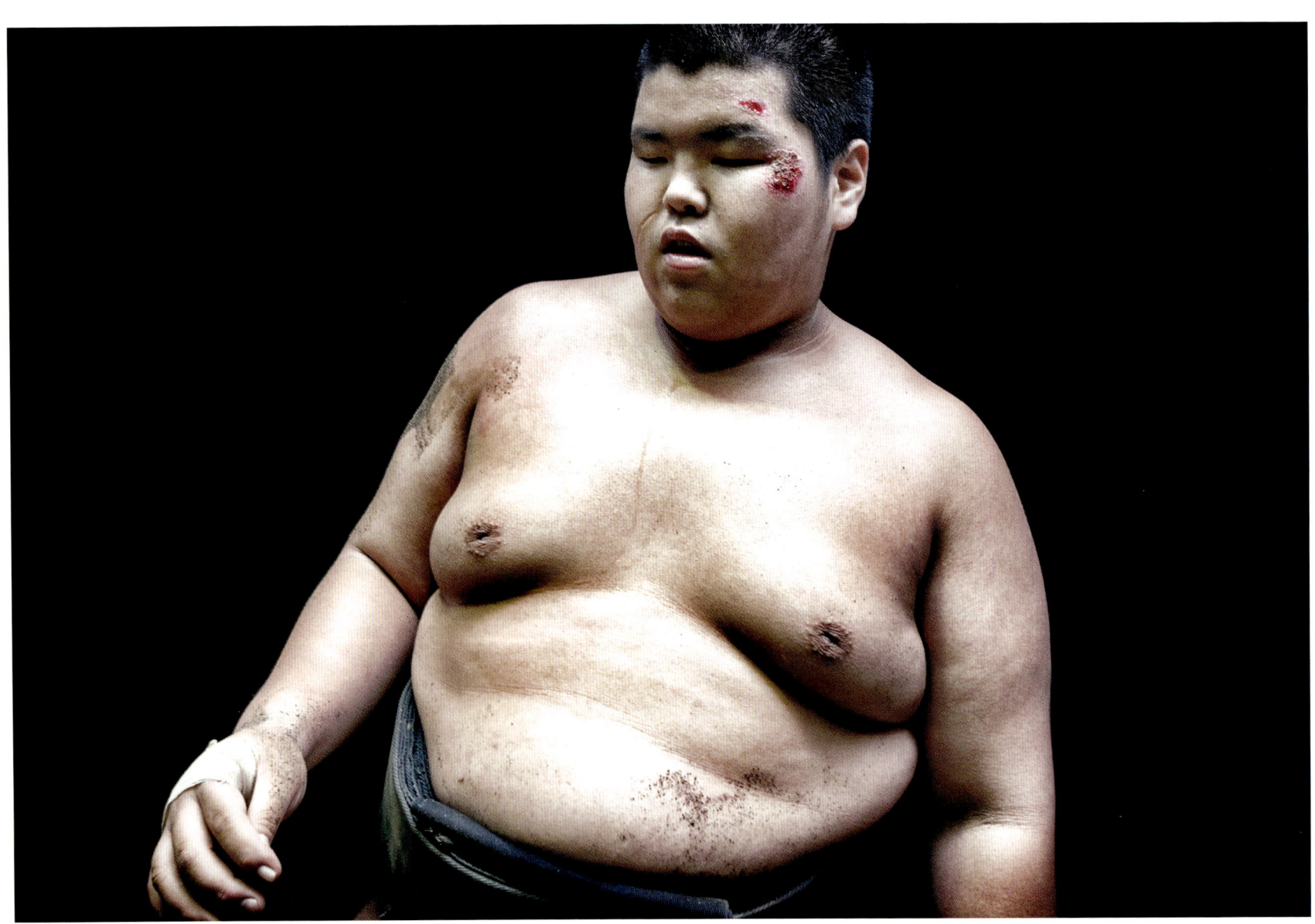

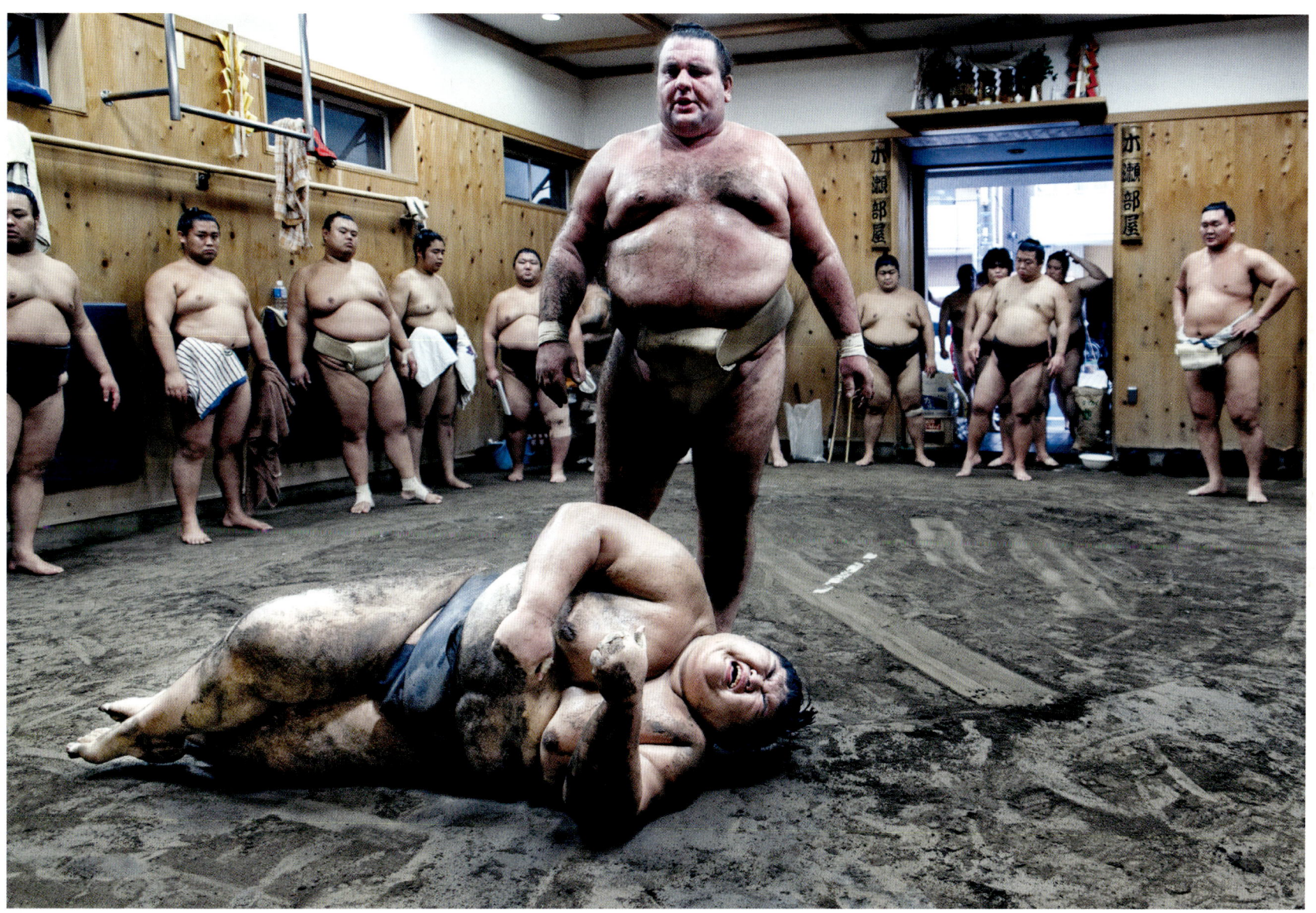

相撲 29

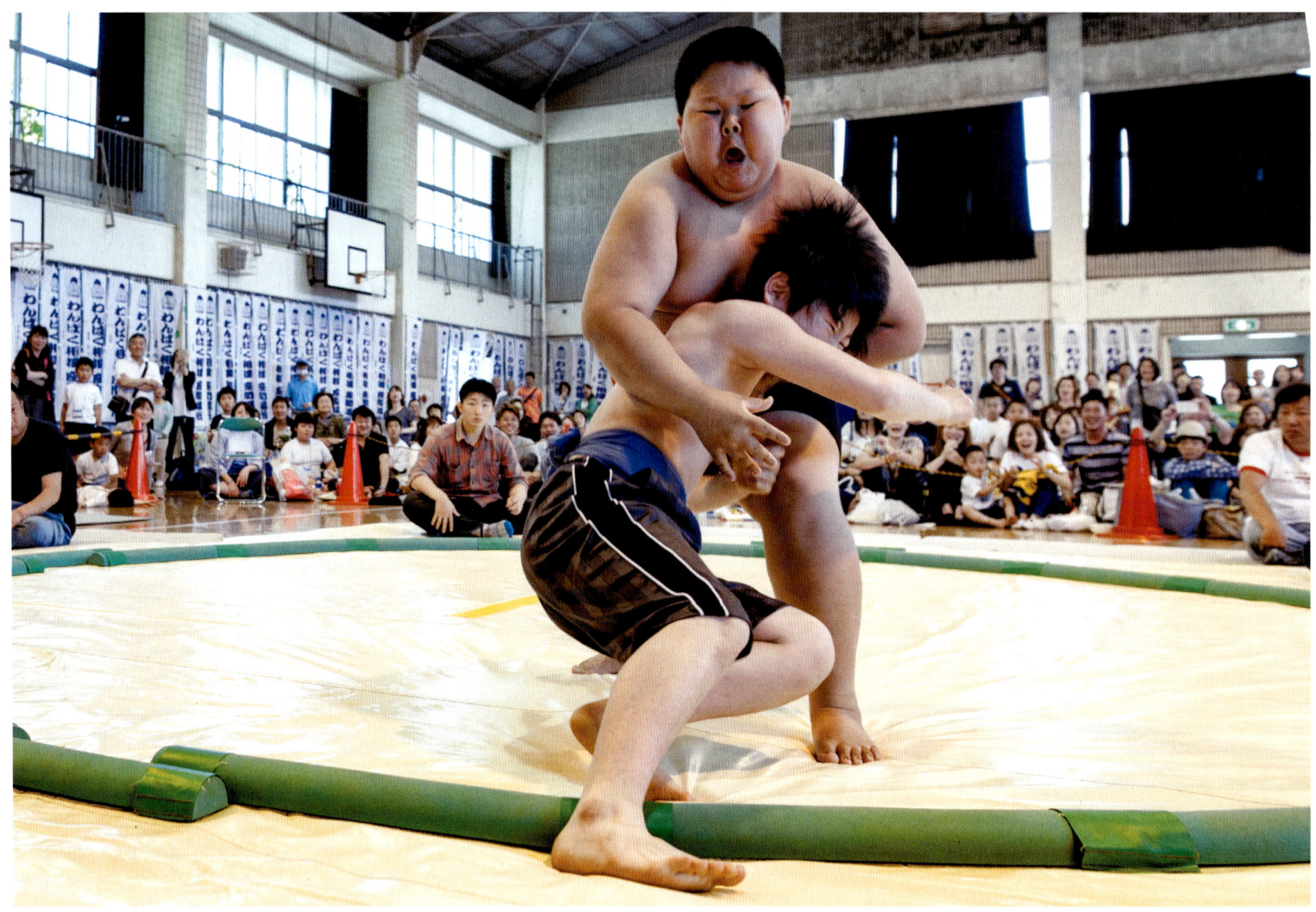

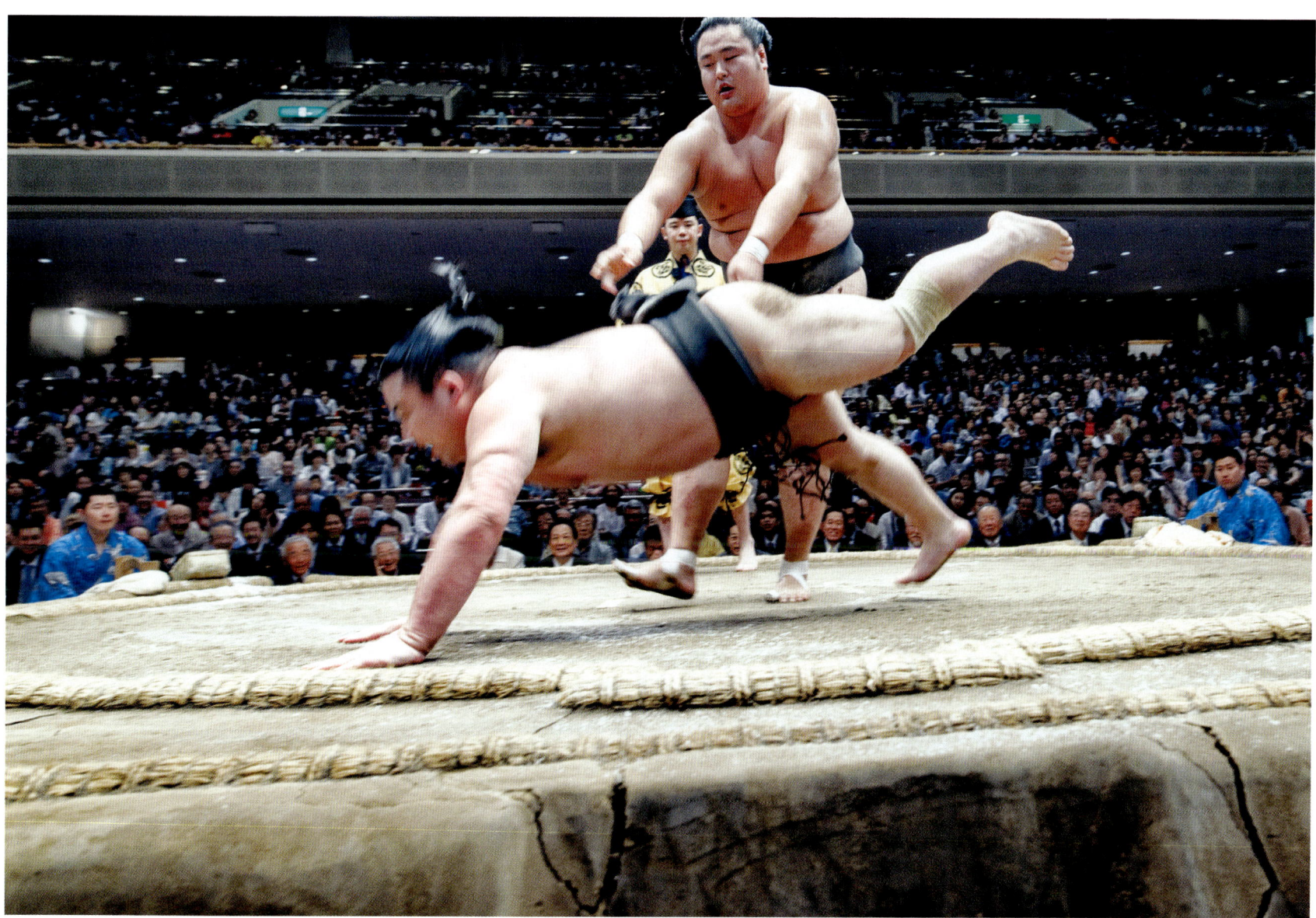

規律
DISCIPLINE

CHILD WRESTLERS WIND DOWN TRAINING WITH PUSH-UPS. THEY ARE GIVEN A TASTE OF THE DISCIPLINE REQUIRED TO BE PROFESSIONAL EARLY ON IN THEIR CAREERS.

子ども力士の稽古は腕立て伏せで終わる。相撲力士に必要な鍛錬を、早い段階から経験させるのだ。

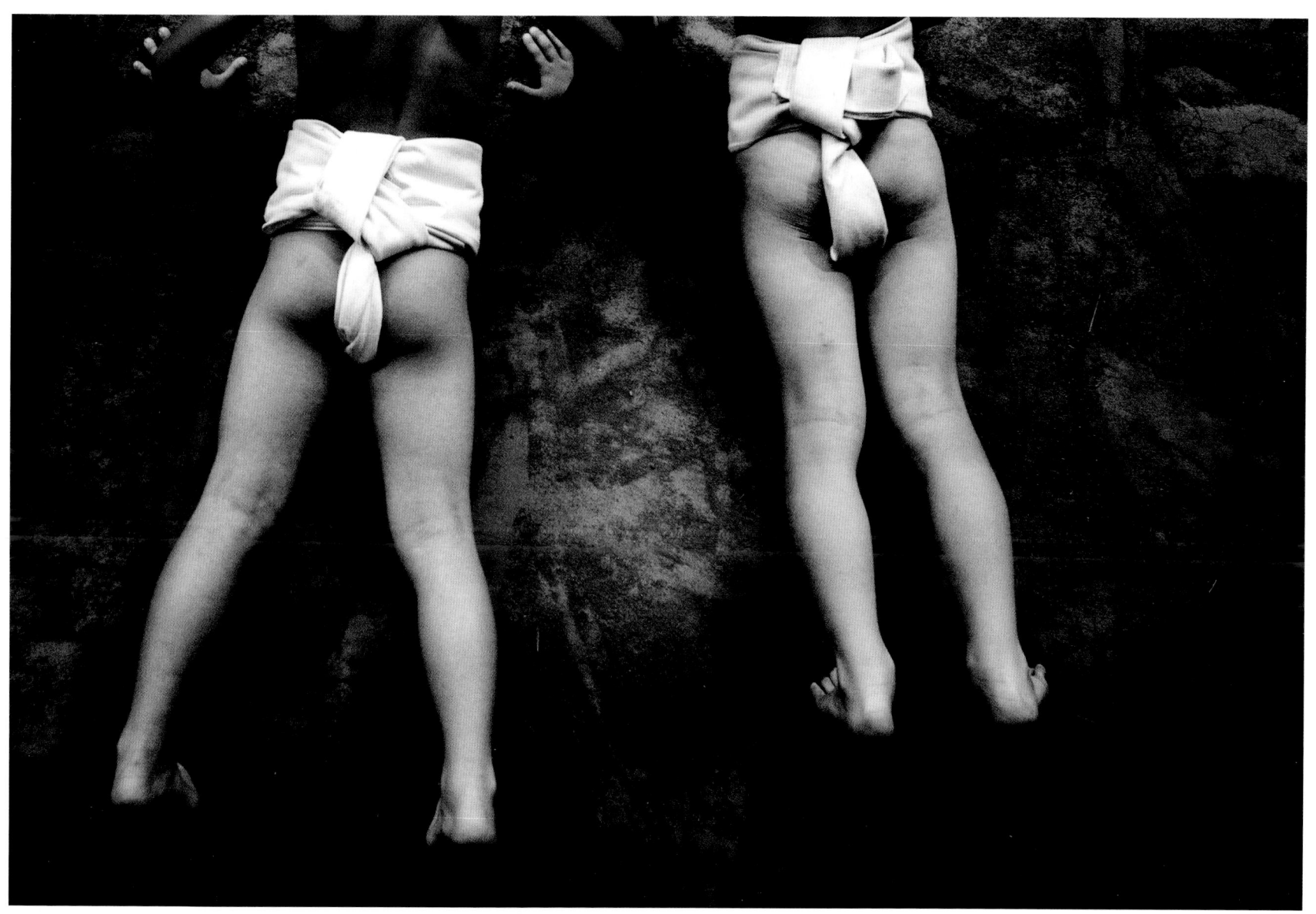

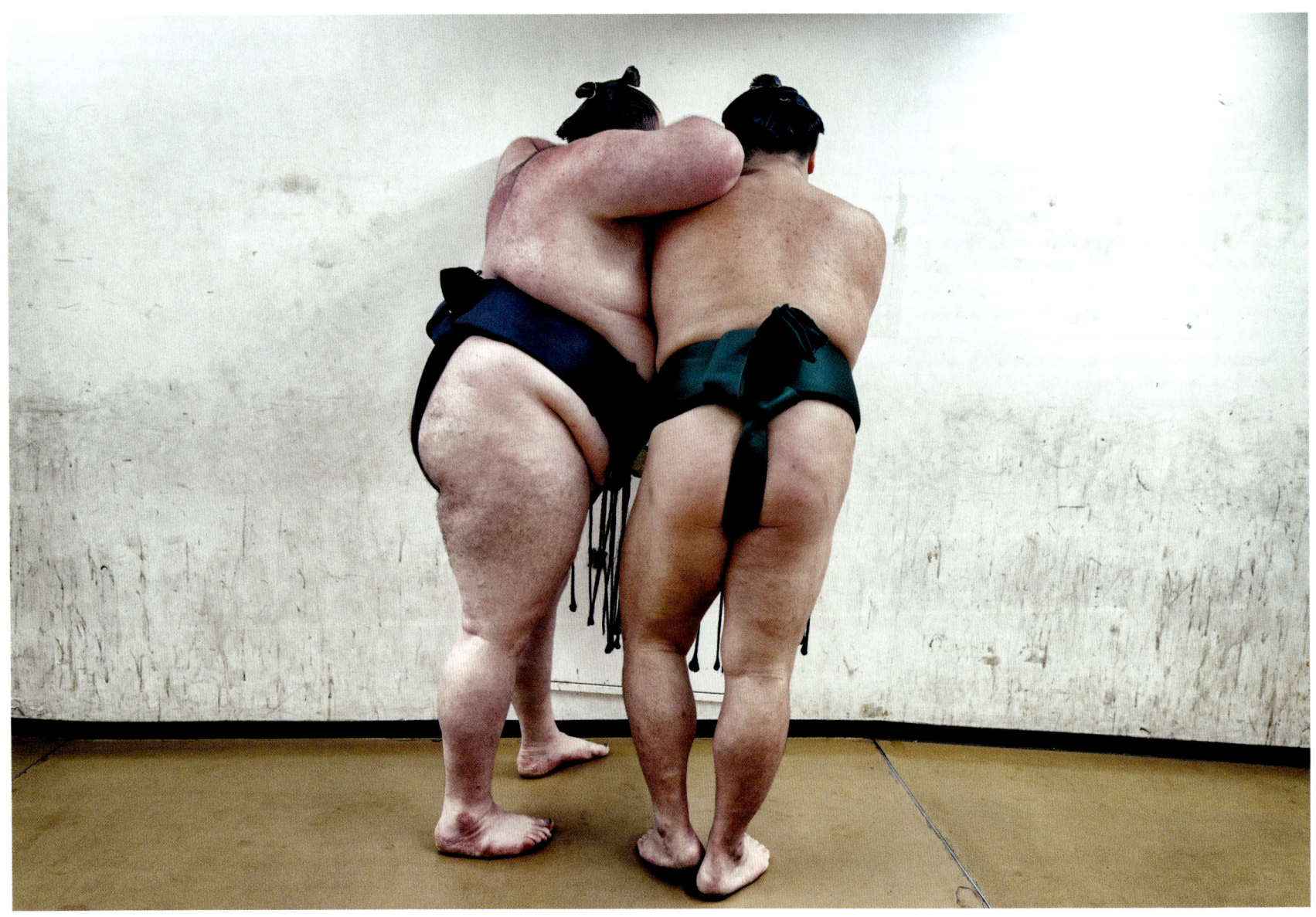

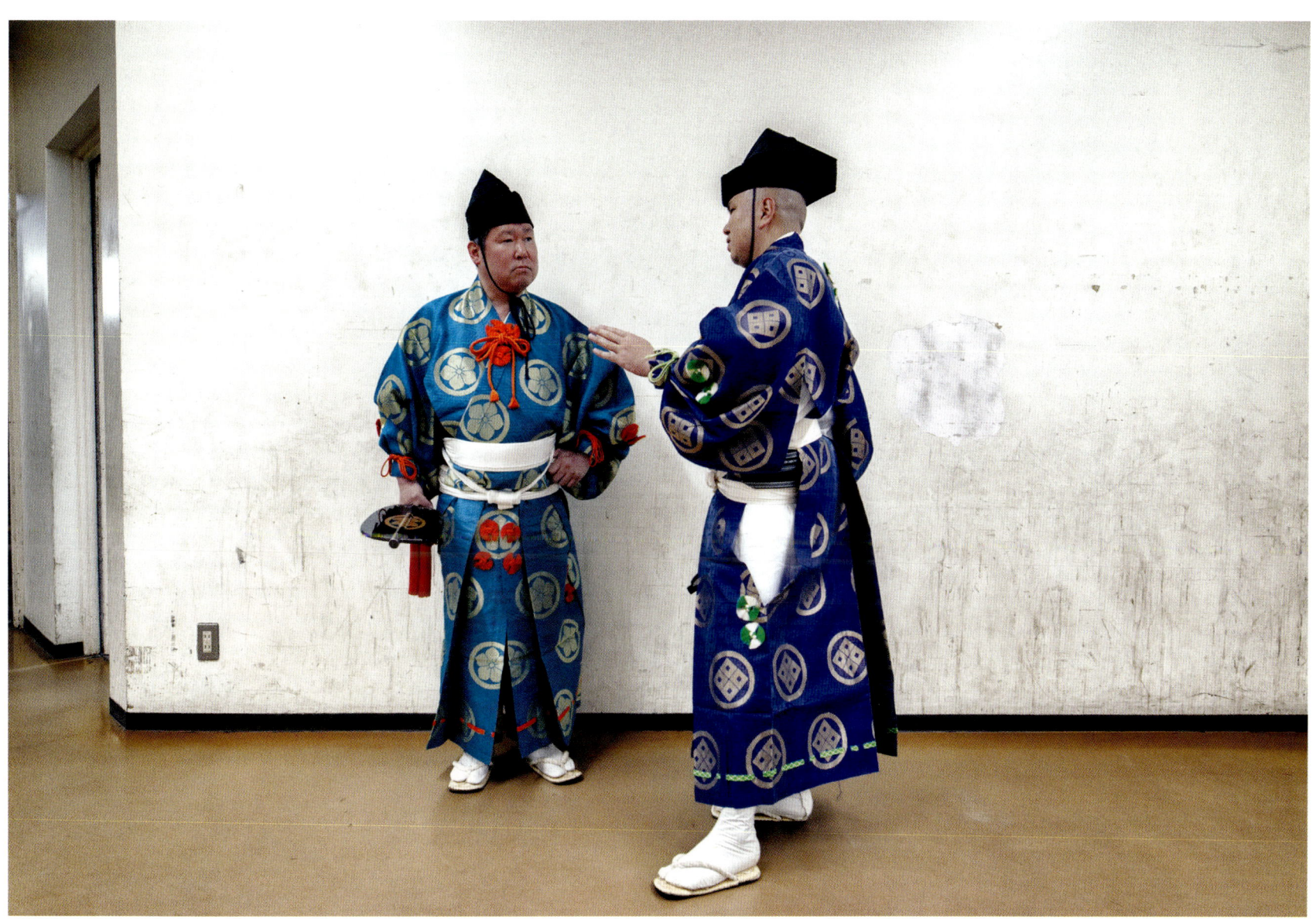

相撲 35

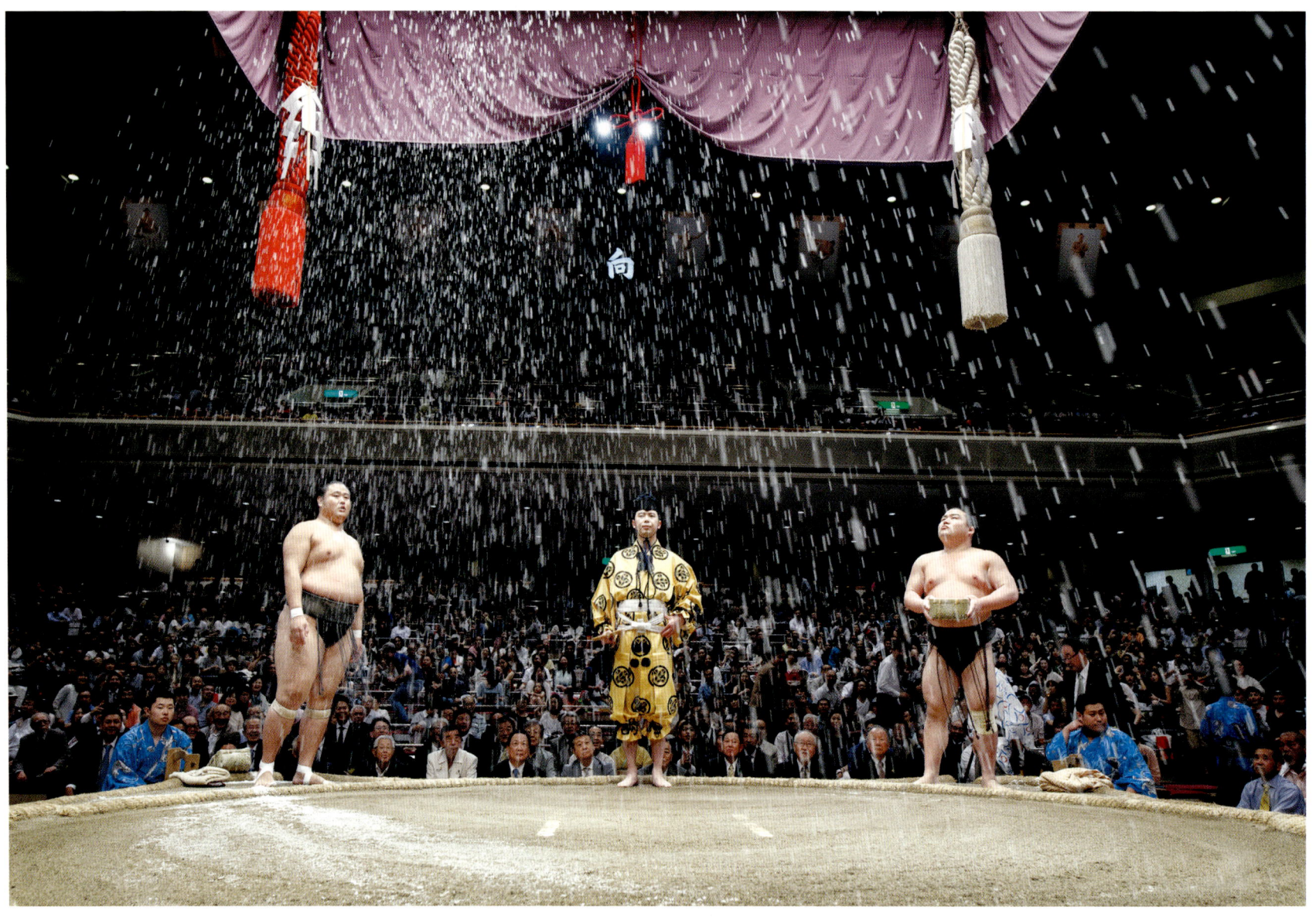

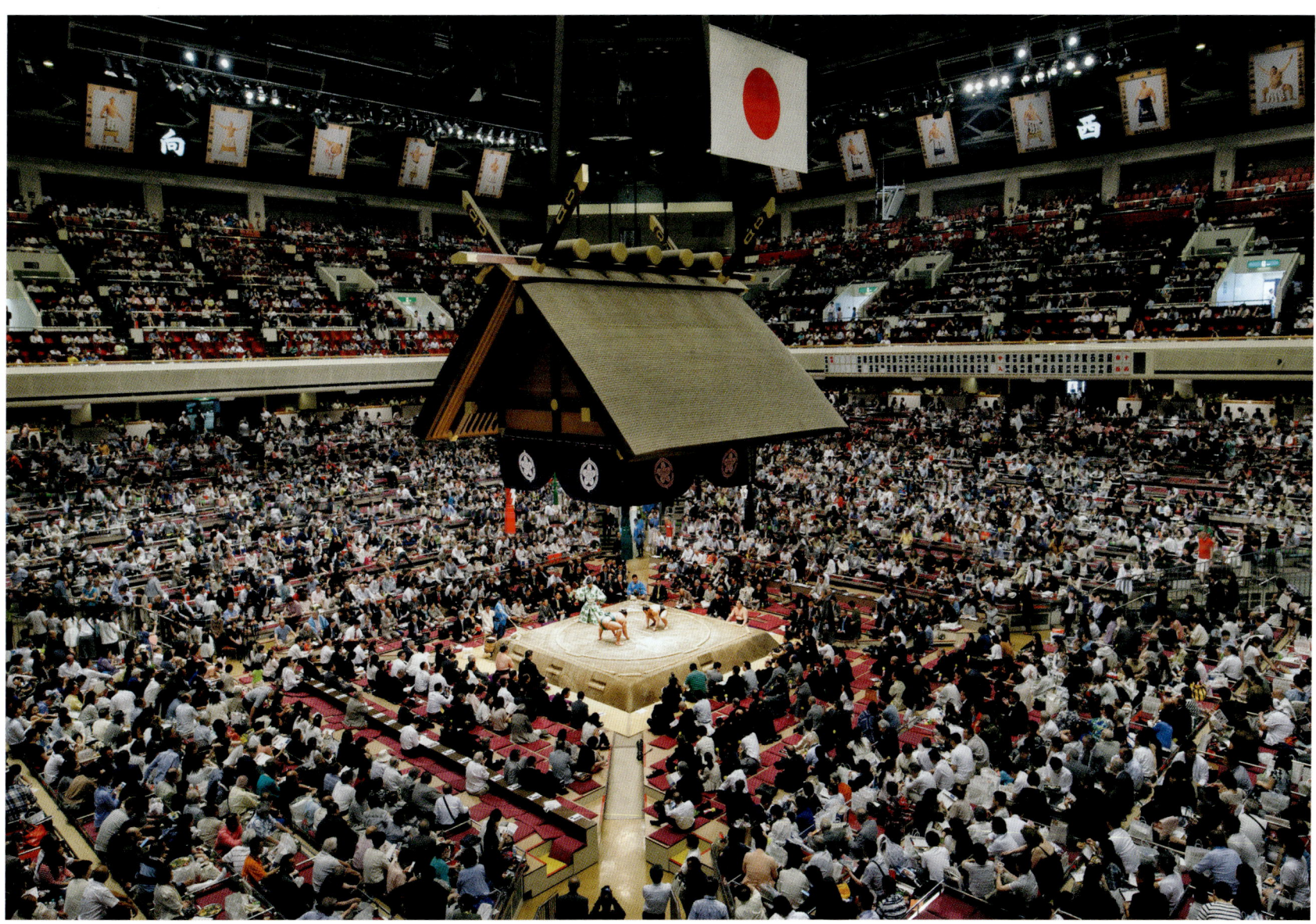

相撲 37

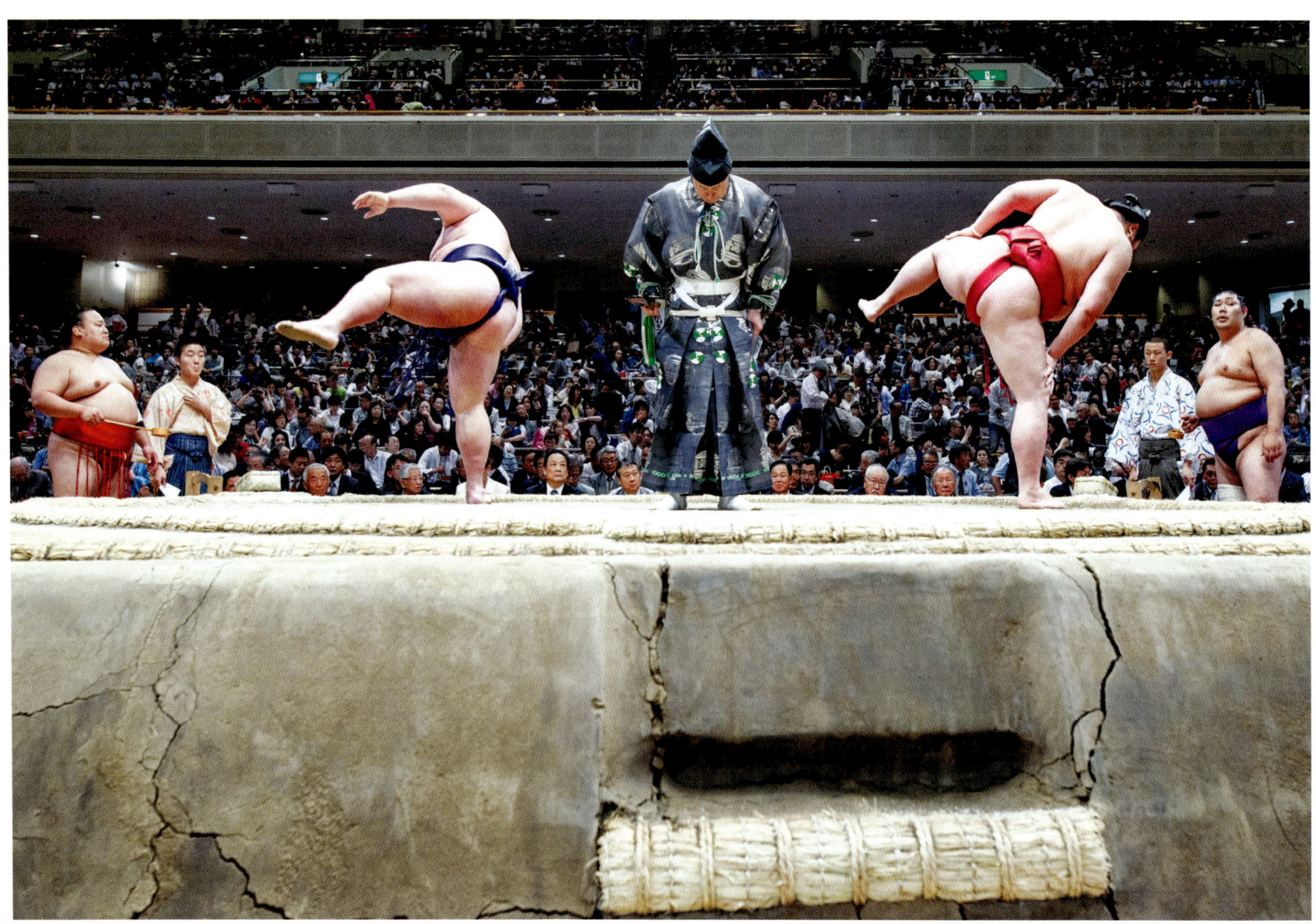

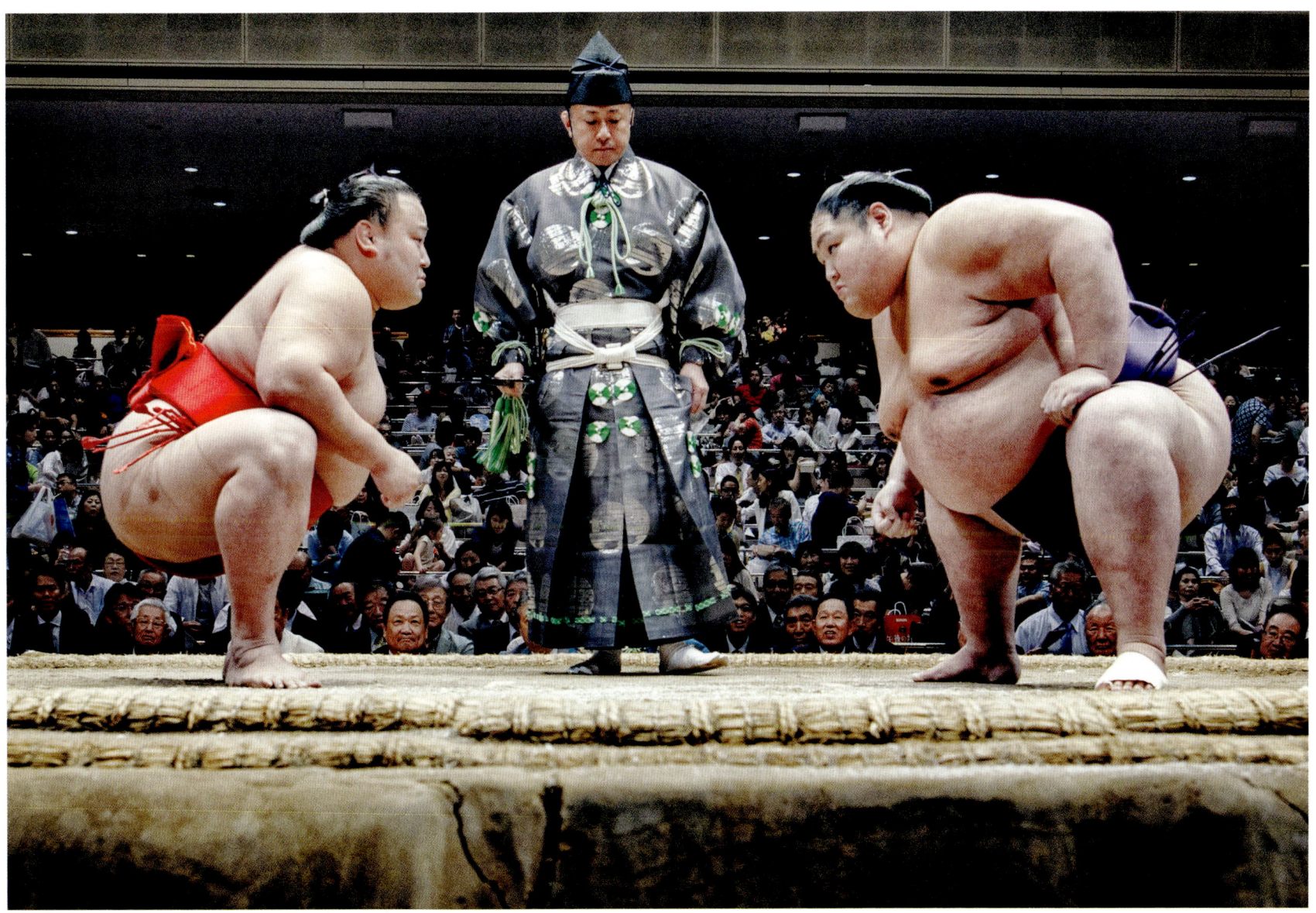

相撲 39

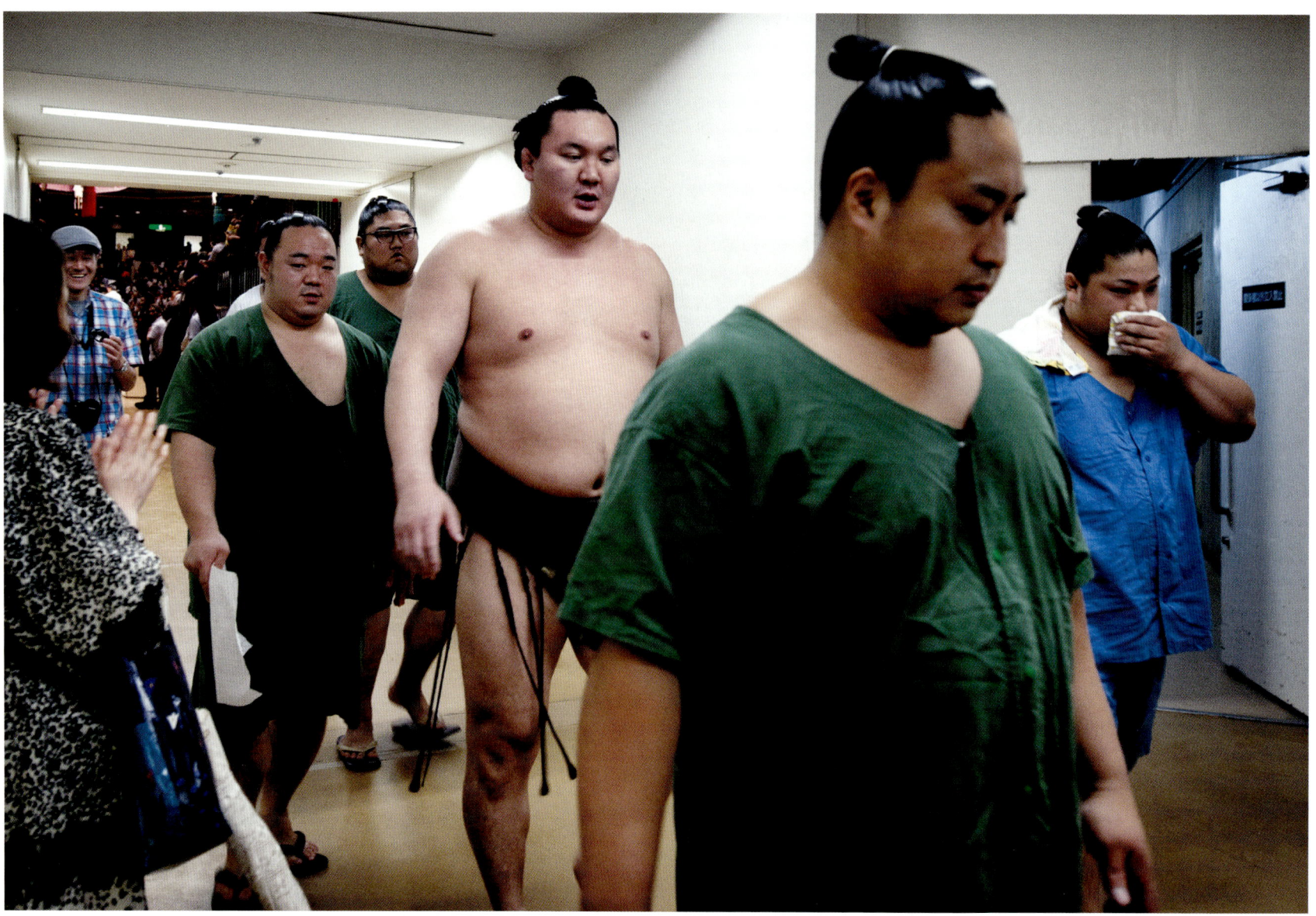

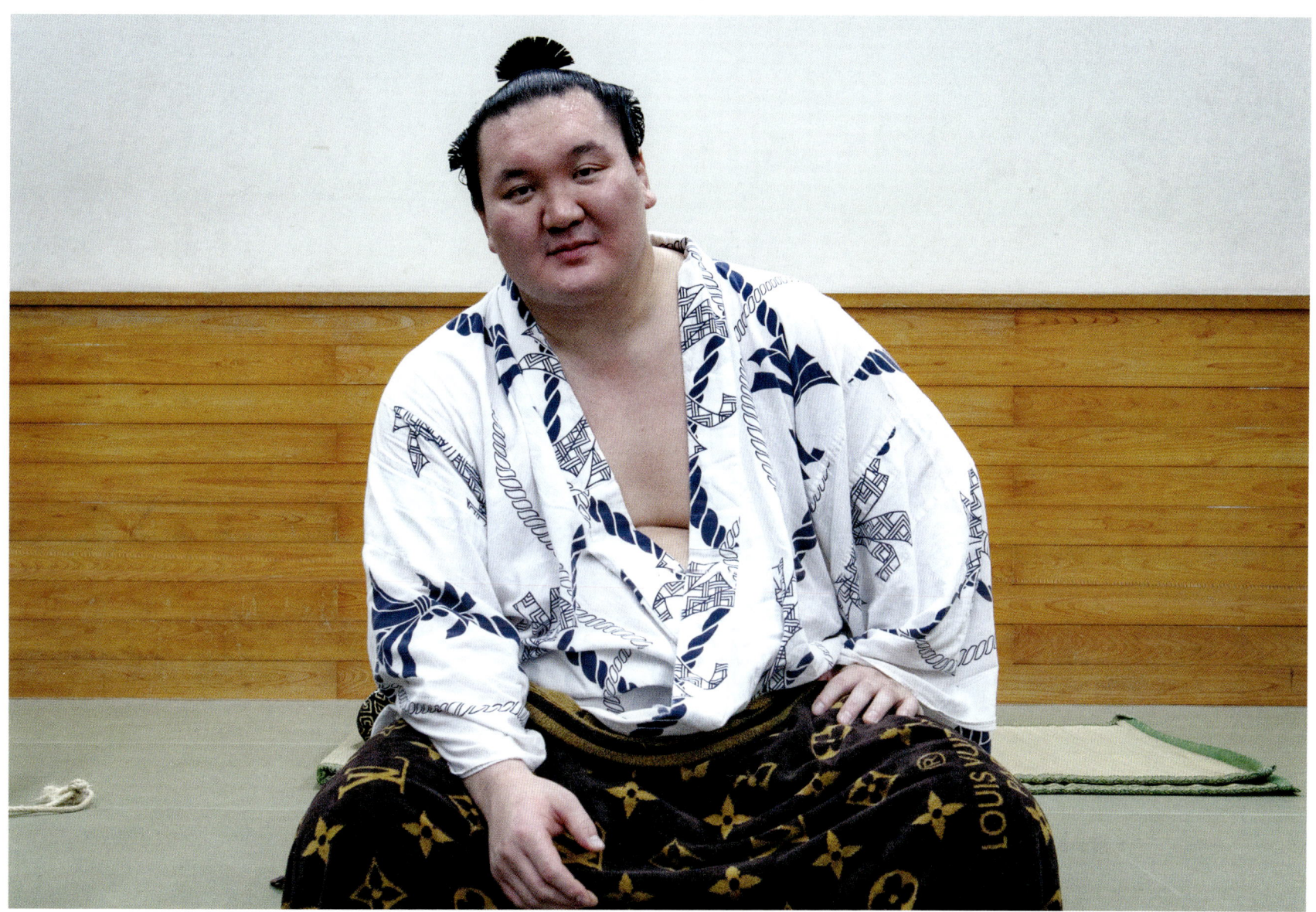

敬意
RESPECT

A STATUETTE FOR SALE OF YOKOZUNA HAKUHŌ SHŌ, THE GREATEST WRESTLER OF ALL TIME, SITS ALONGSIDE THOSE OF OTHER RESPECTED WRESTLERS AT KOKUGIKAN STADIUM.

国技館では、他の有名力士に並んで、史上最高力士、横綱・白鵬翔のフィギュアが販売されている。

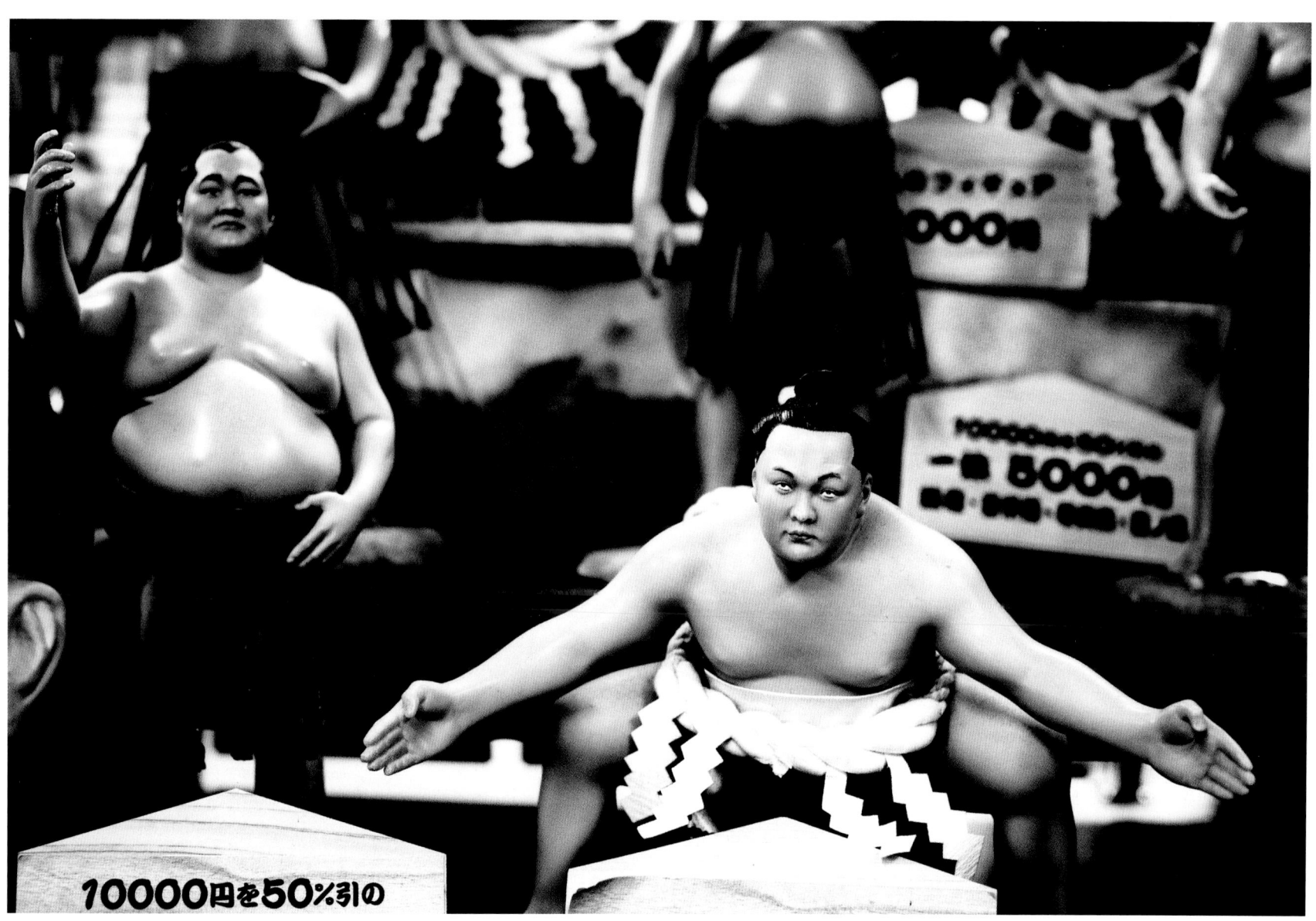

相撲　43

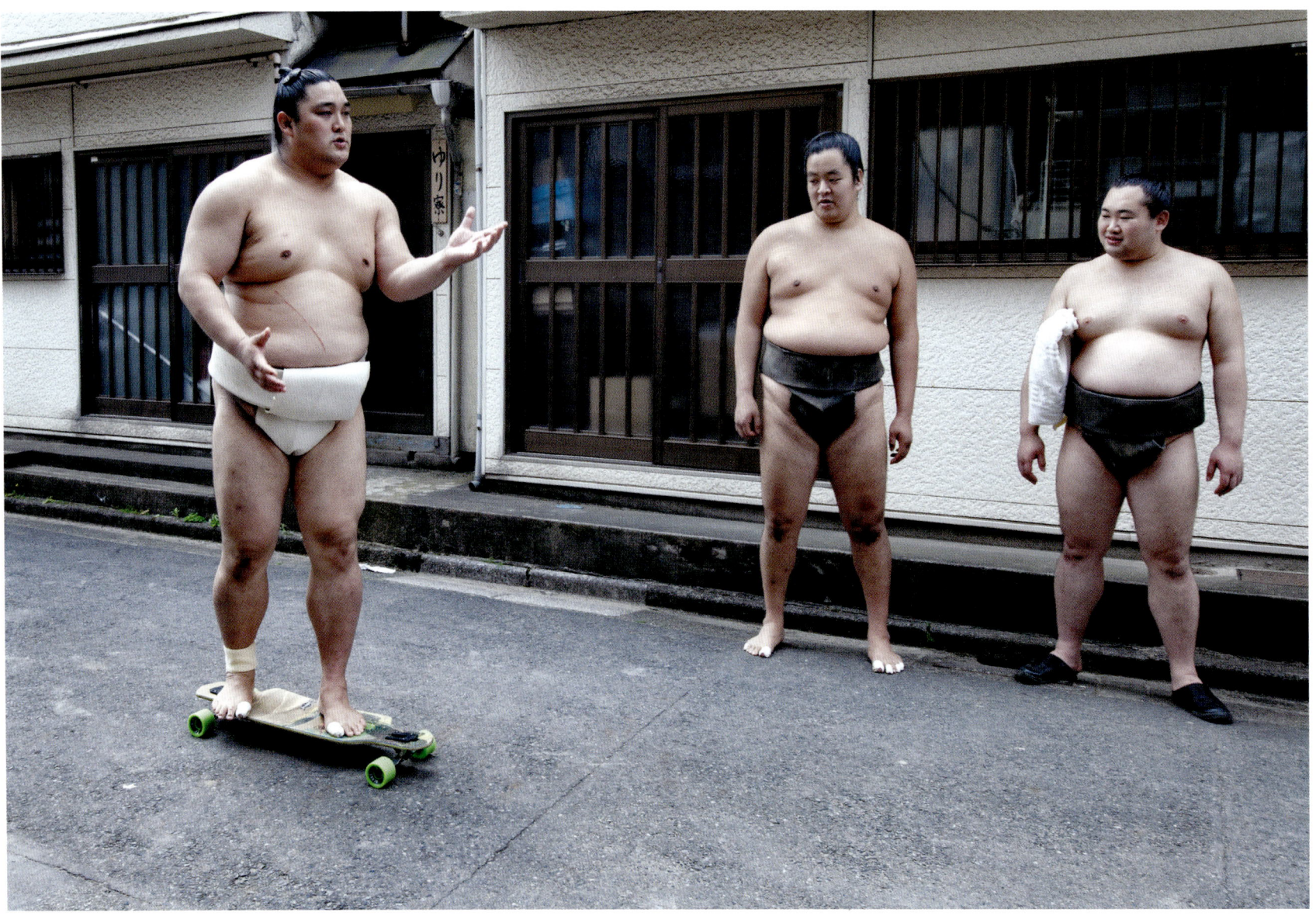

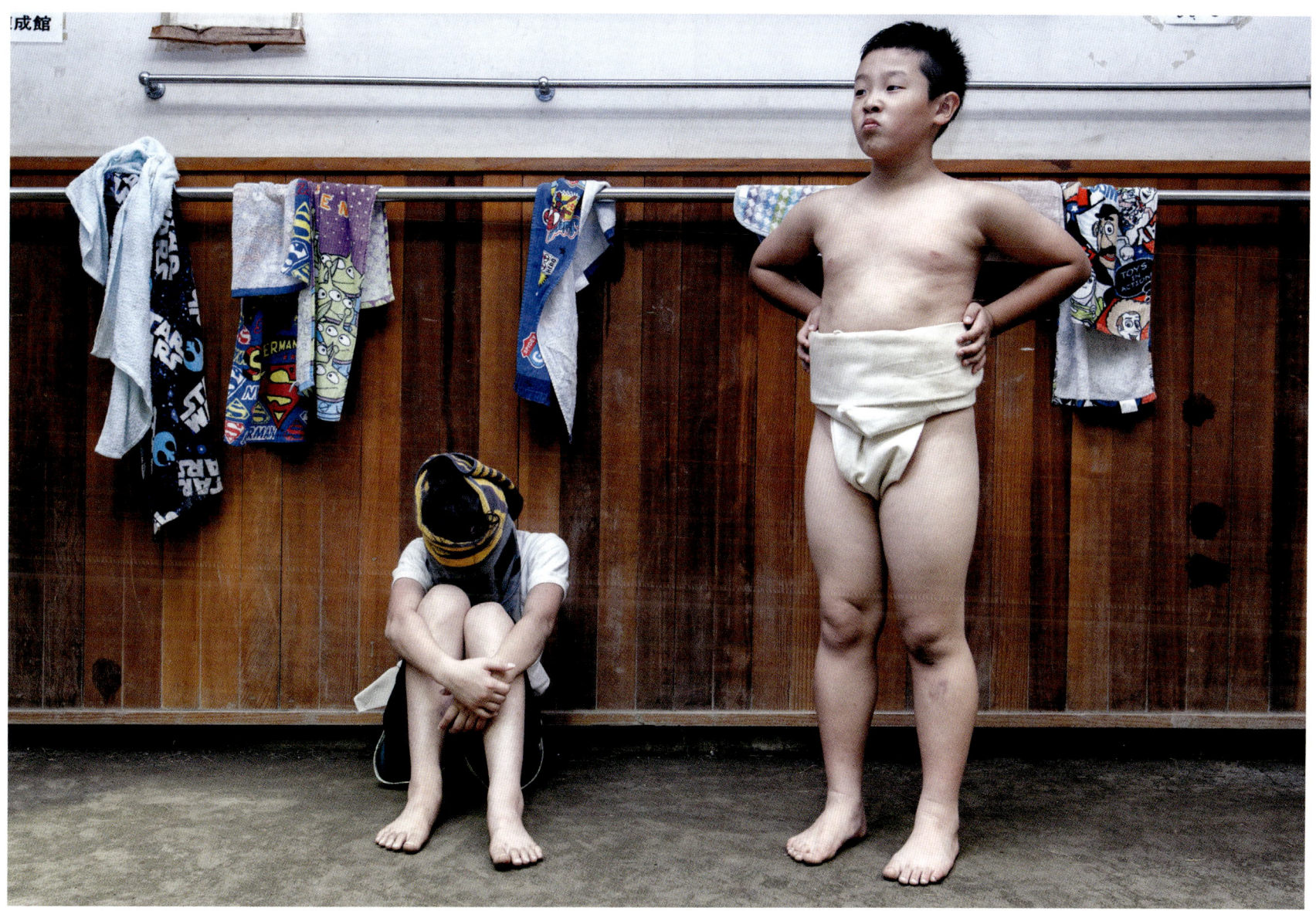

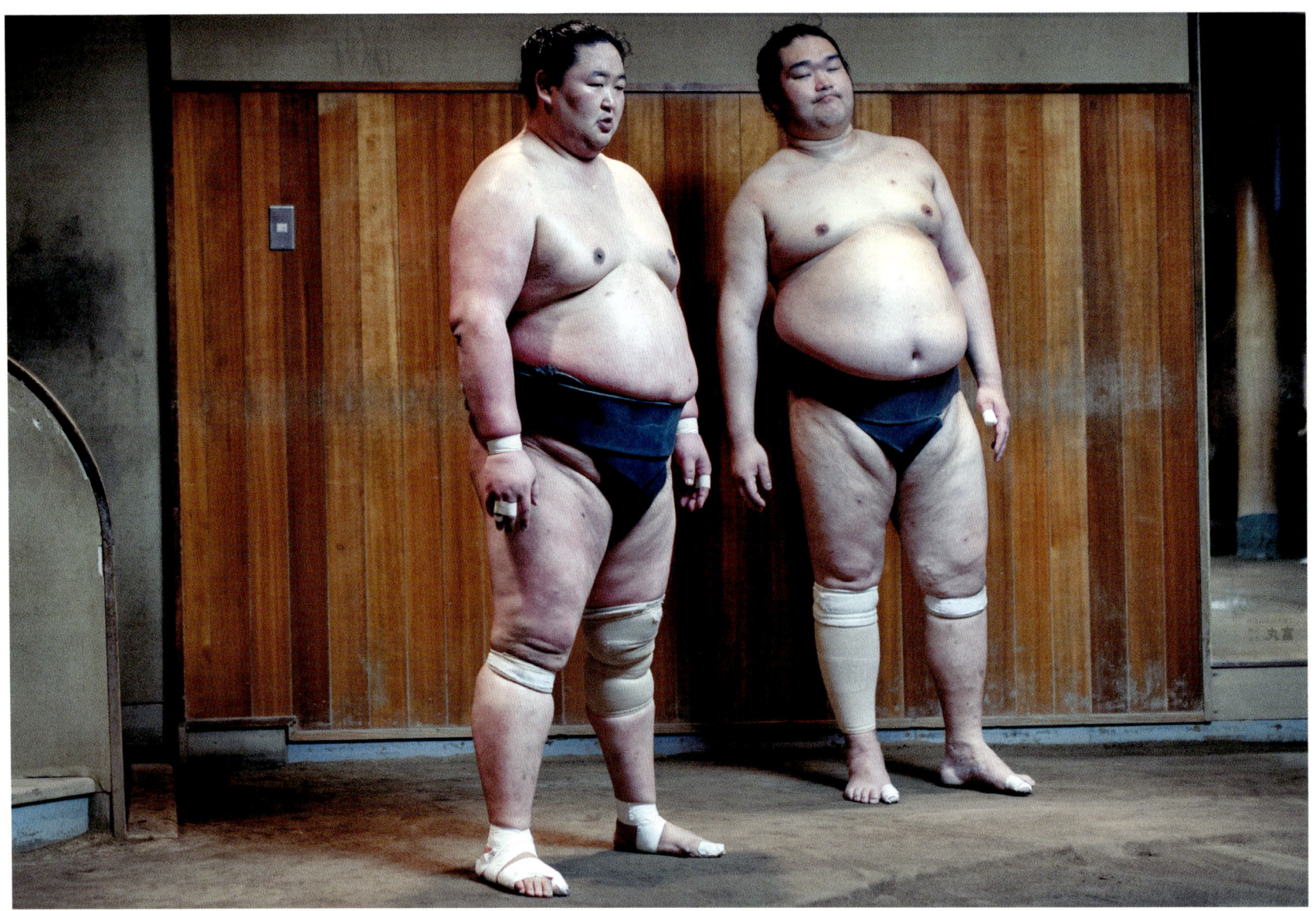

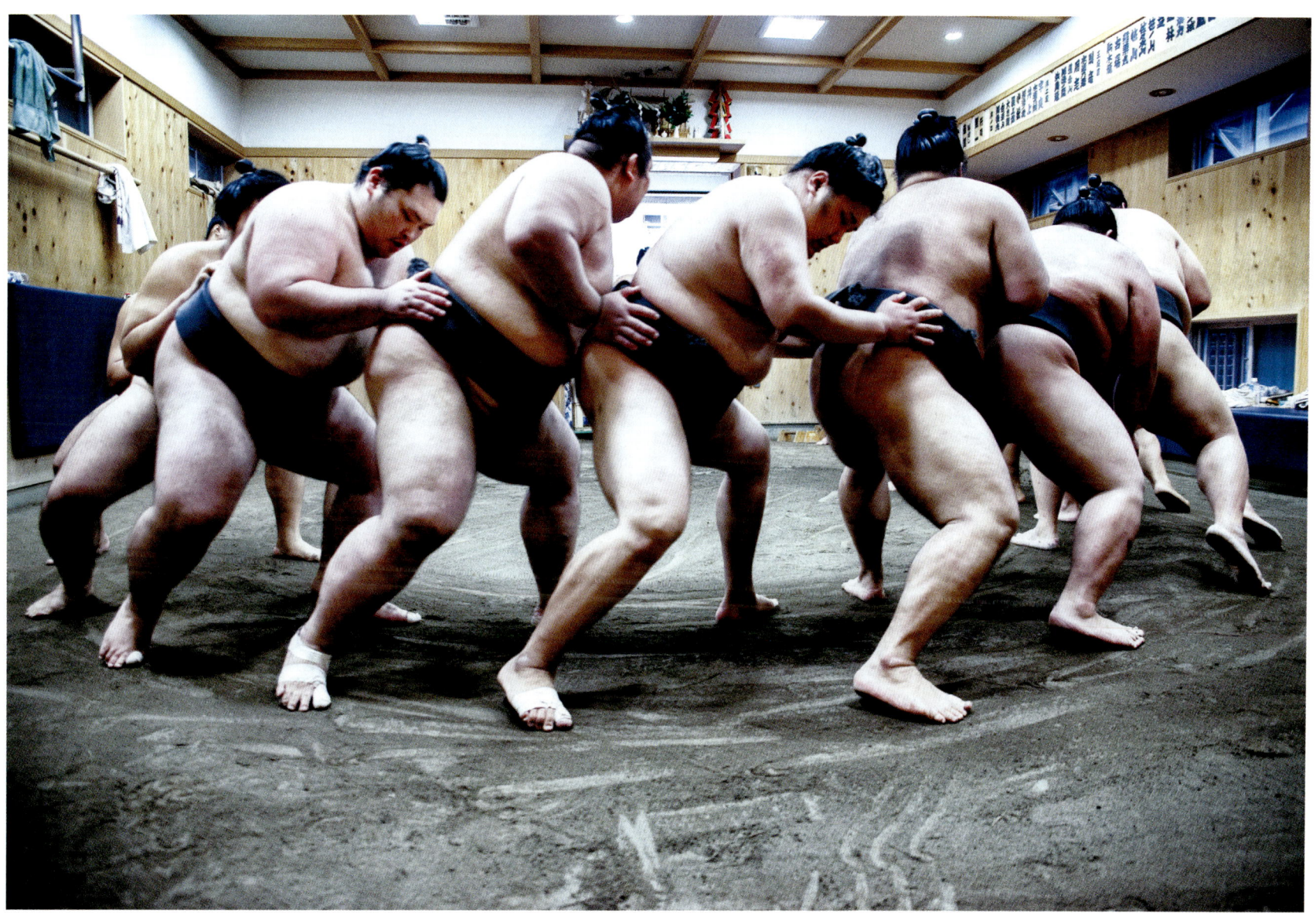

相撲 47

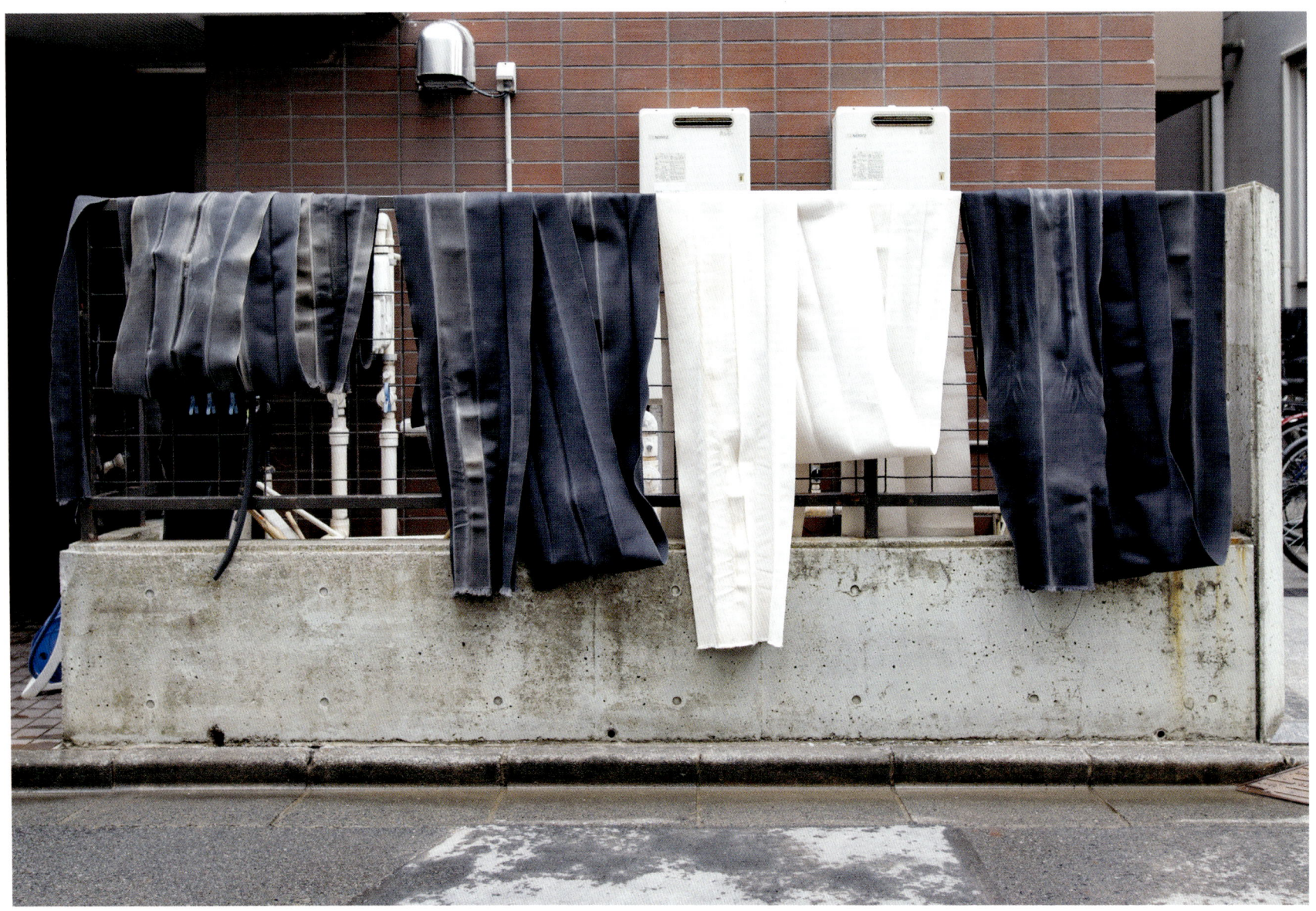

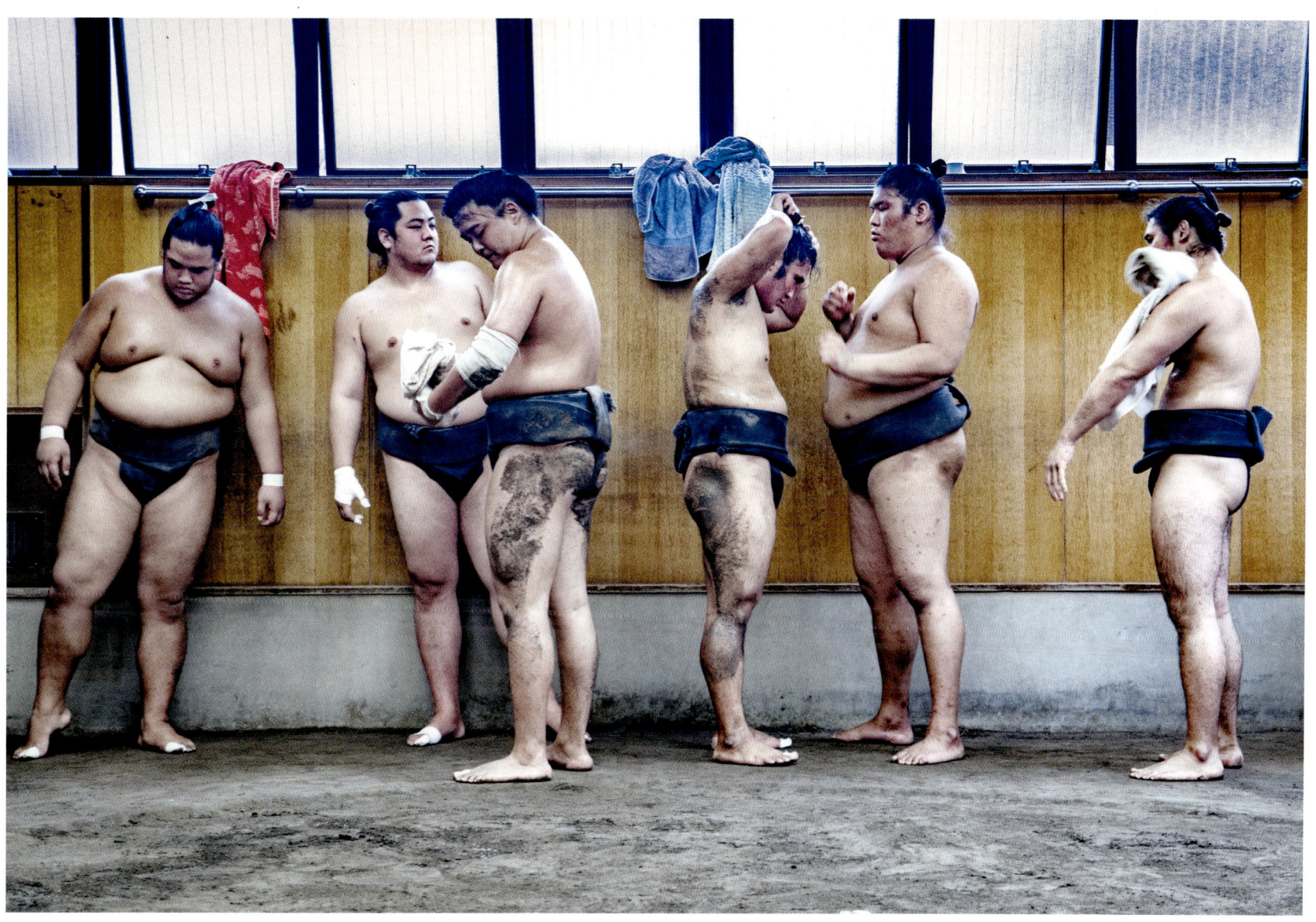

相撲　49

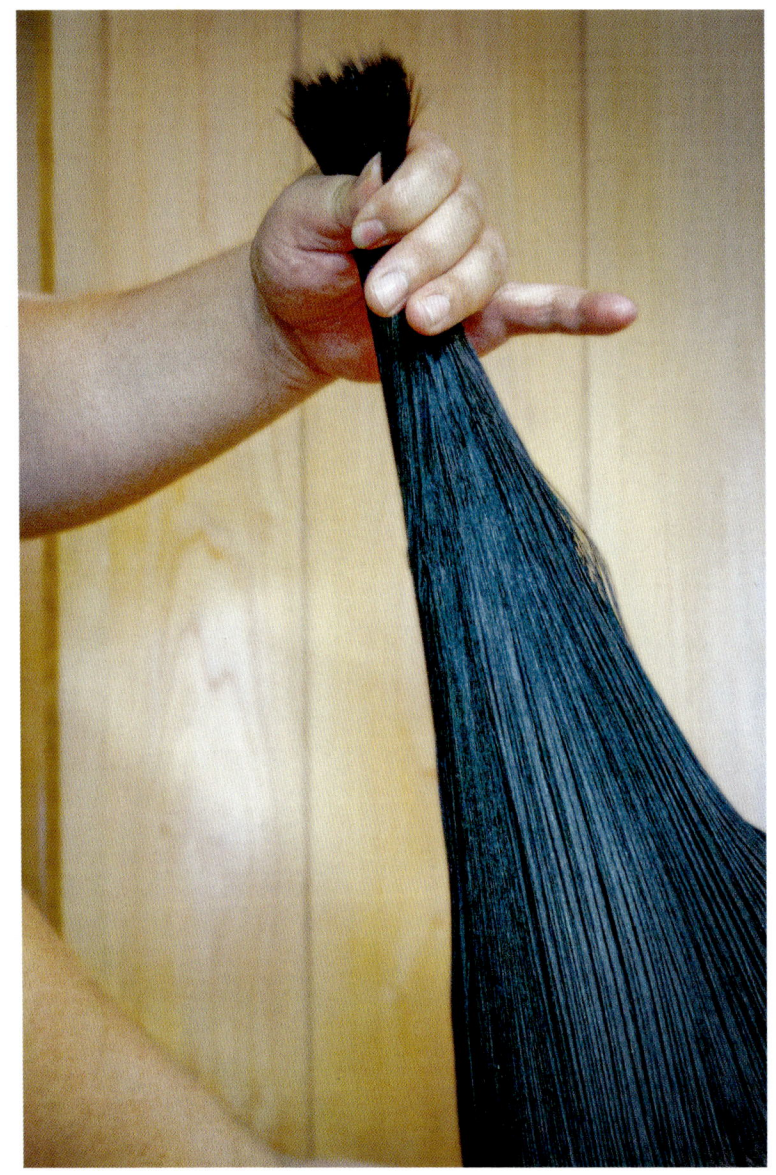

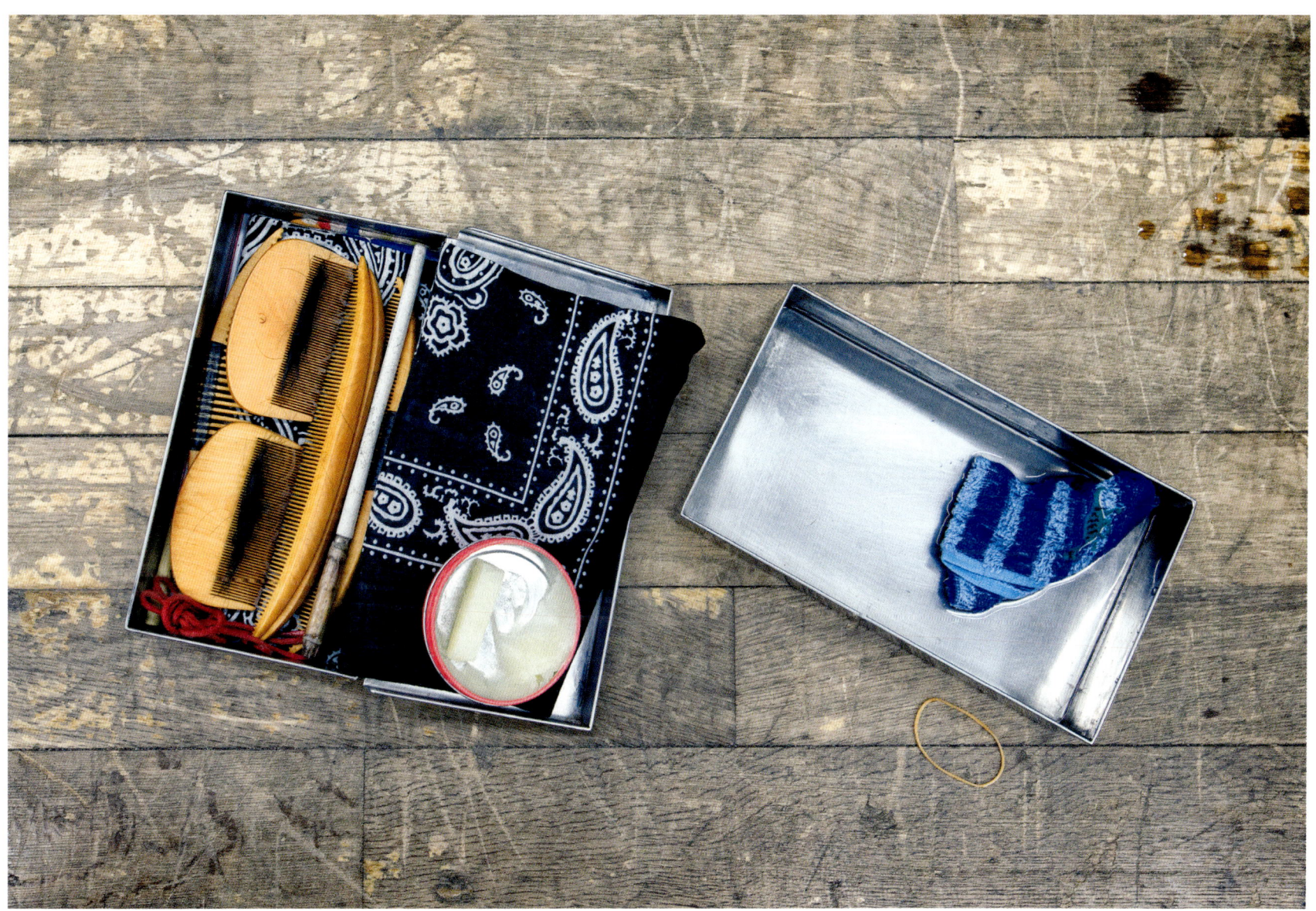

相撲 51

柔軟性

FLEXIBILITY

EXCEPTIONAL FLEXIBILITY IS REQUIRED TO PERFORM *MATAWARI*, A STRETCH THAT IS PRACTISED IN VIRTUALLY EVERY TRAINING SESSION.

稽古中ほぼ毎回練習される股割りは、多大な運動能力を必要とする。

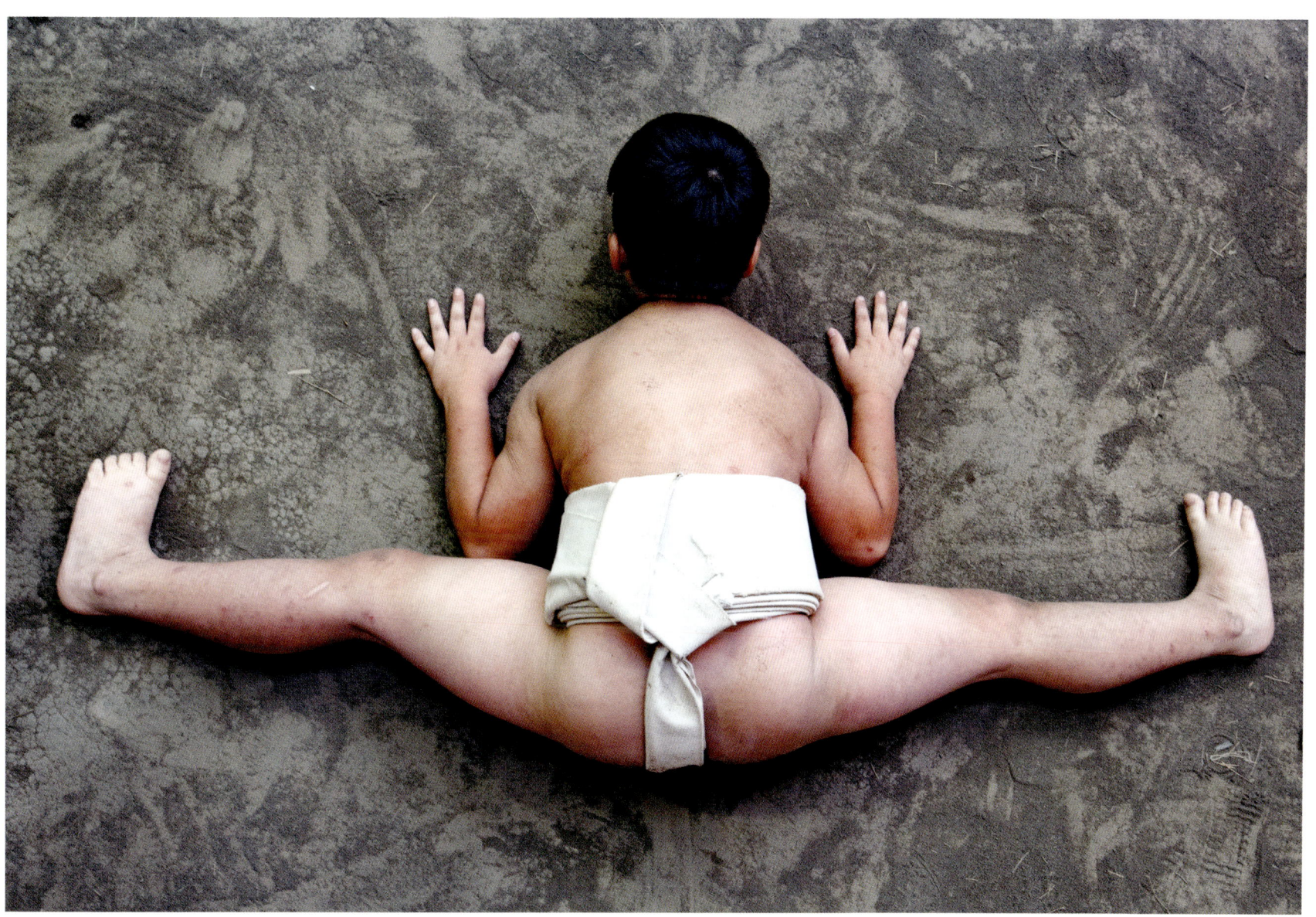

相撲 53

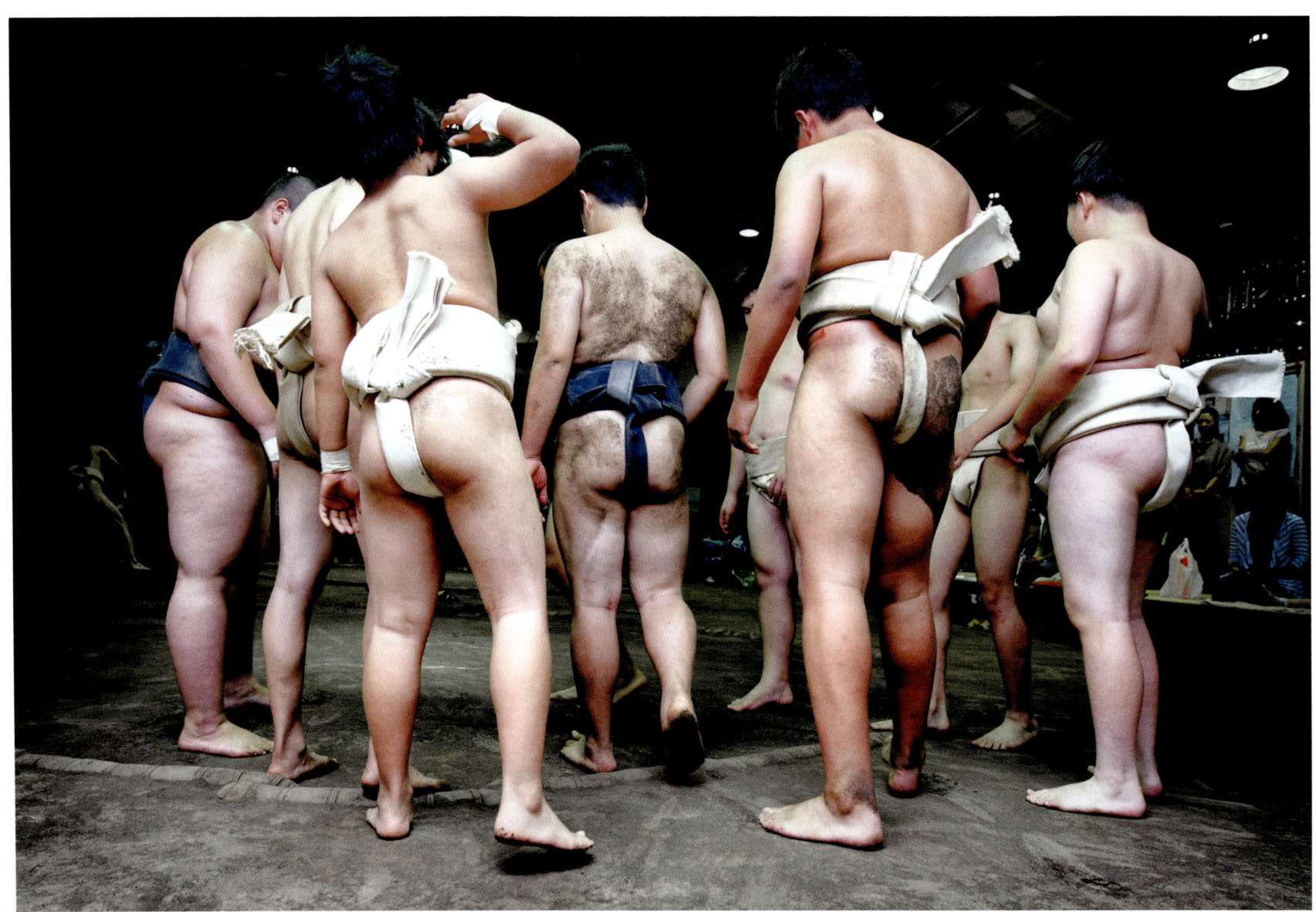

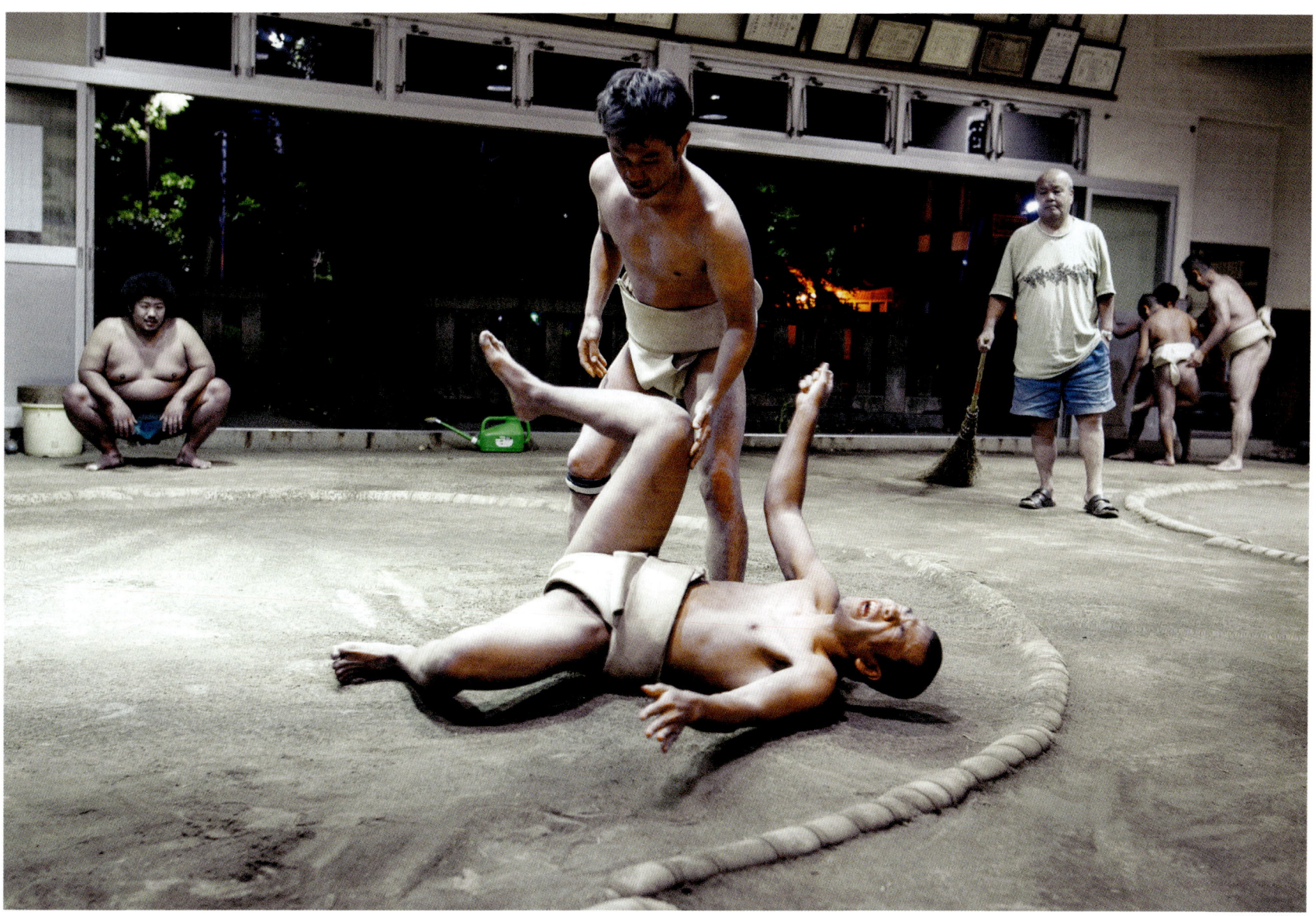

相撲 55

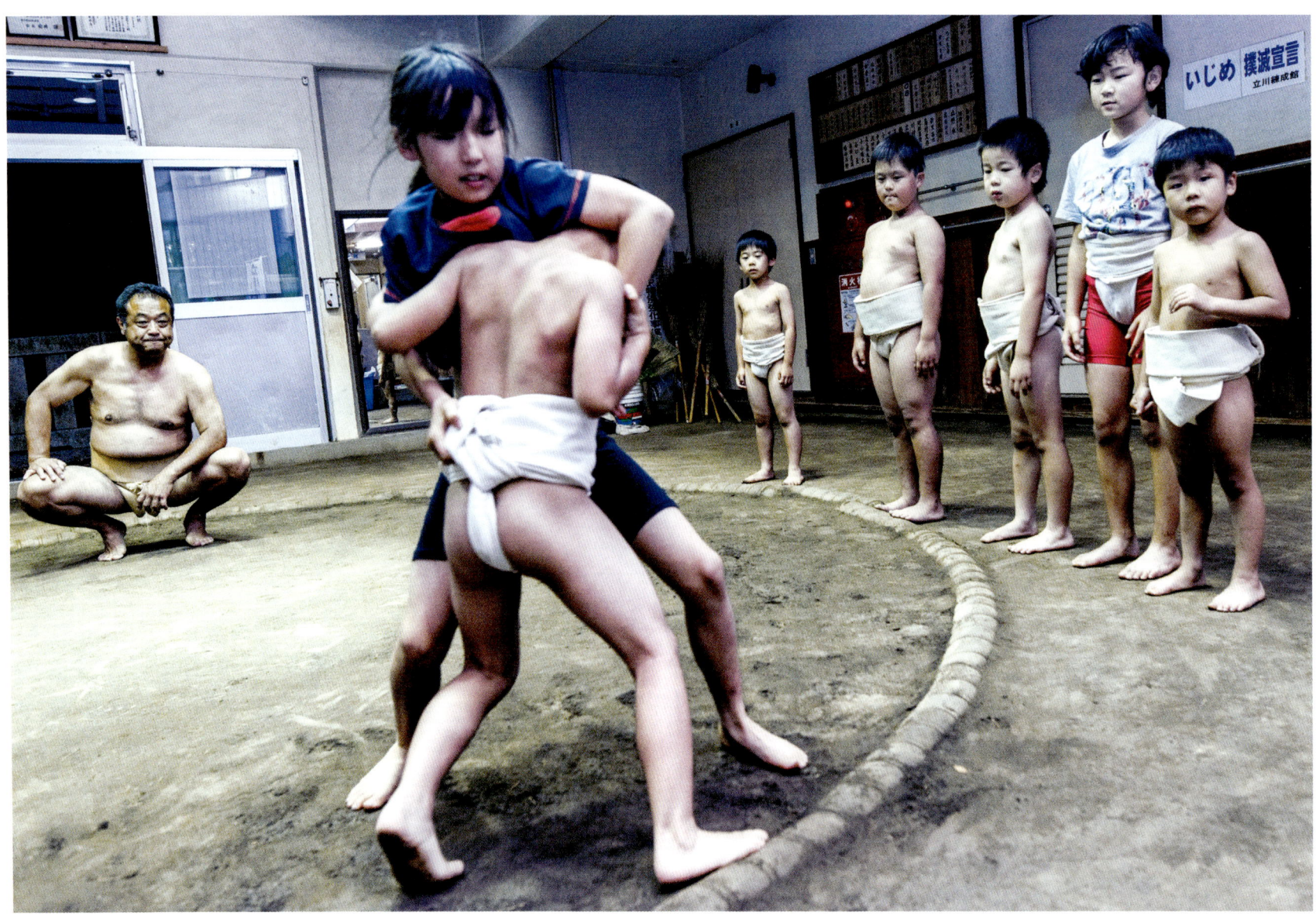

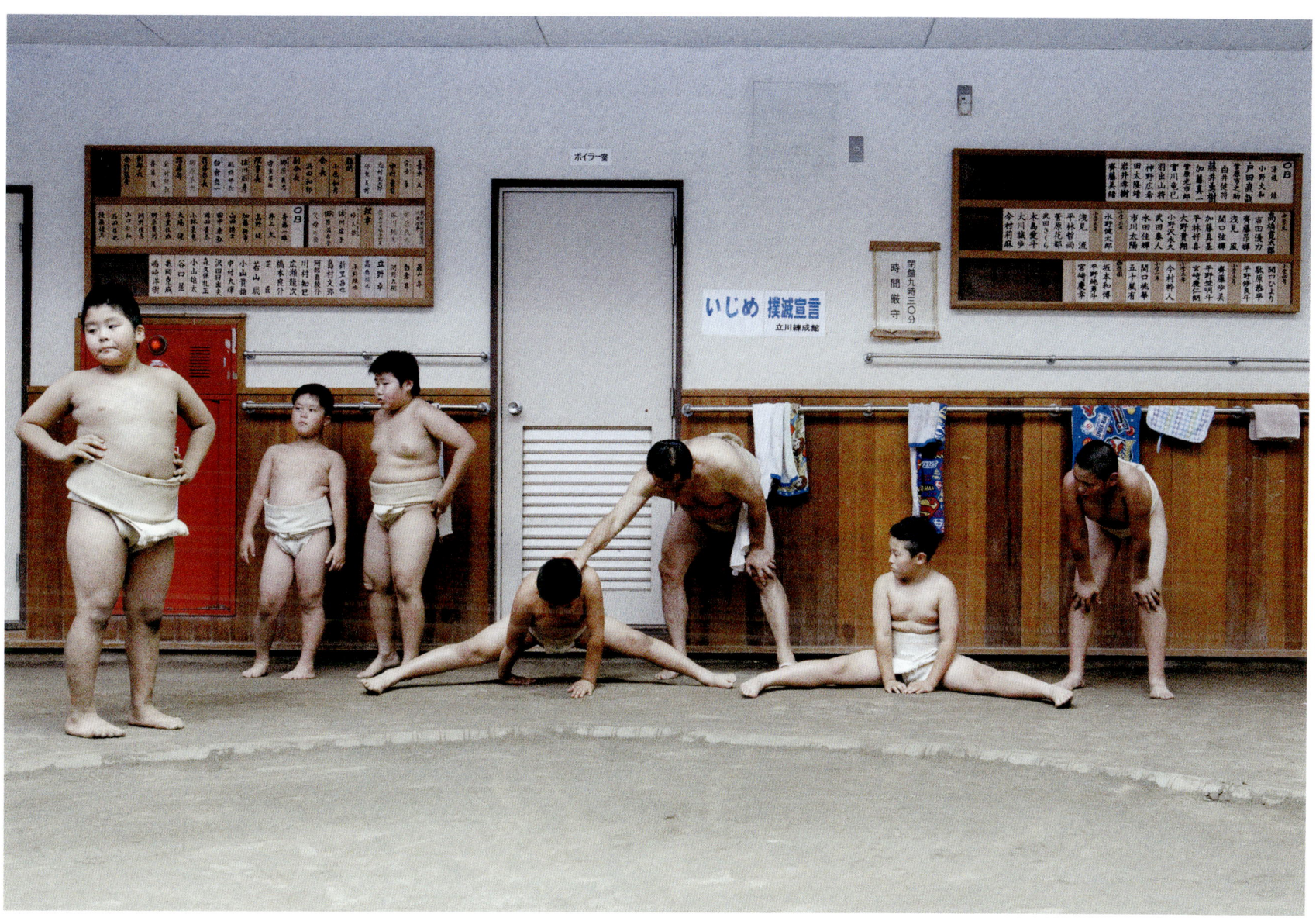

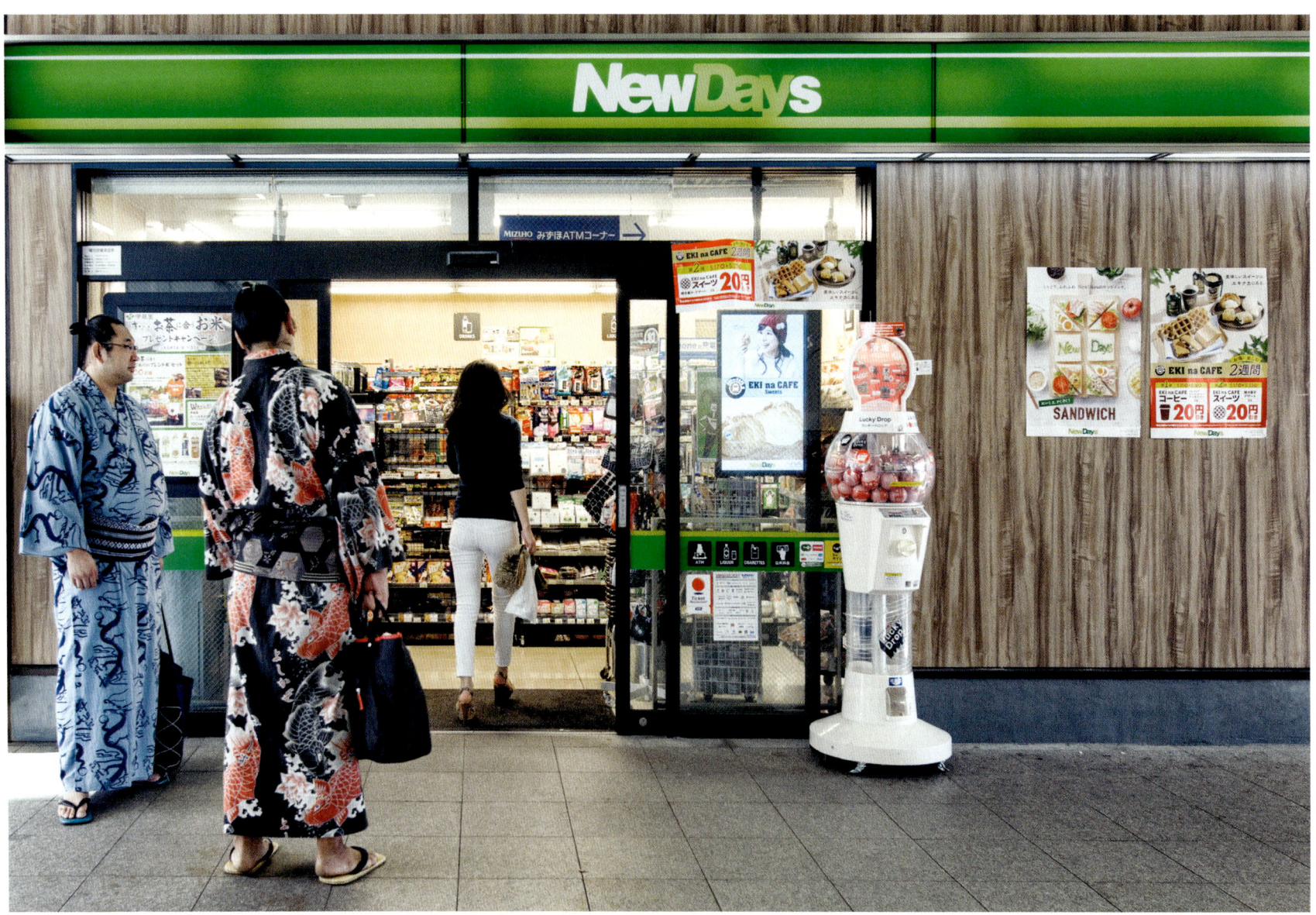

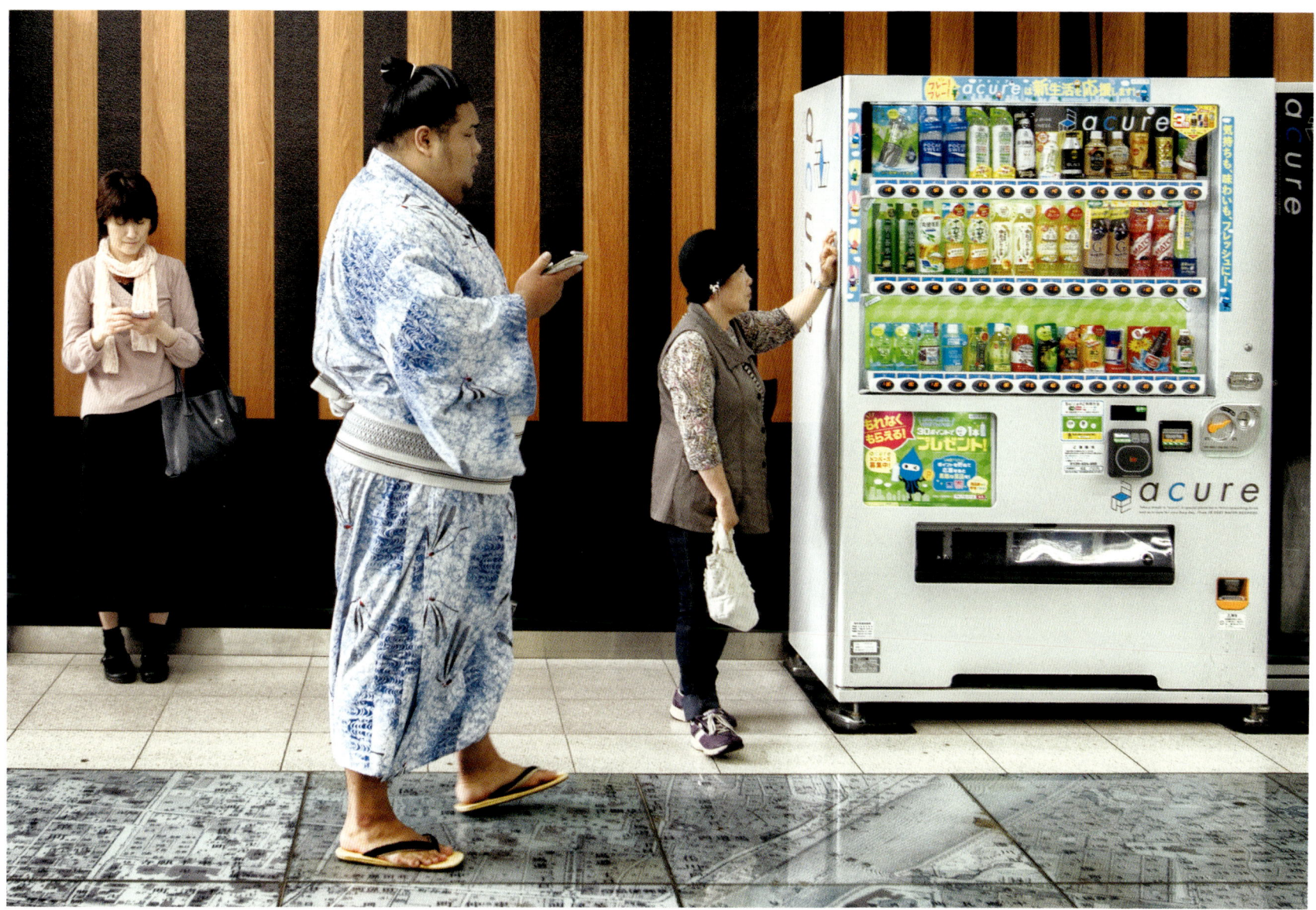

相撲

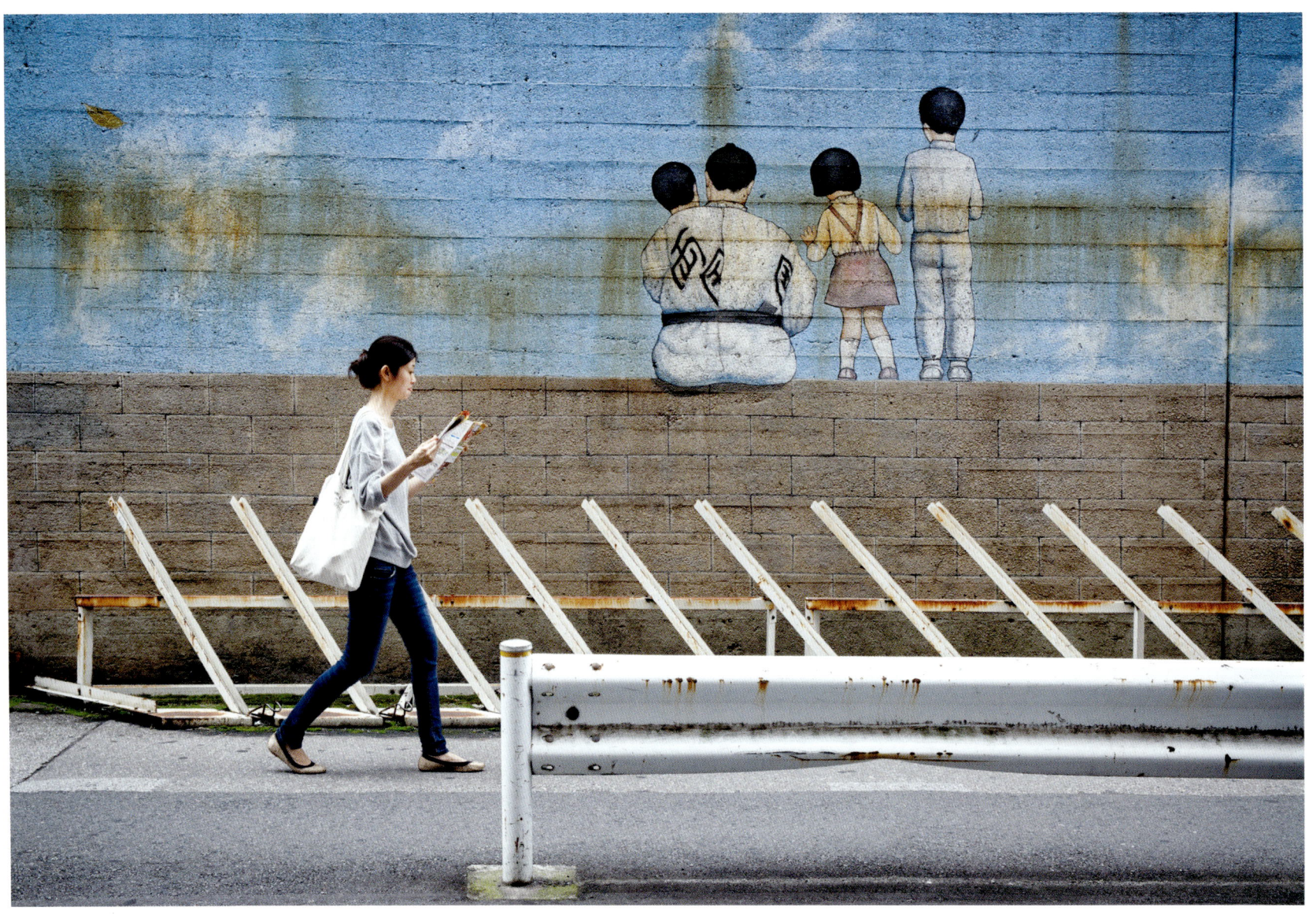

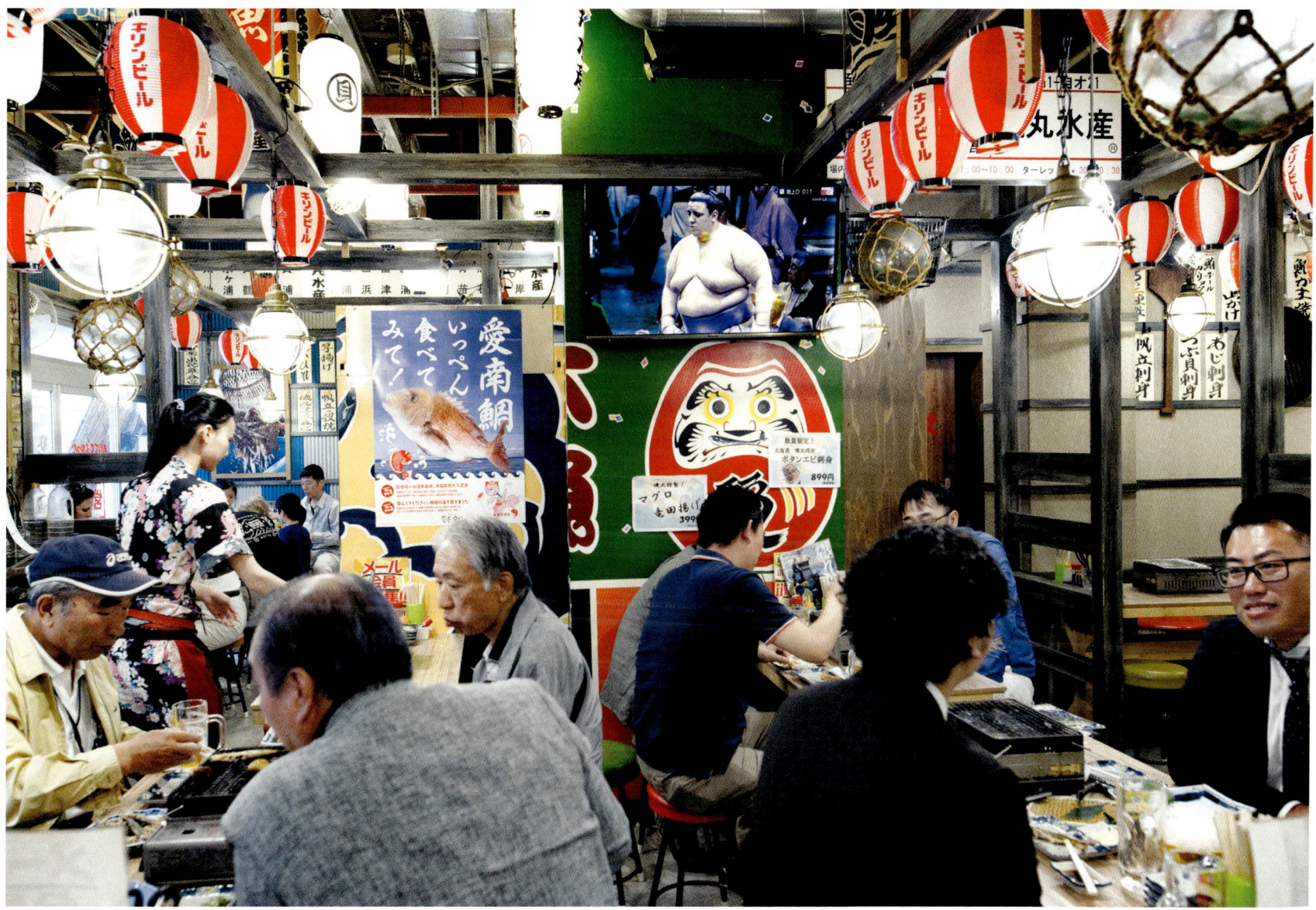

相撲 61

伝統
TRADITION

A *DOHYŌ-IRI* IS A RING ENTERING CEREMONY, PERFORMED ONLY BY HIGH RANKING WRESTLERS BEFORE THE MAIN EVENT IN SUMO TOURNAMENTS.

土俵入りとは、大相撲本場所の取組前に、上位力士だけが行う土俵入りのことである。

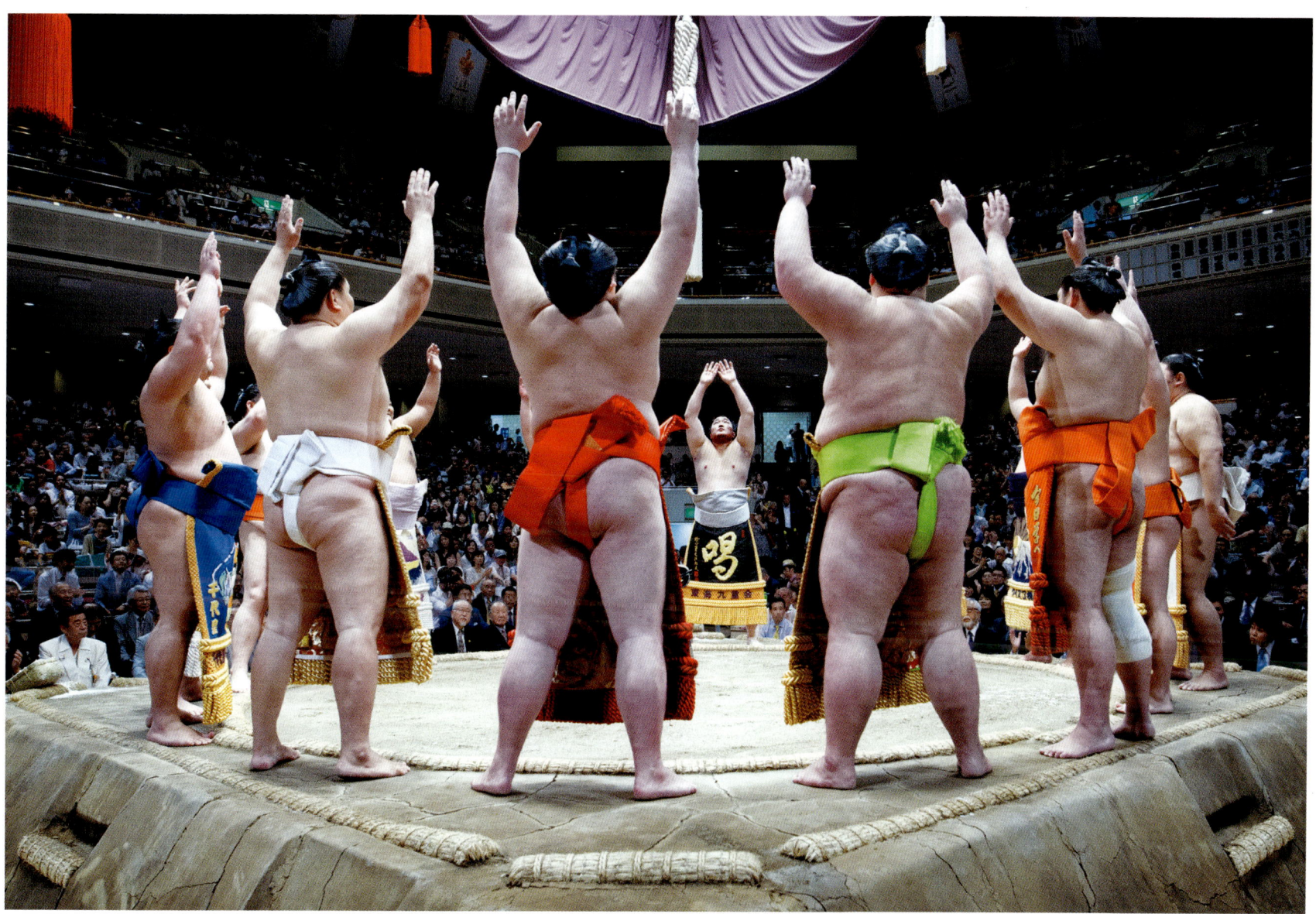

相撲 63

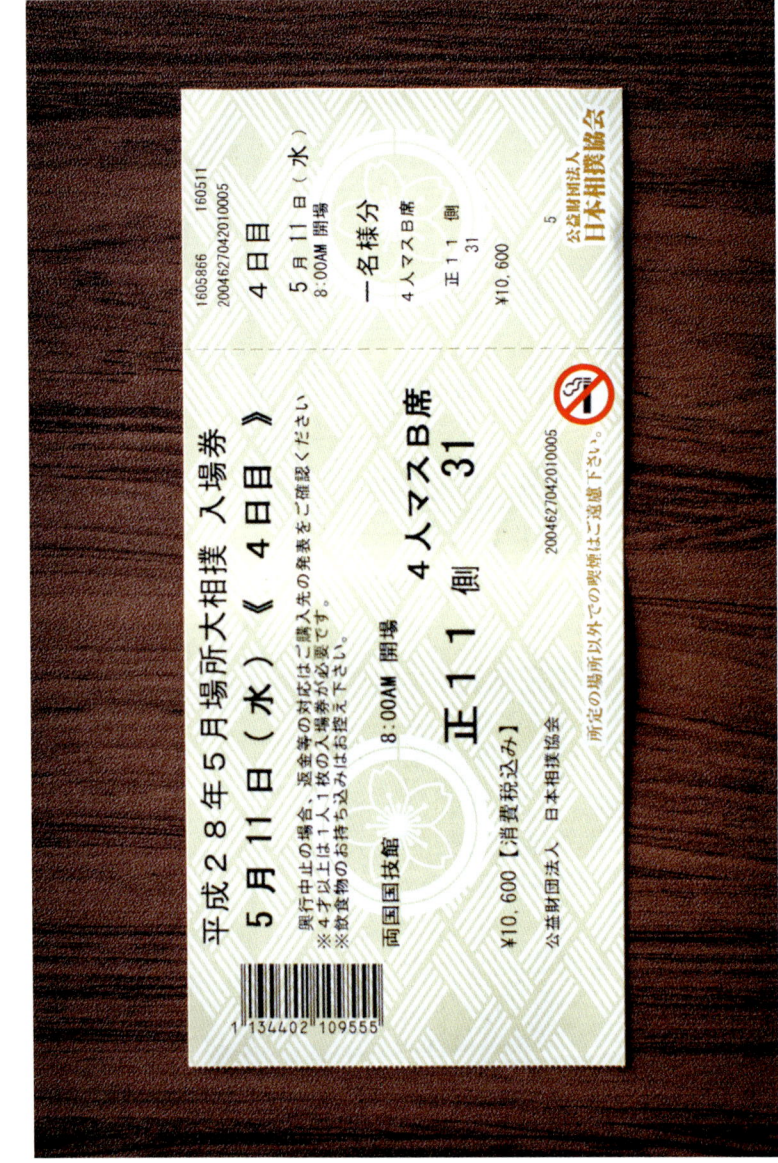

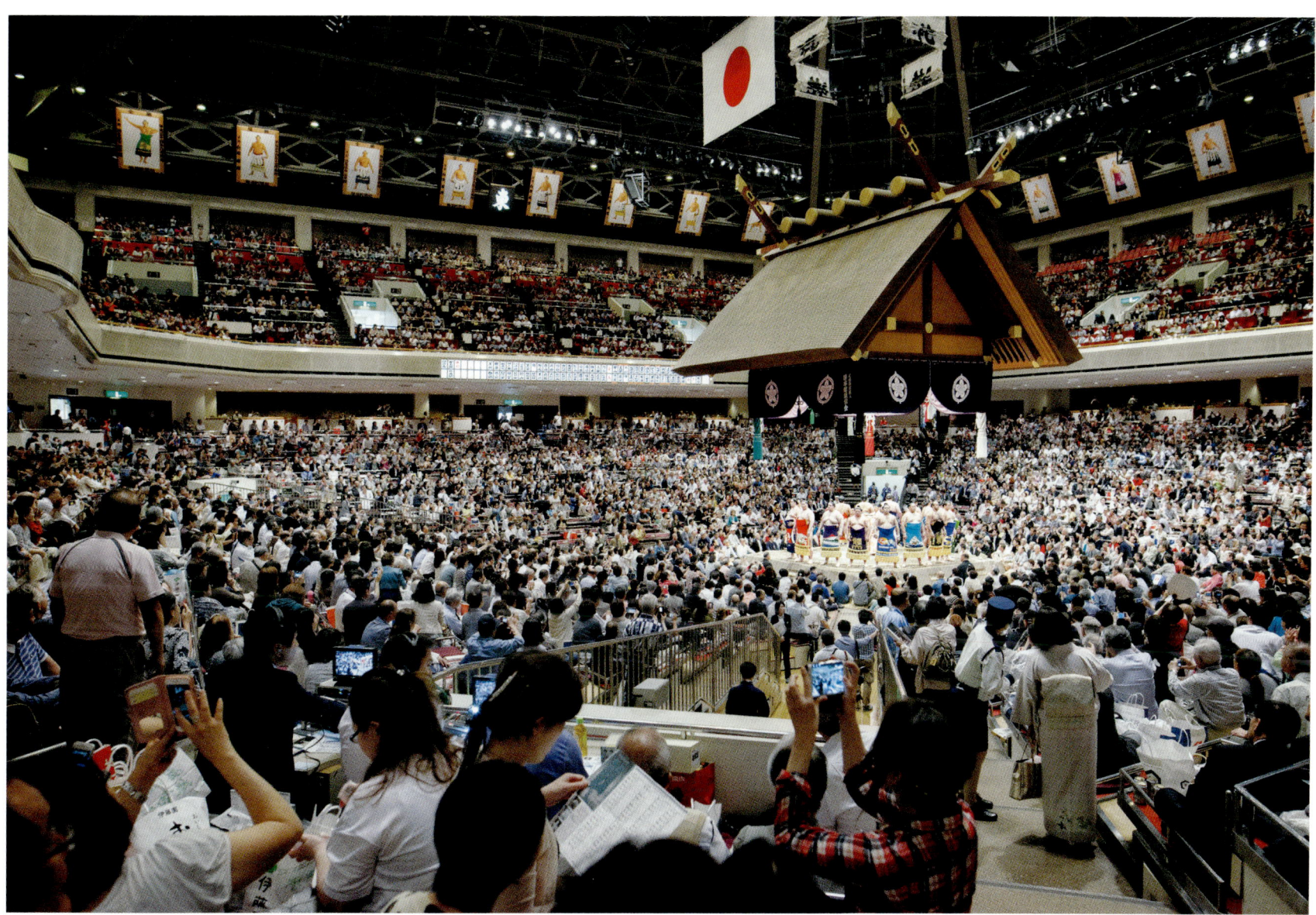

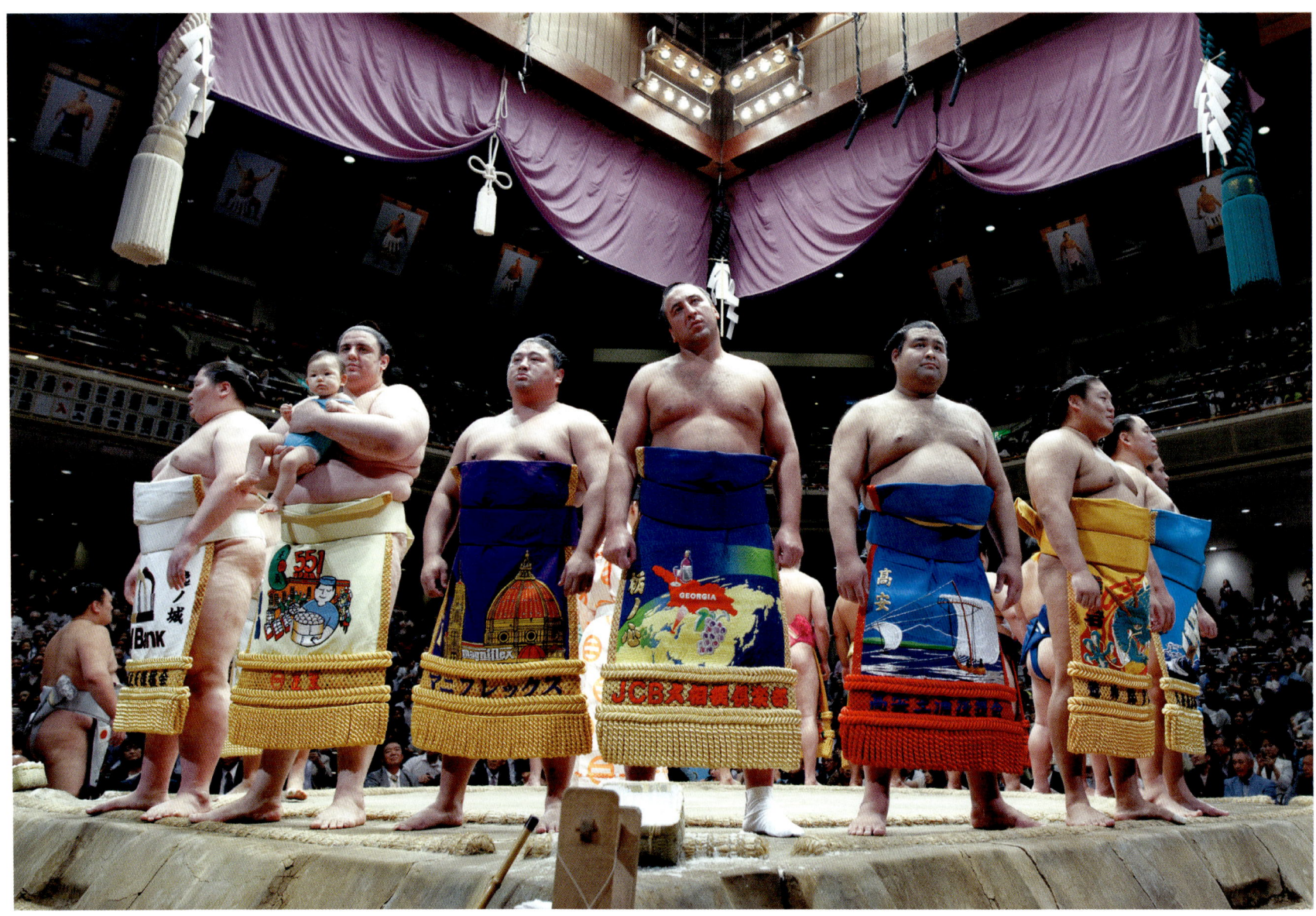

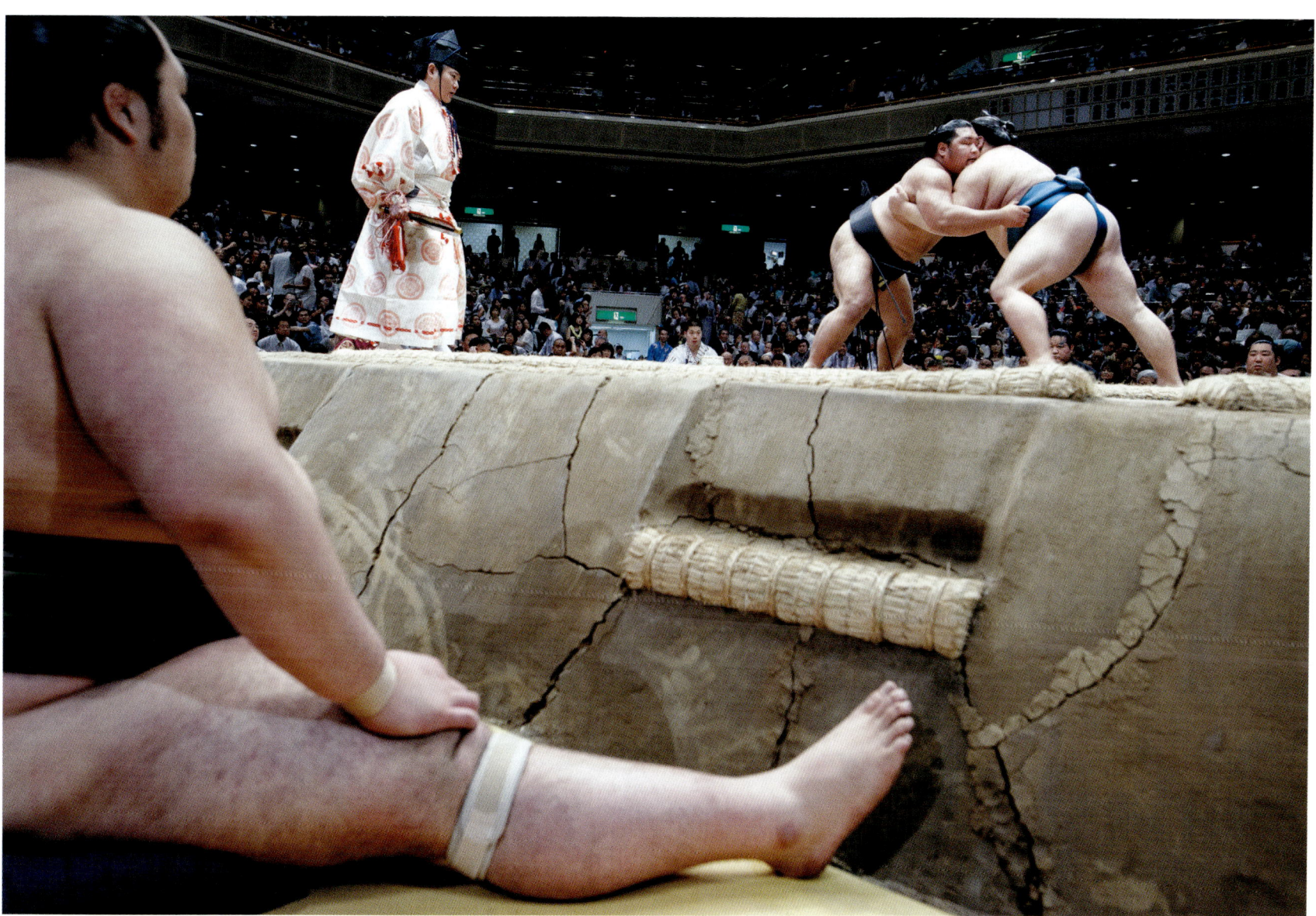

相撲 67

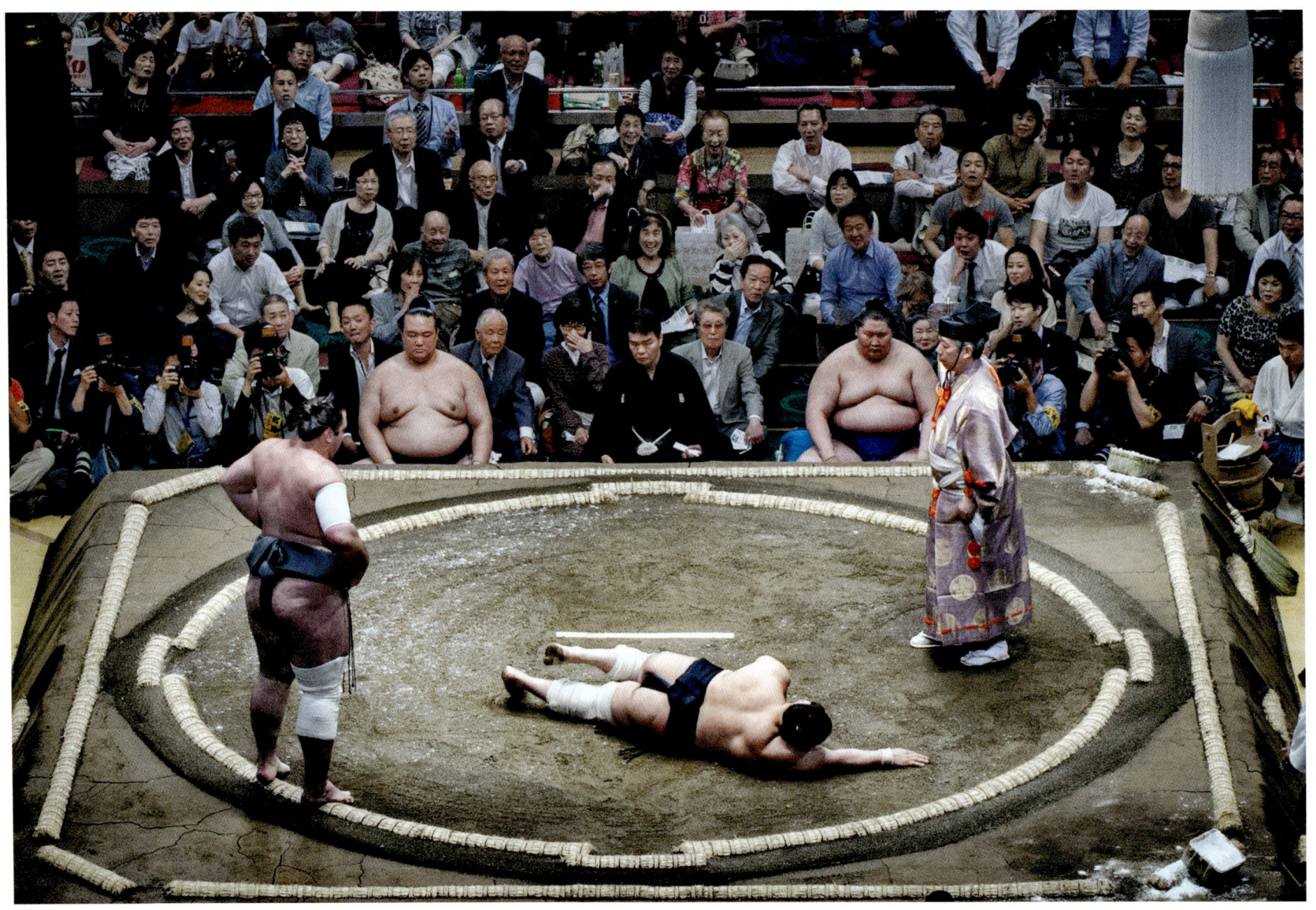

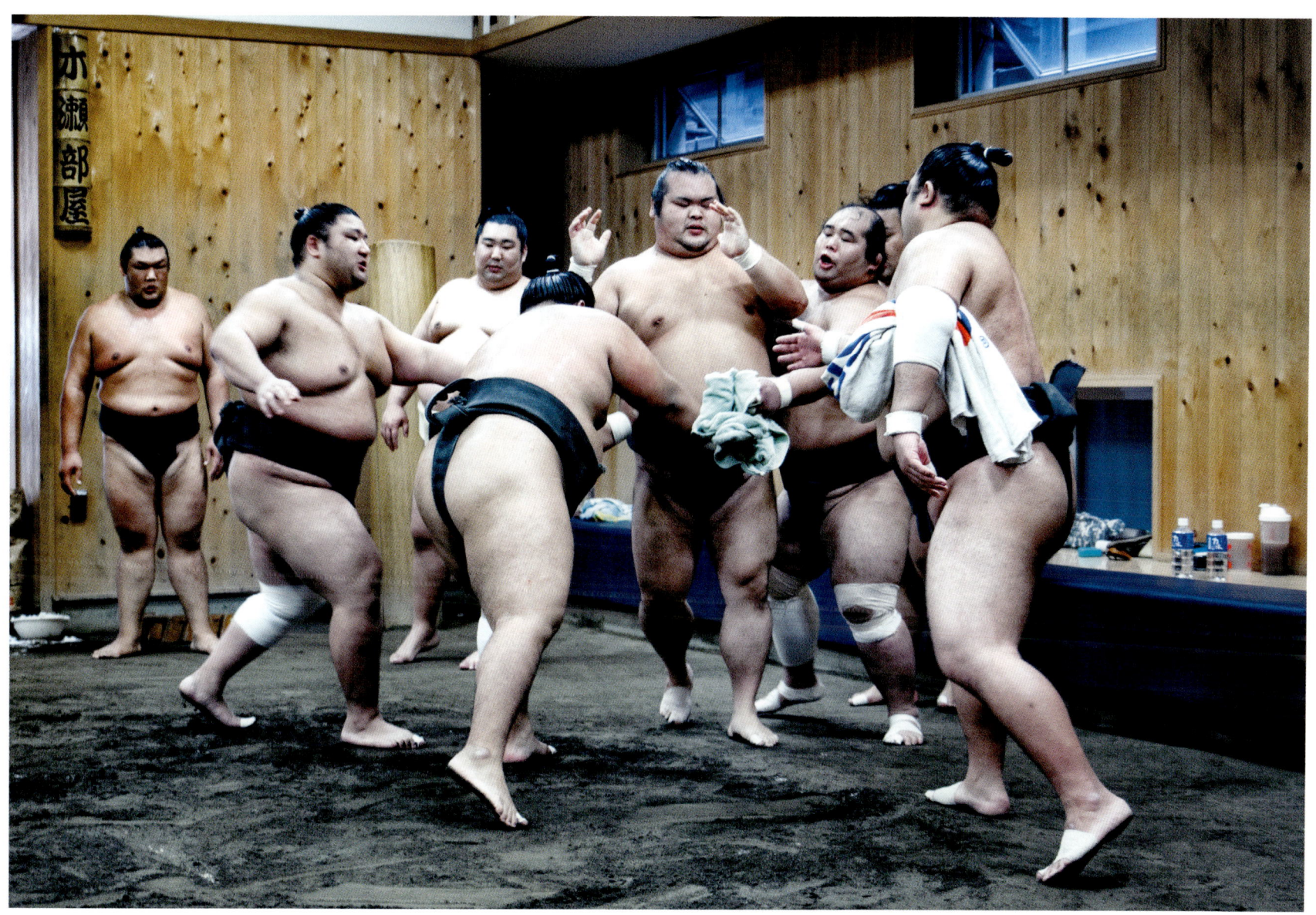

相撲　69

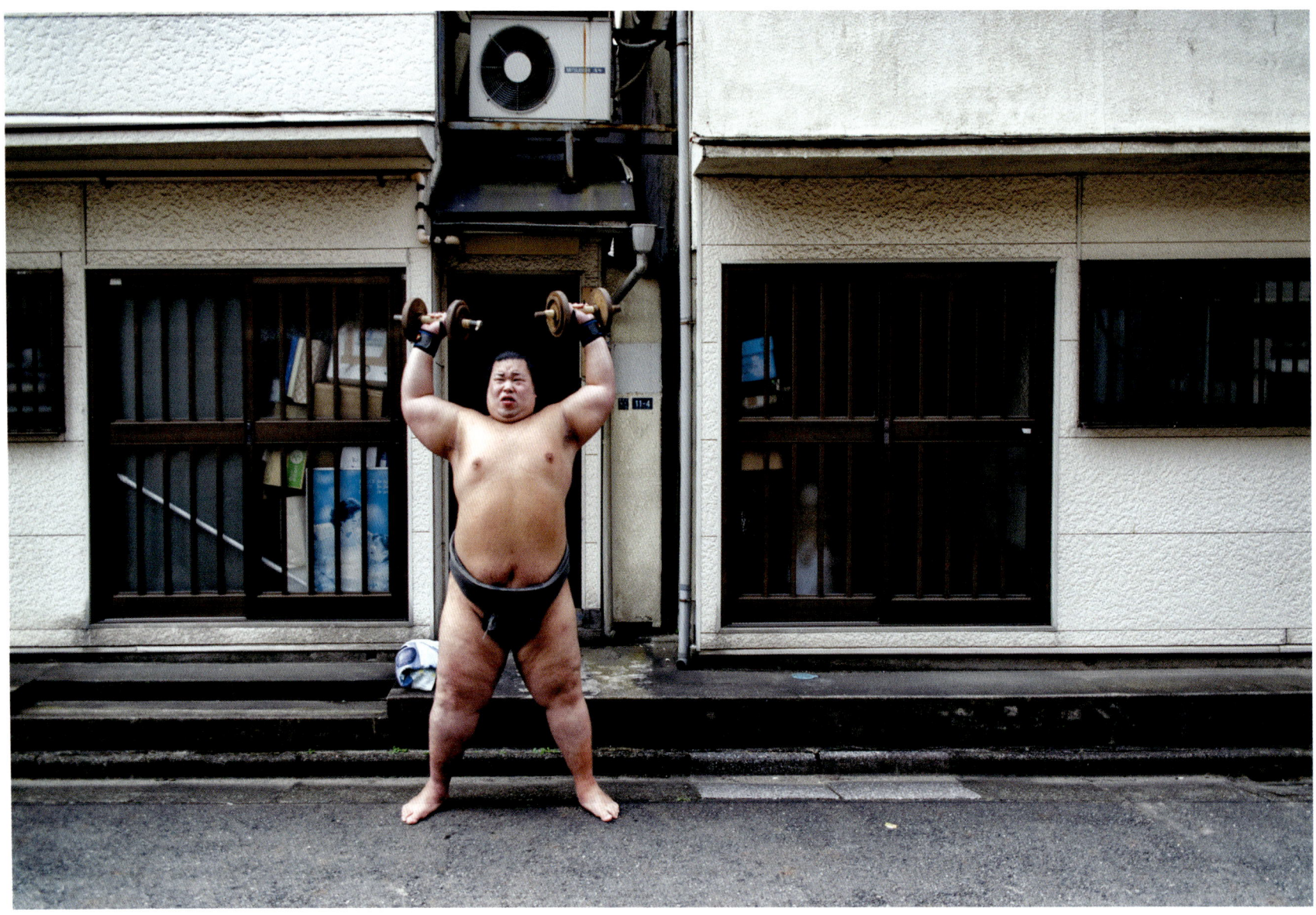

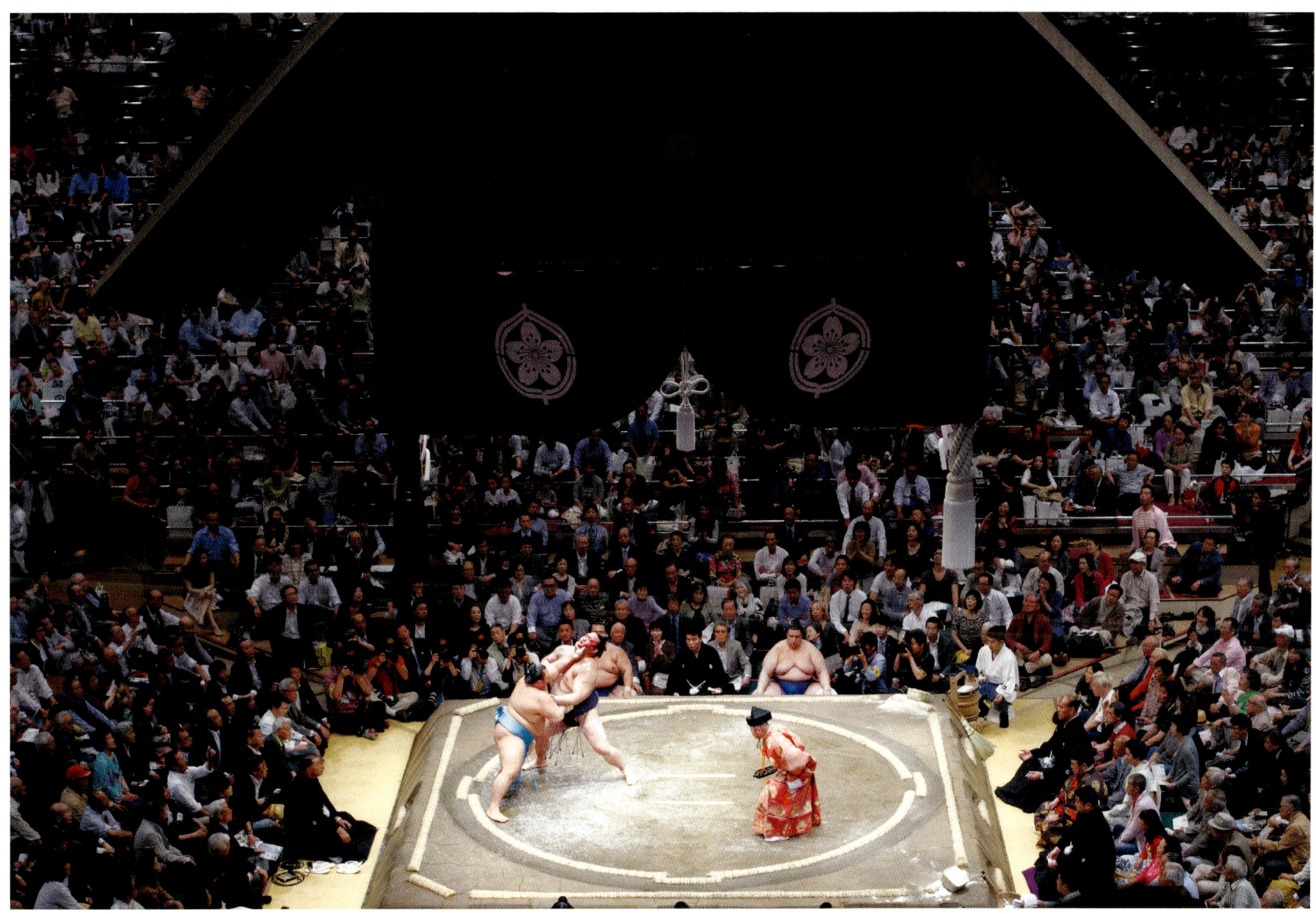

相撲 71

勇士
WARRIOR

A *RIKISHI* STRUGGLES TO HIS FEET DURING A *BUTSUKARI-GEIKO* SESSION. WRESTLERS REGULARLY PUSH EACH OTHER TO THE LIMITS OF THEIR PHYSICAL ENDURANCE IN TRAINING SESSIONS IN ORDER TO BECOME FORMIDABLE WARRIORS.

ぶつかり稽古で奮闘する力士。稽古中、力士達は互いに強靭な戦士を目指し、体力の限界まで互いに刺激し合う。

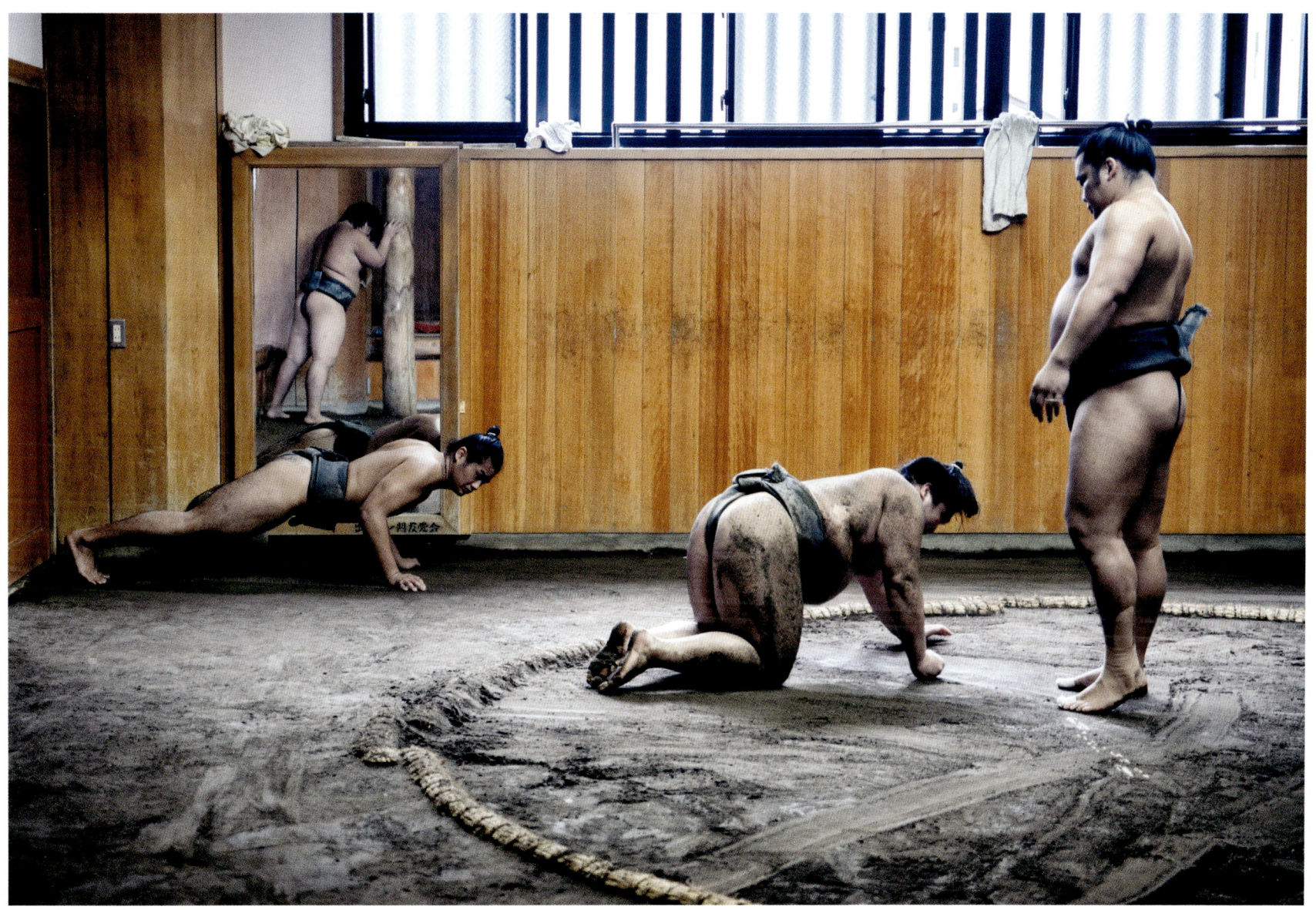

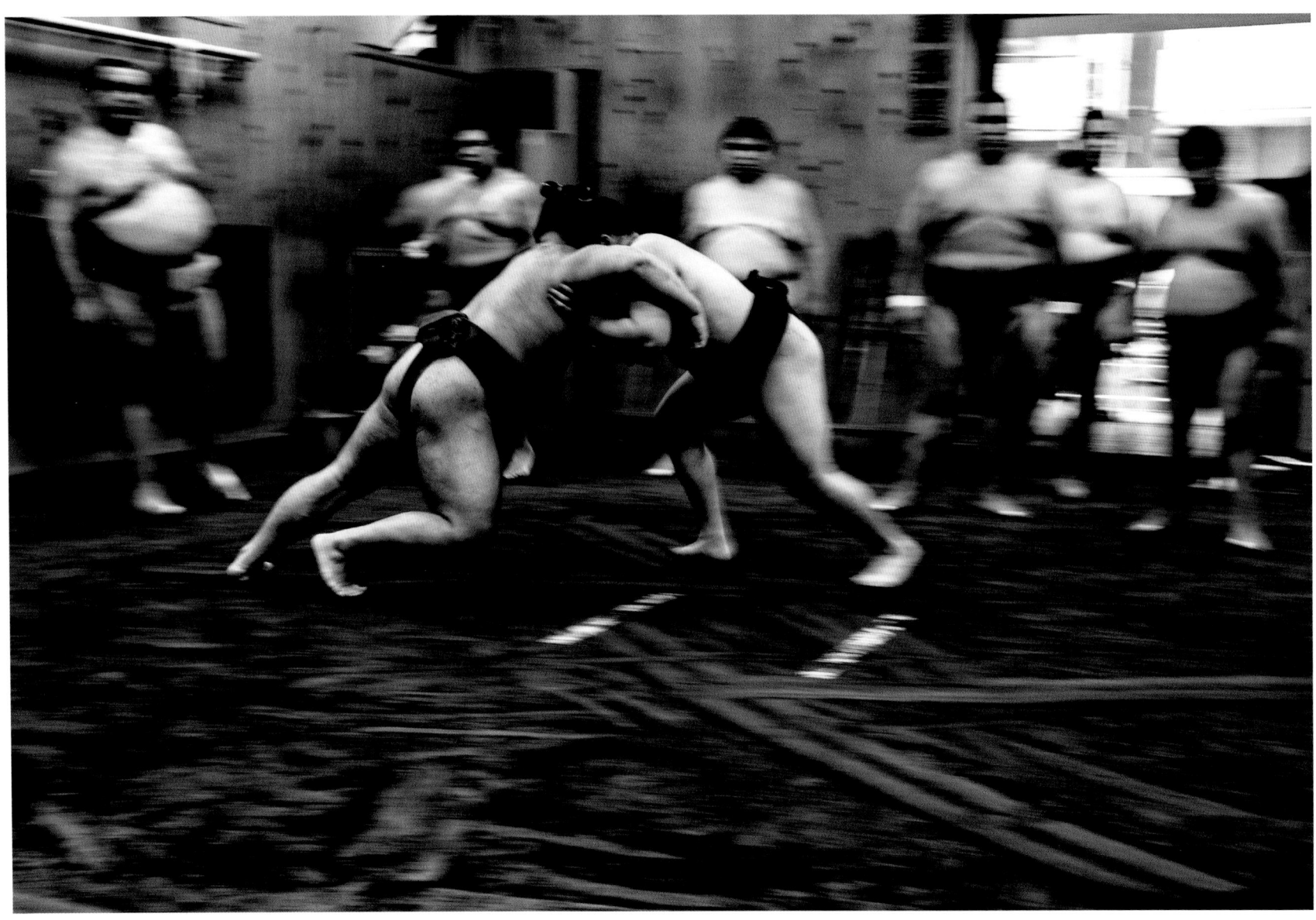

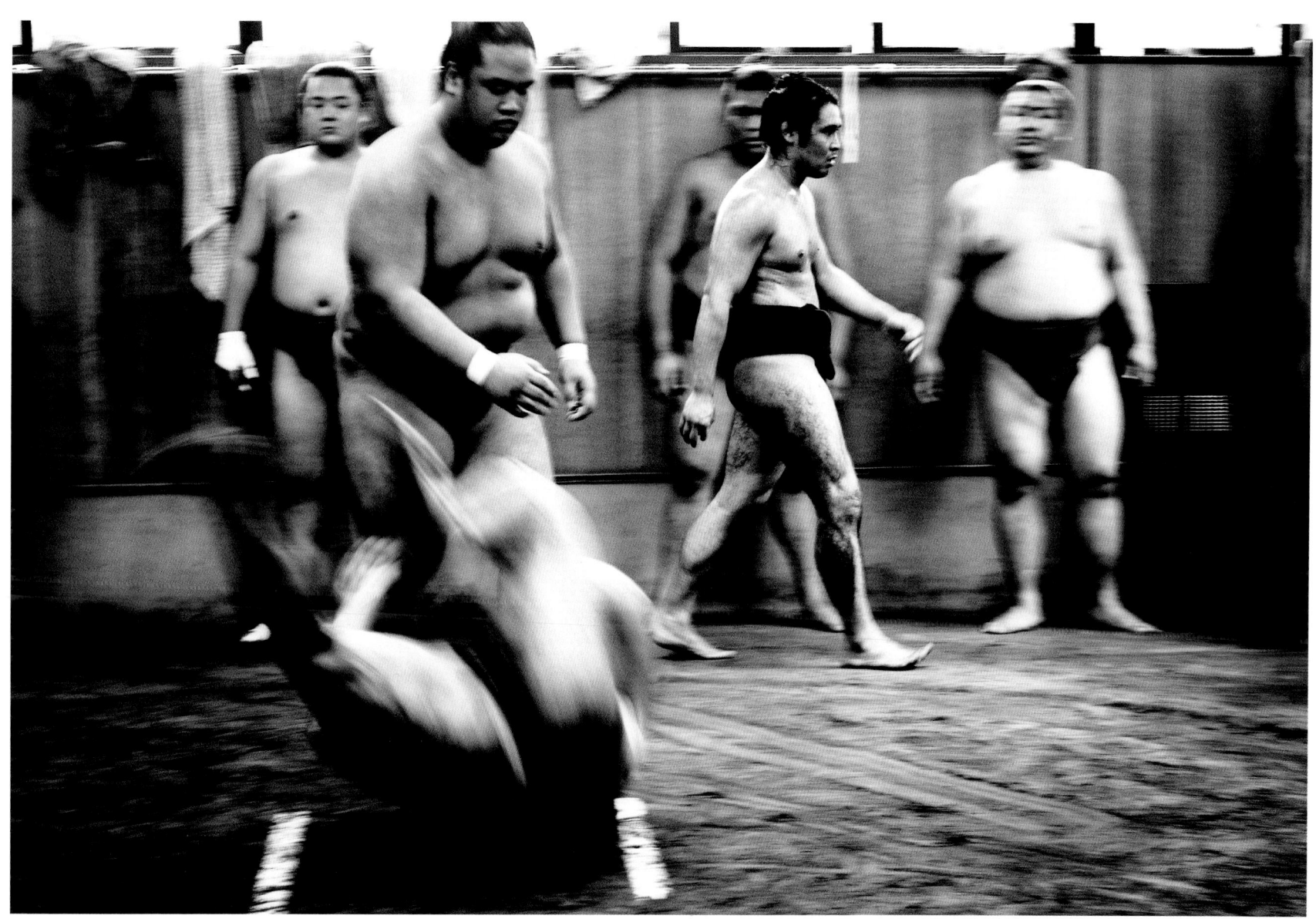

相撲 75

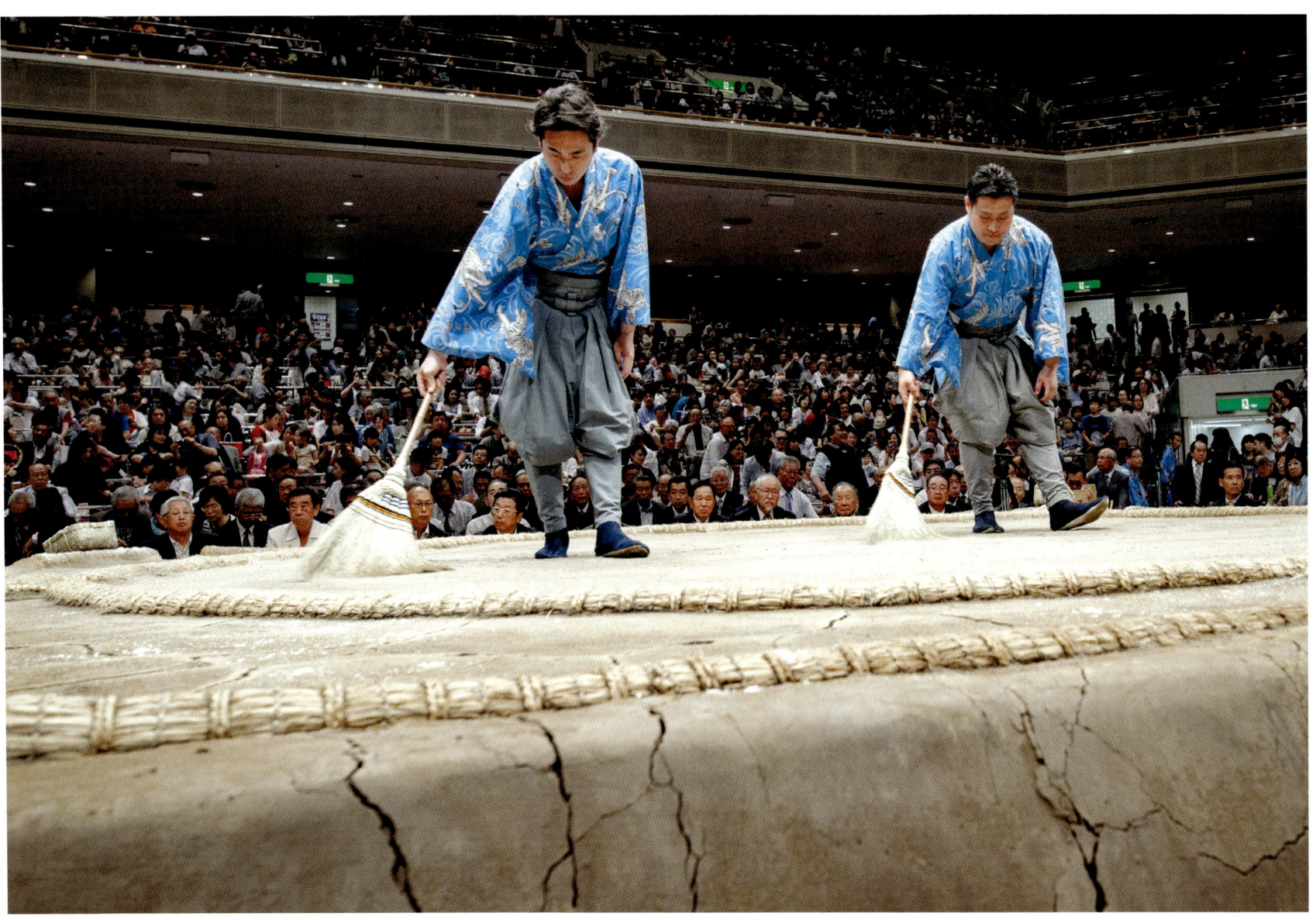

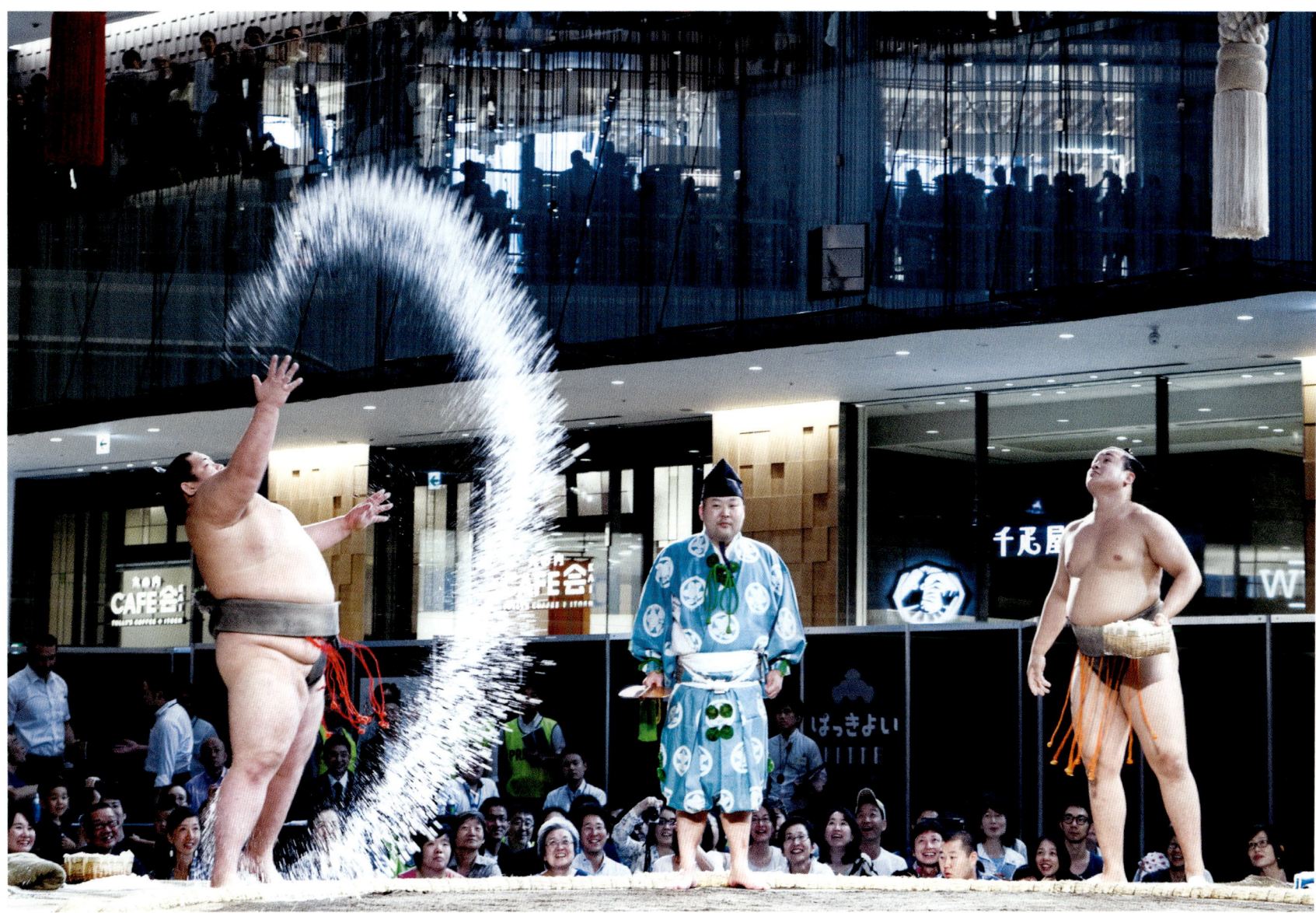

相撲 77

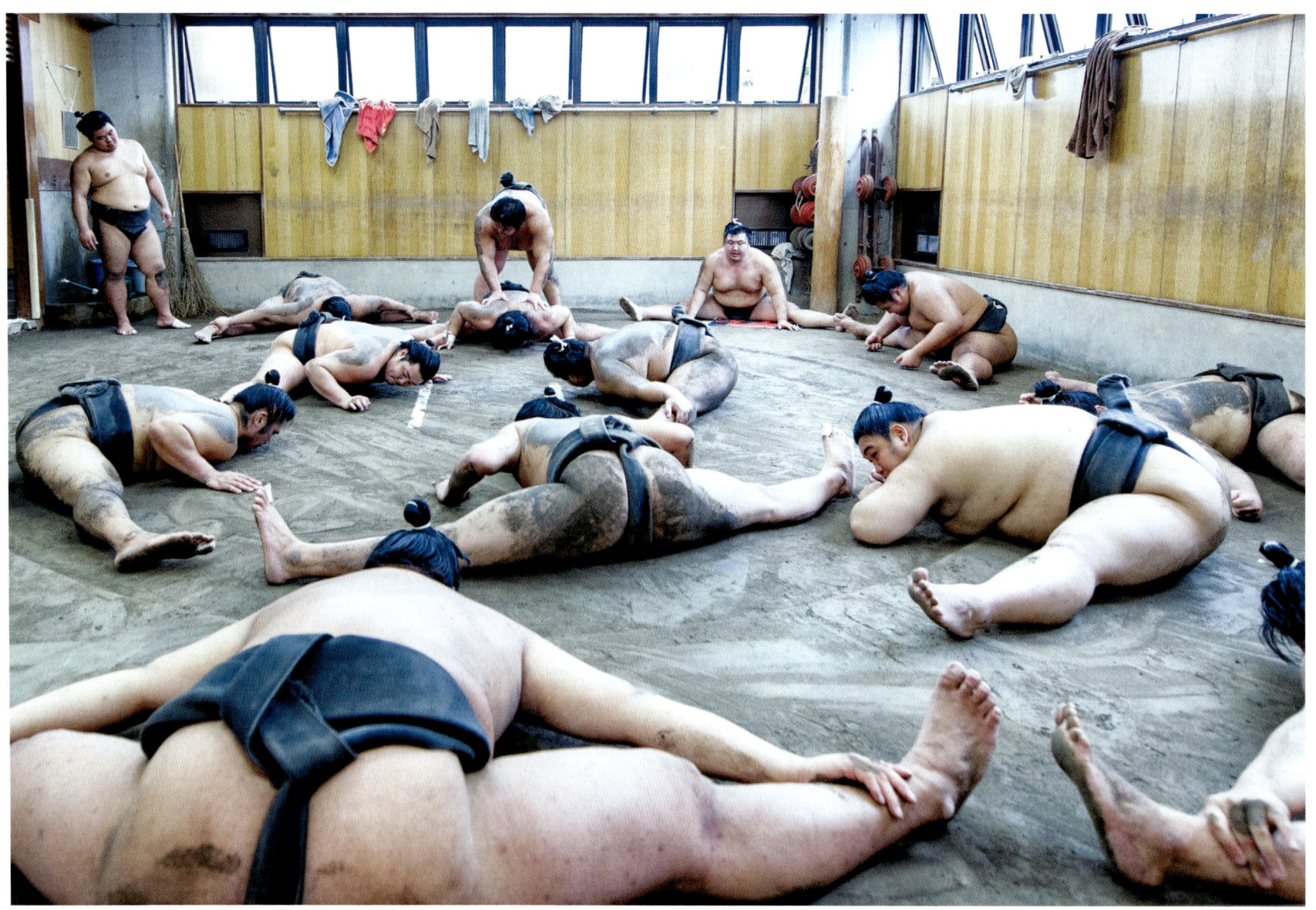

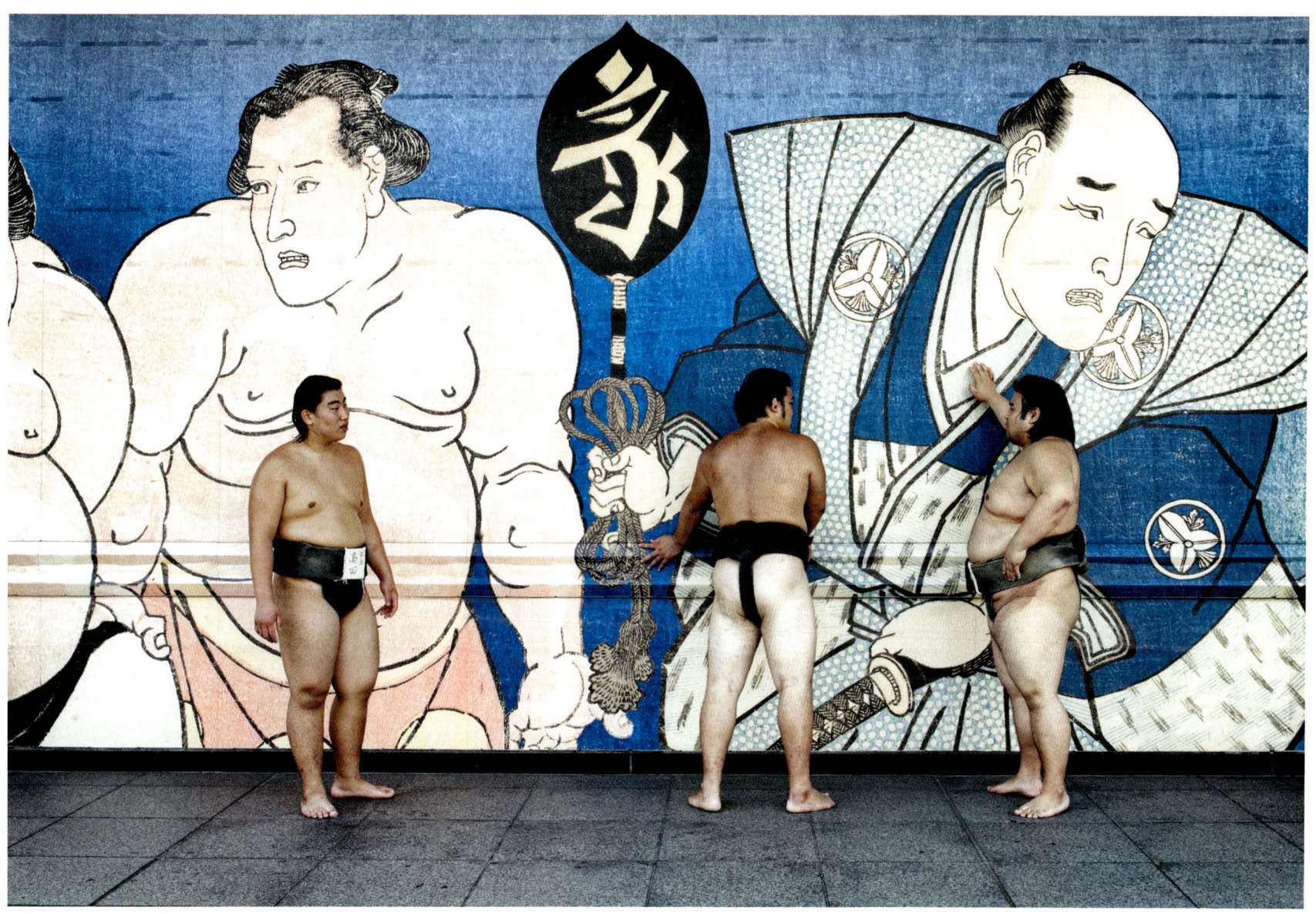

相撲 79

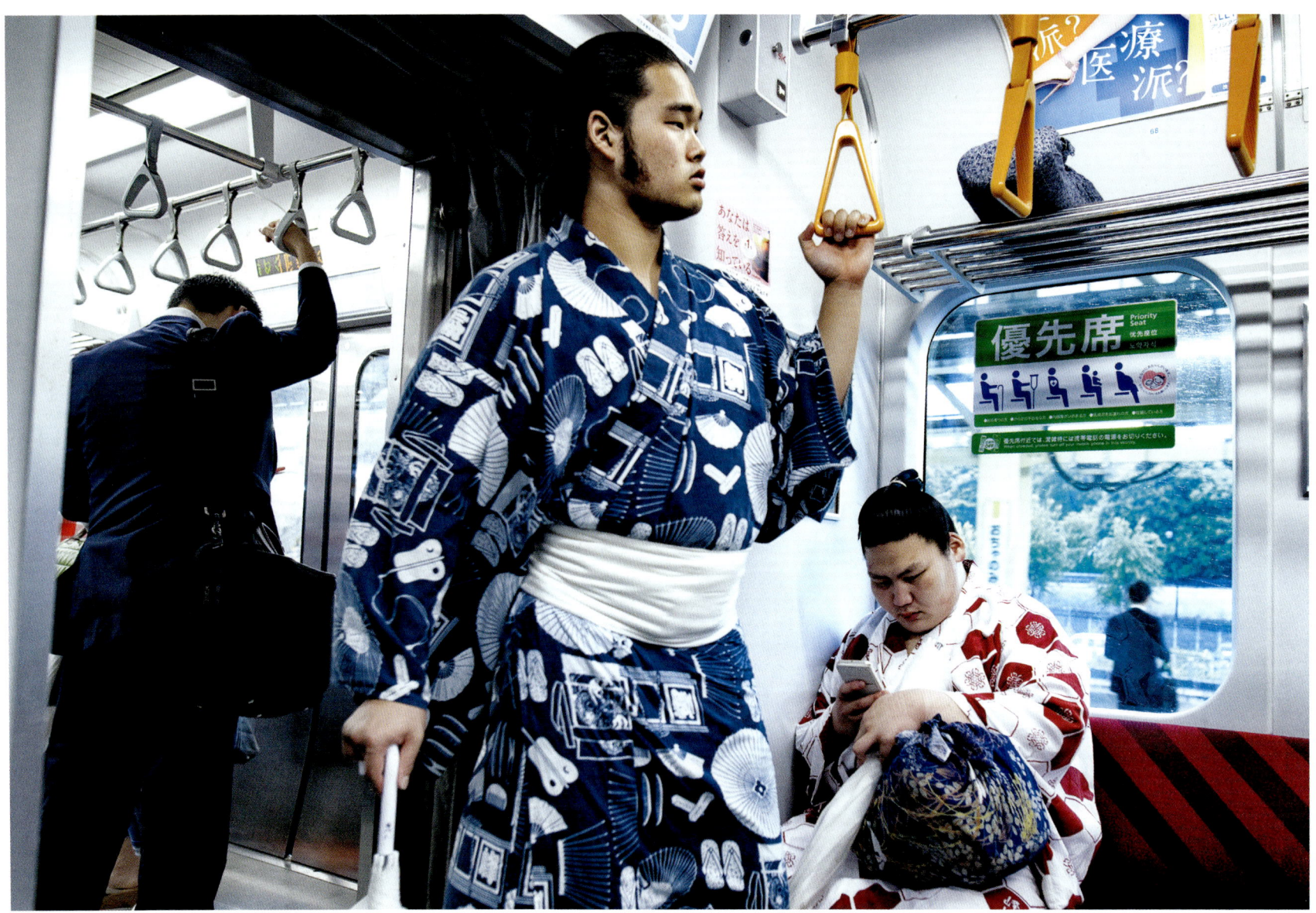

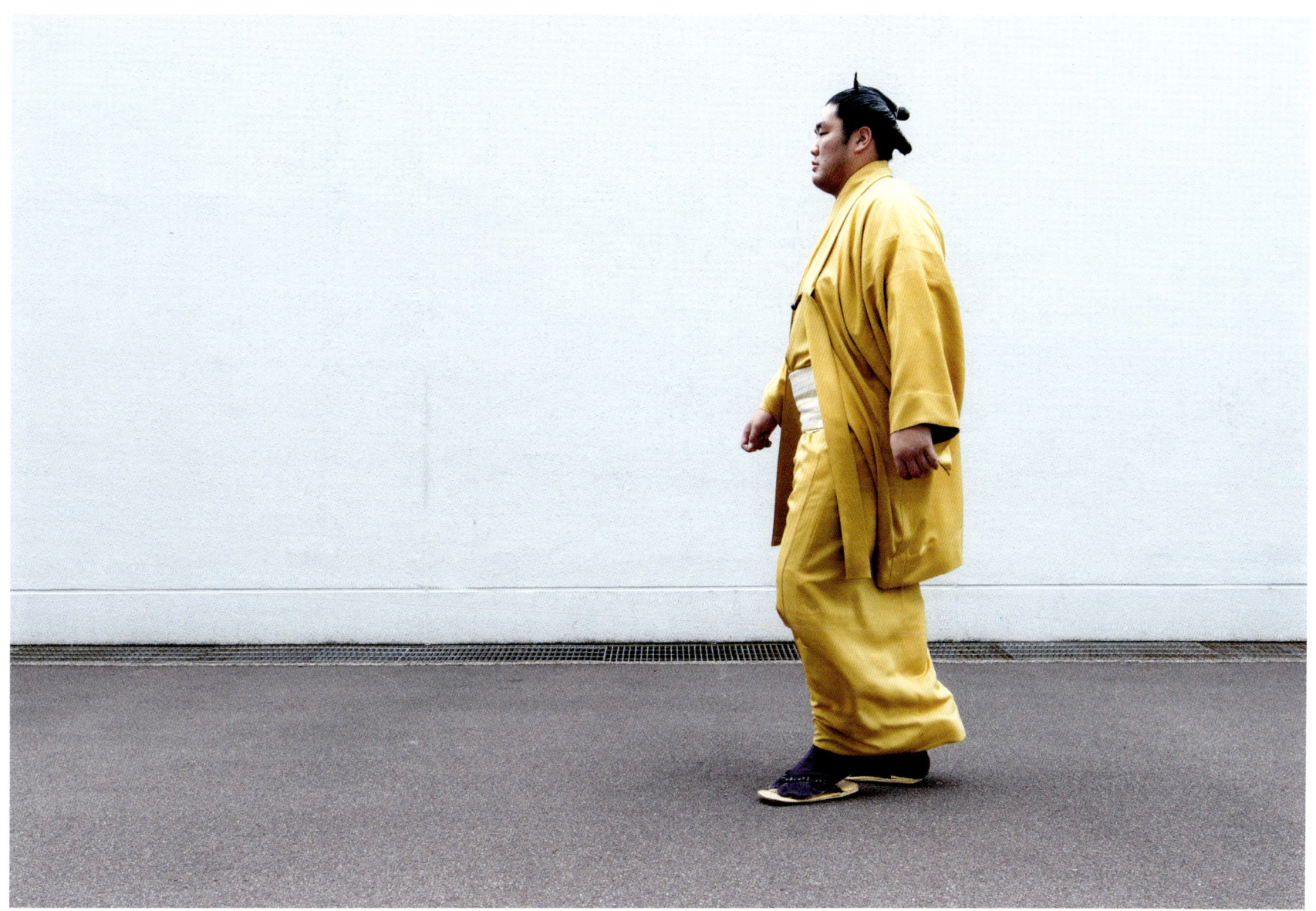

相撲　81

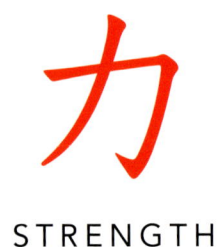

STRENGTH

A *RIKISHI* AT FUJISHIMA *BEYA* PERFORMS *SHIKO* DURING TRAINING IN ORDER TO STRENGTHEN HIS STANCE.

構えを強くするために四股を踏む藤島部屋の力士。

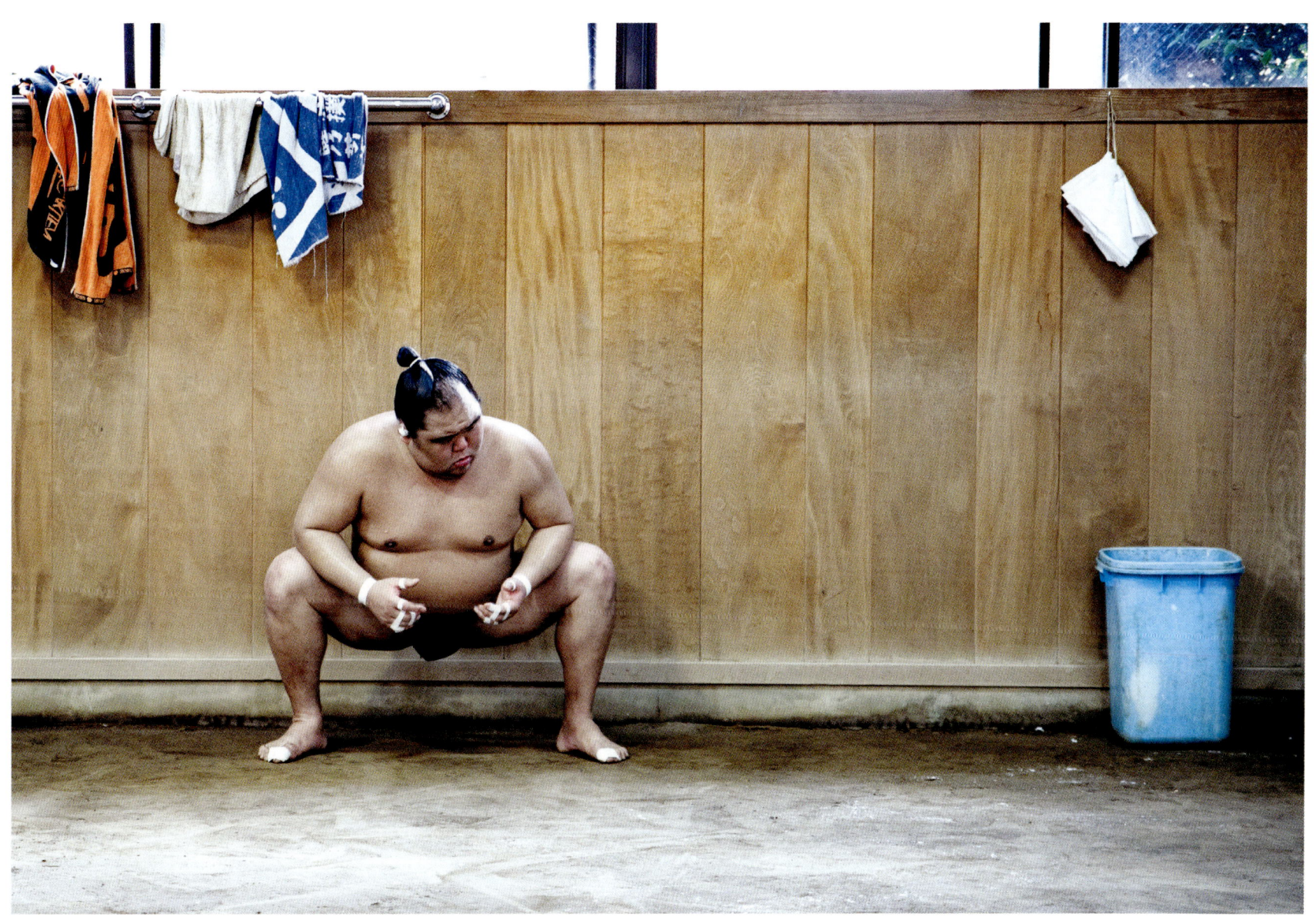

相撲 83

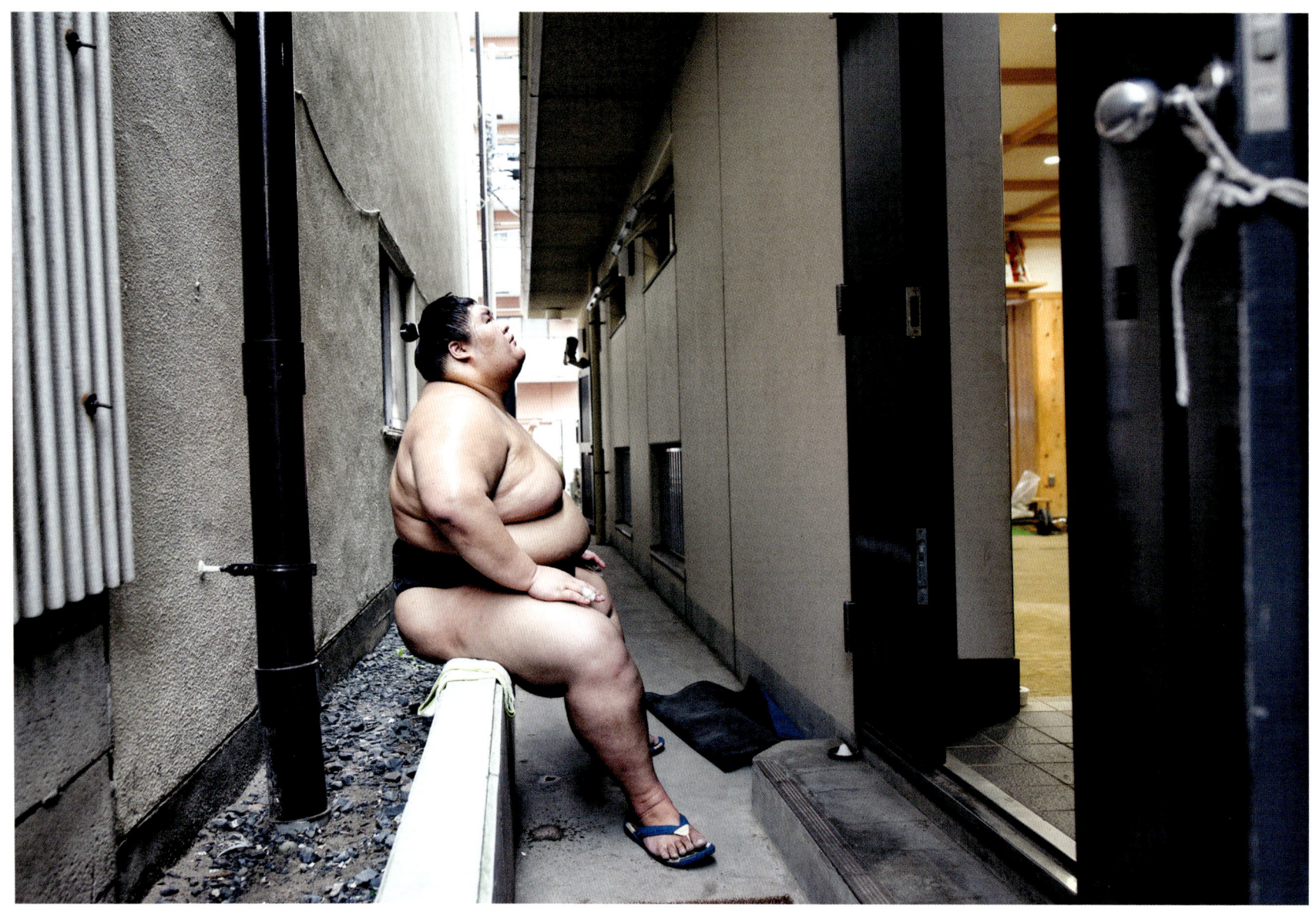

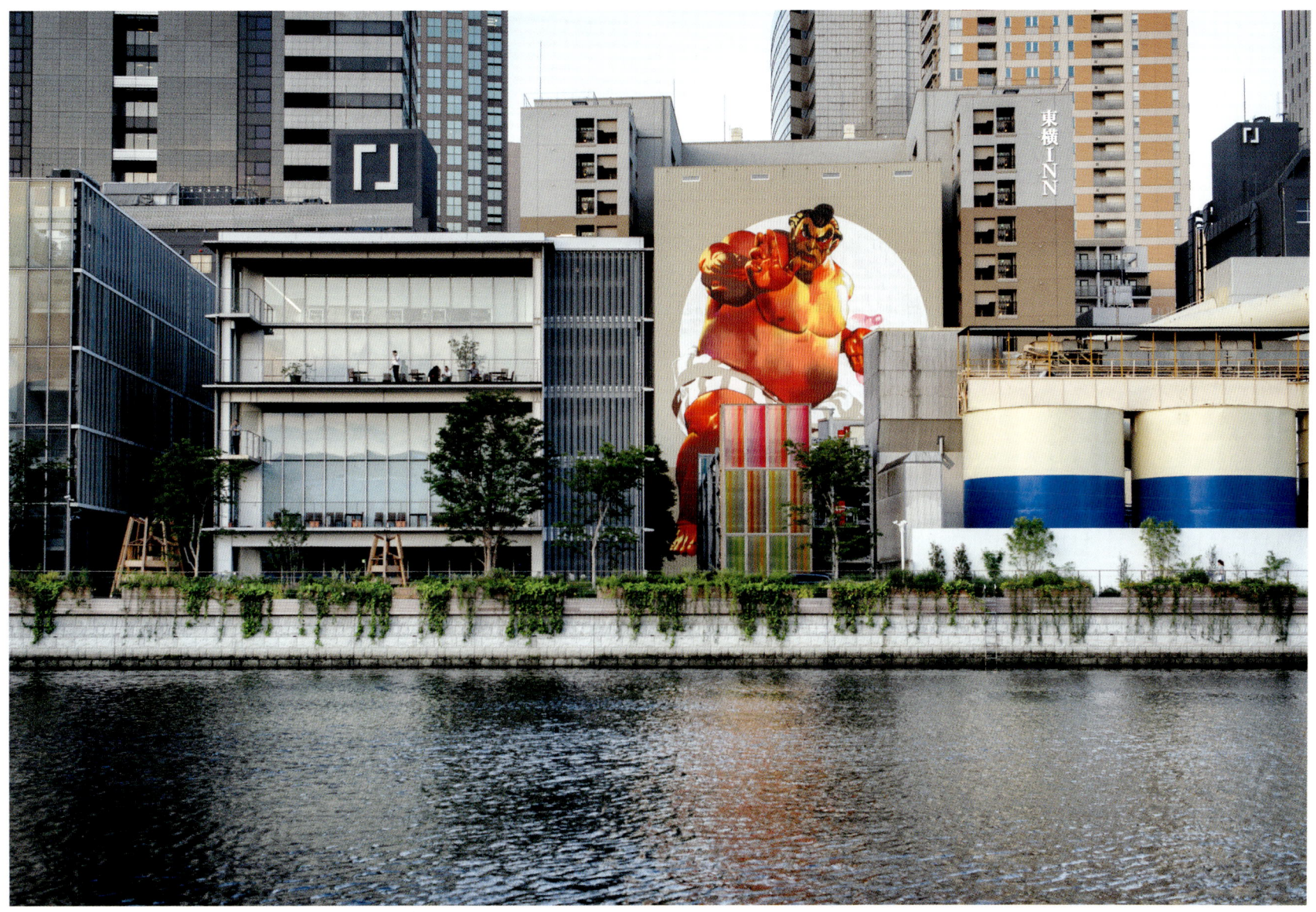

相撲　85

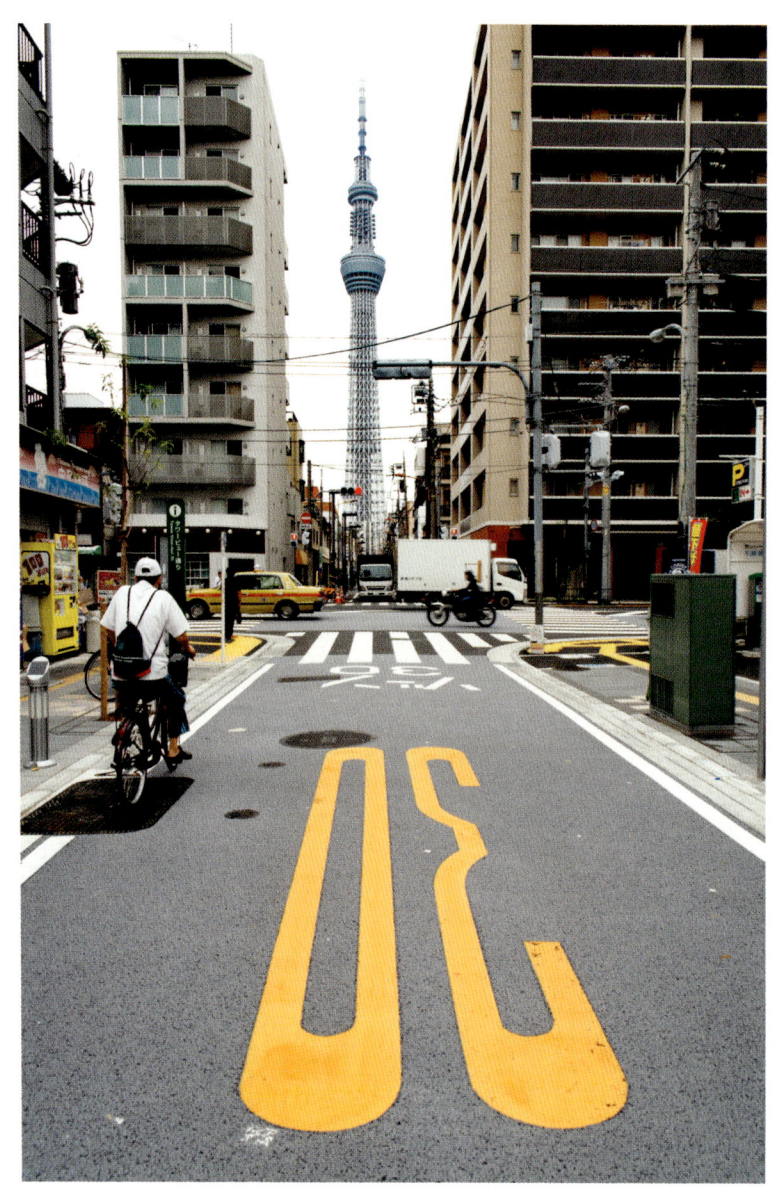

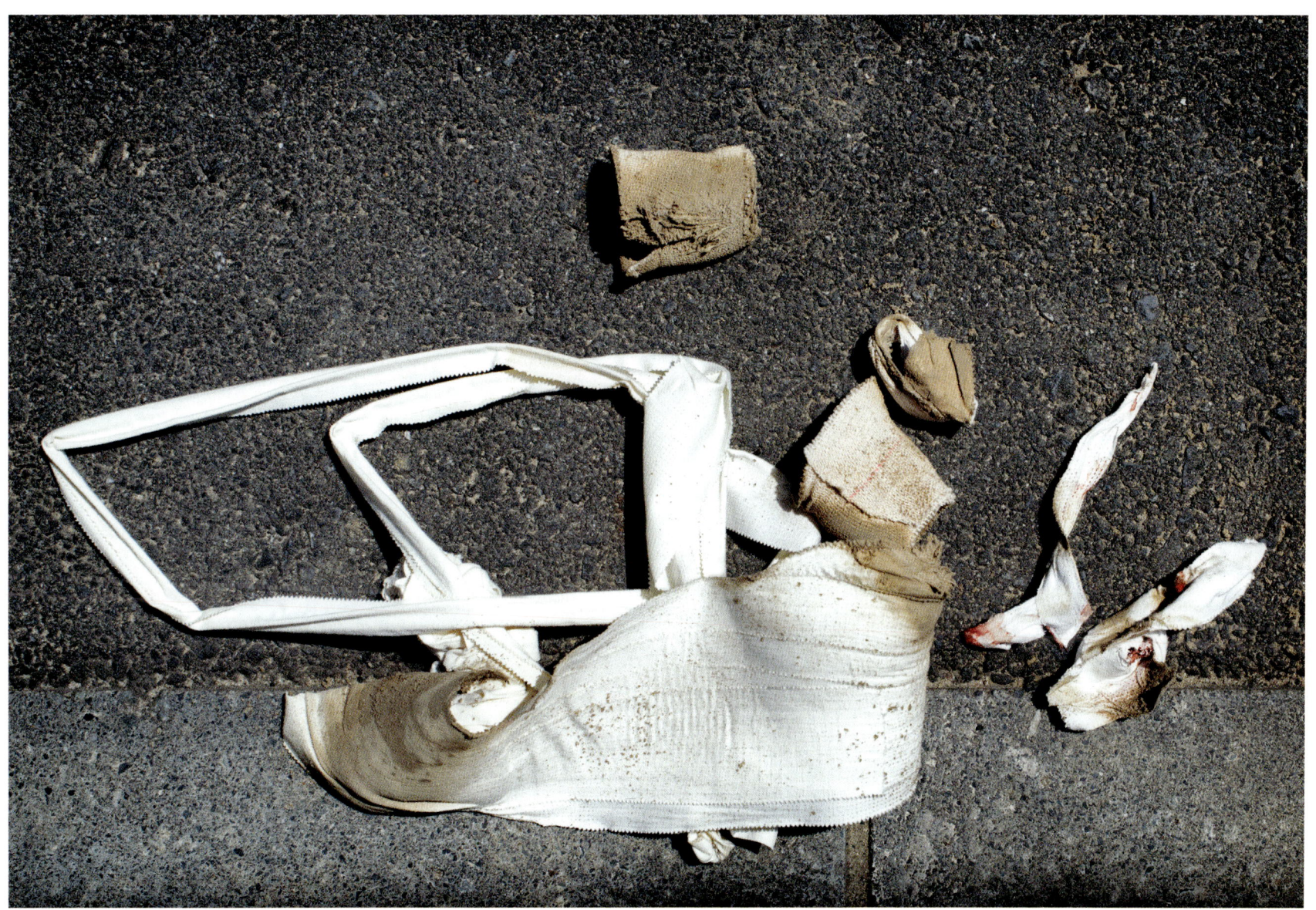

相撲 87

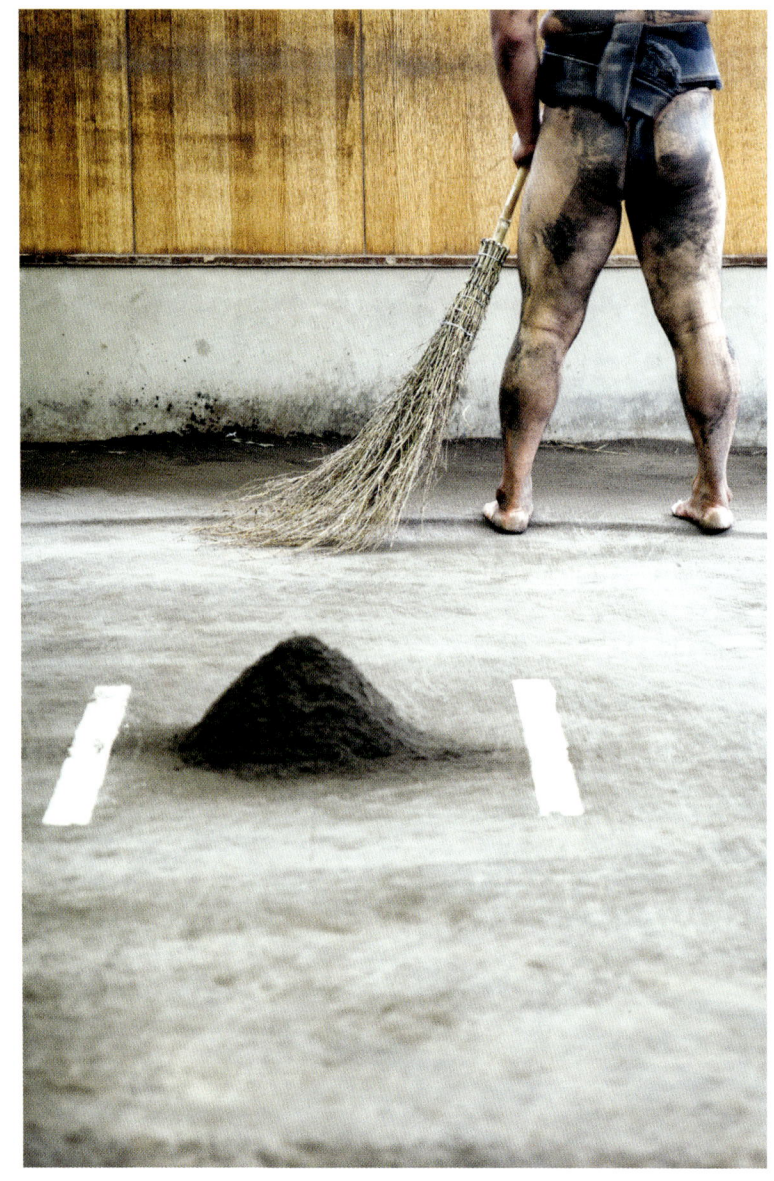

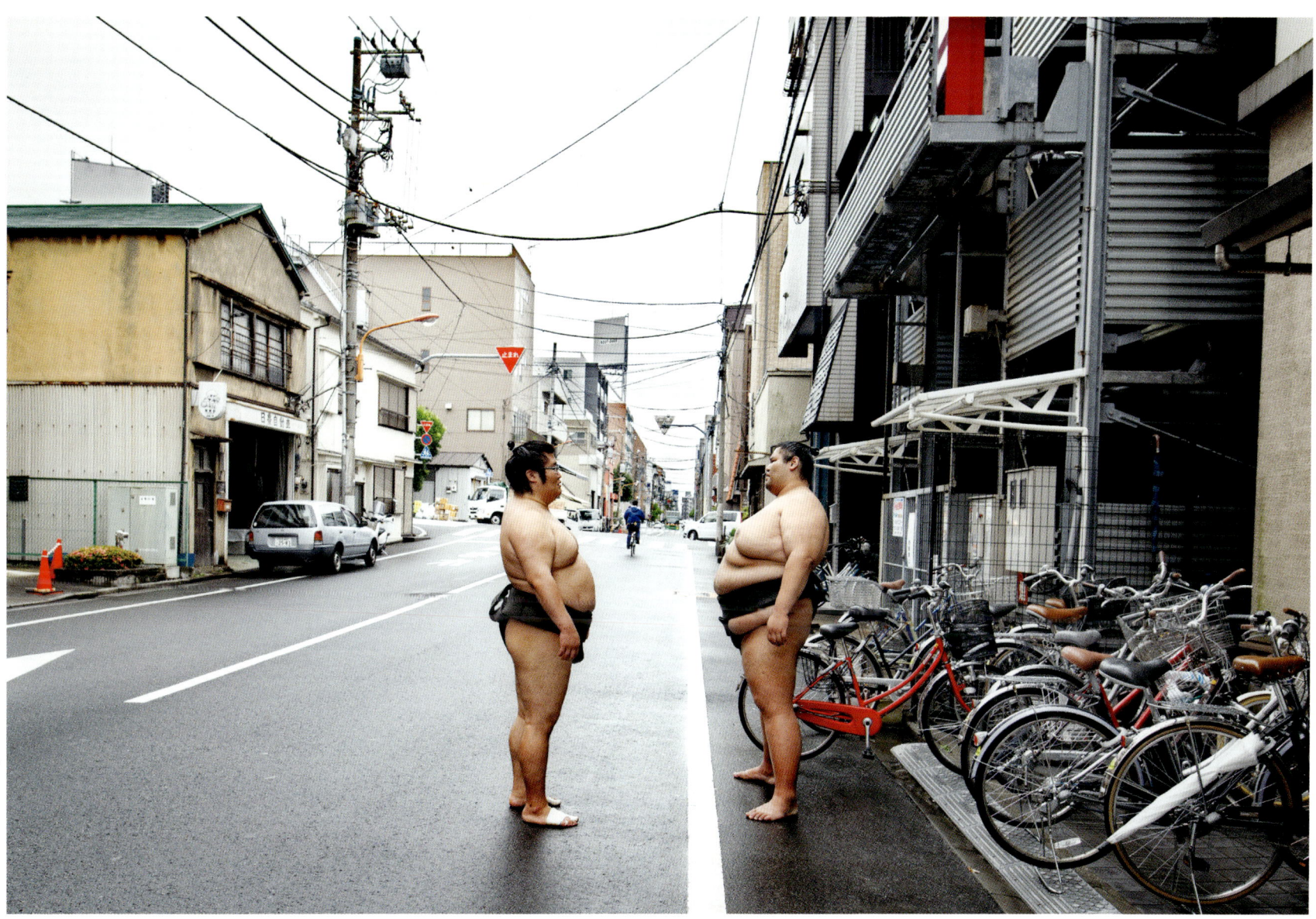

相撲 89

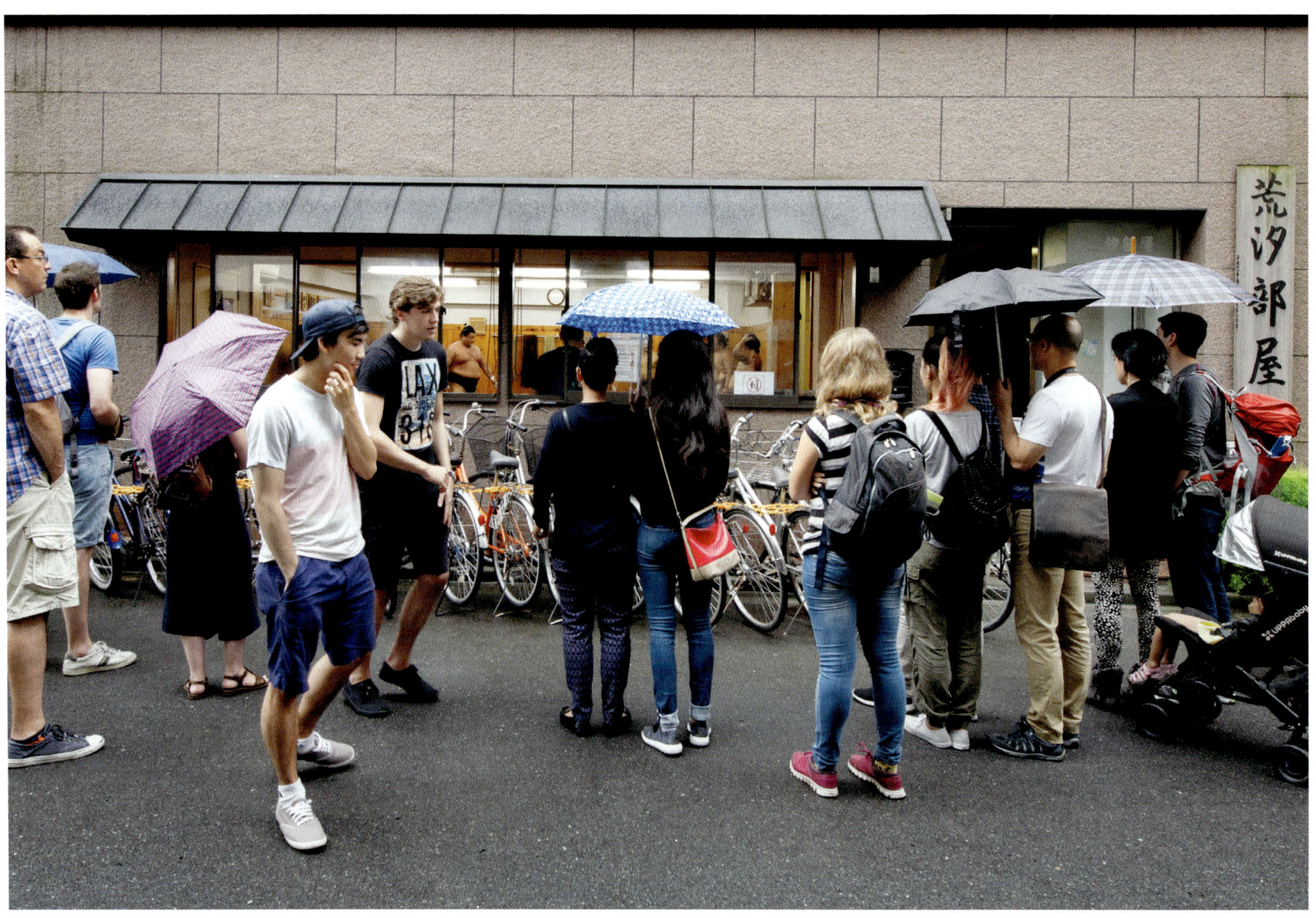

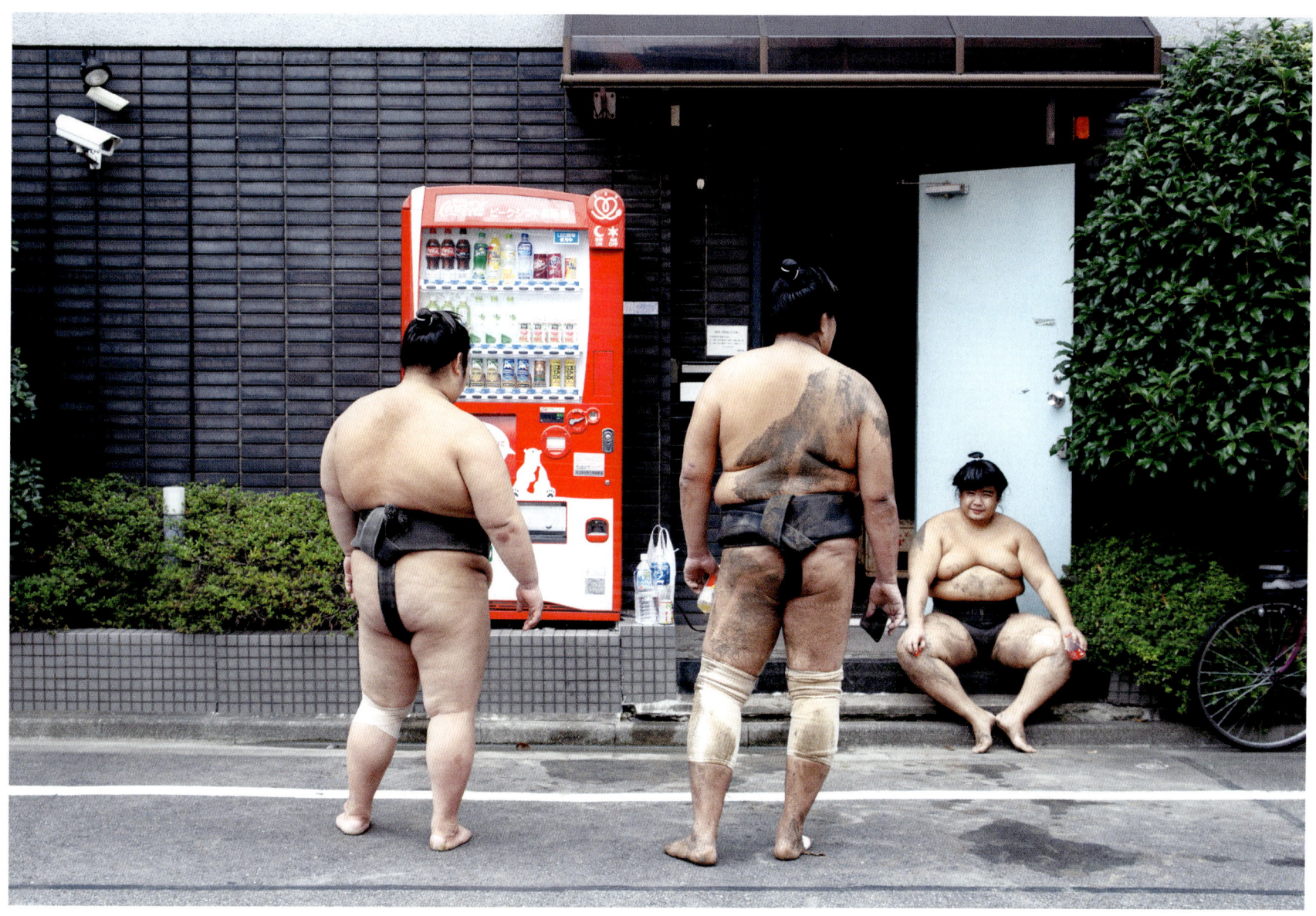

相撲 91

栄誉
HONOR

FANS FILL THE KOKUGIKAN STADIUM TO CAPACITY IN ORDER TO HONOUR KYOKUTENHŌ DURING HIS *DANPATSU-SHIKI*. THE NEXT GENERATION LOOKS UP IN AWE AT ONE OF THE ALL-TIME FAVOURITES.

旭天鵬を称えて、断髪式には国技館は多くのファンで埋め尽くされた。次世代の子ども達が史上最高の力士の一人として畏敬の念で彼を見上げている。

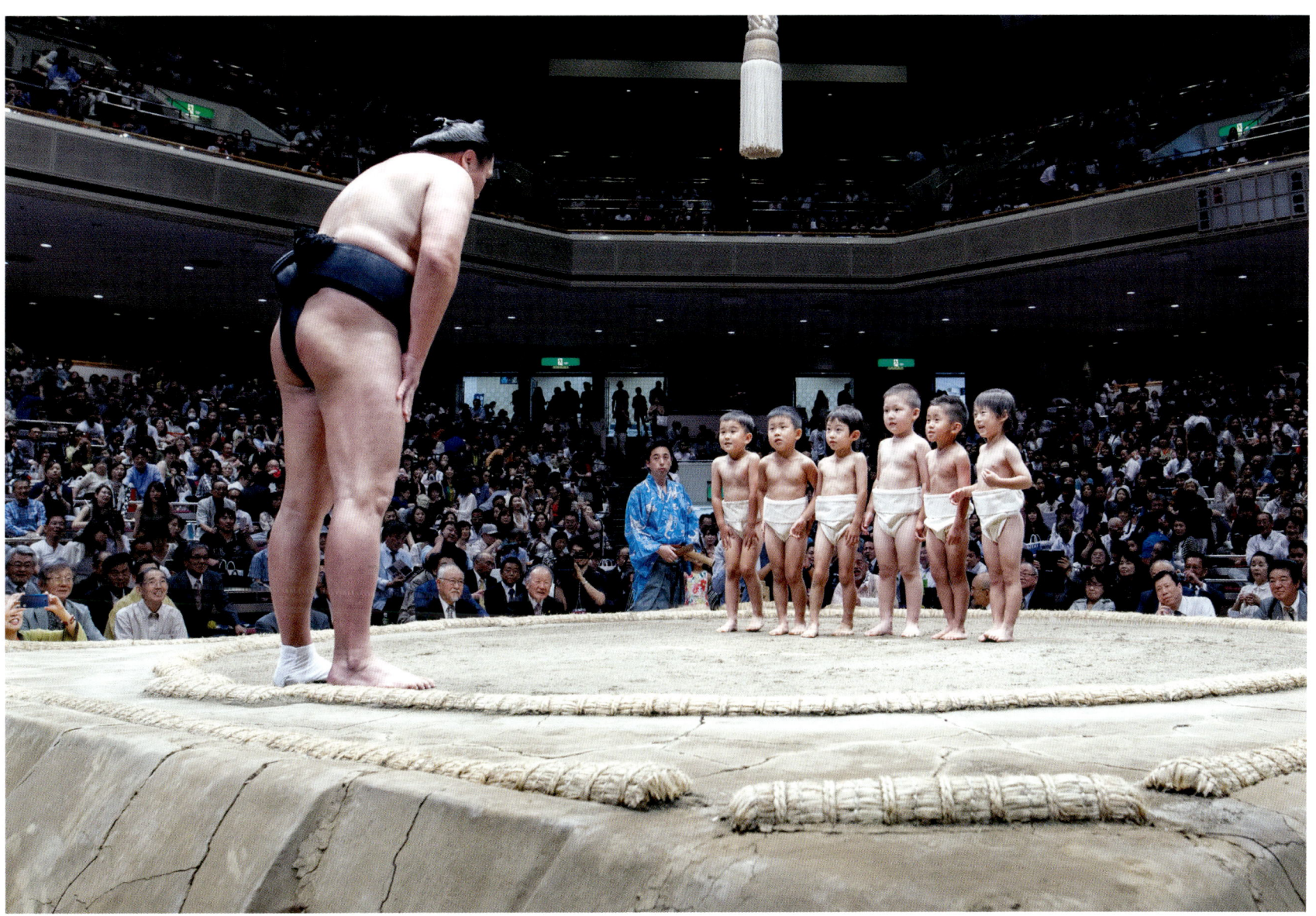

相撲 93

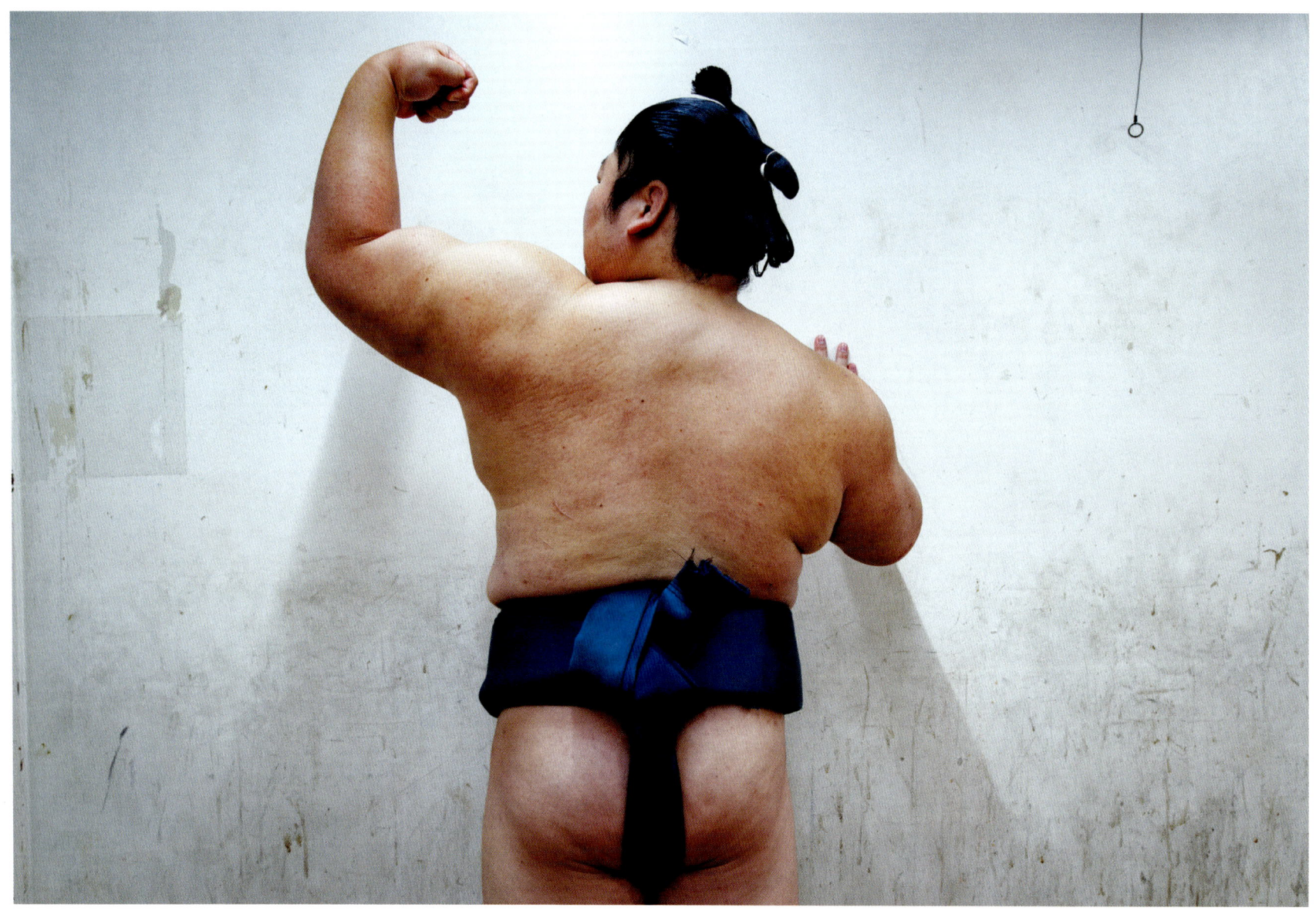

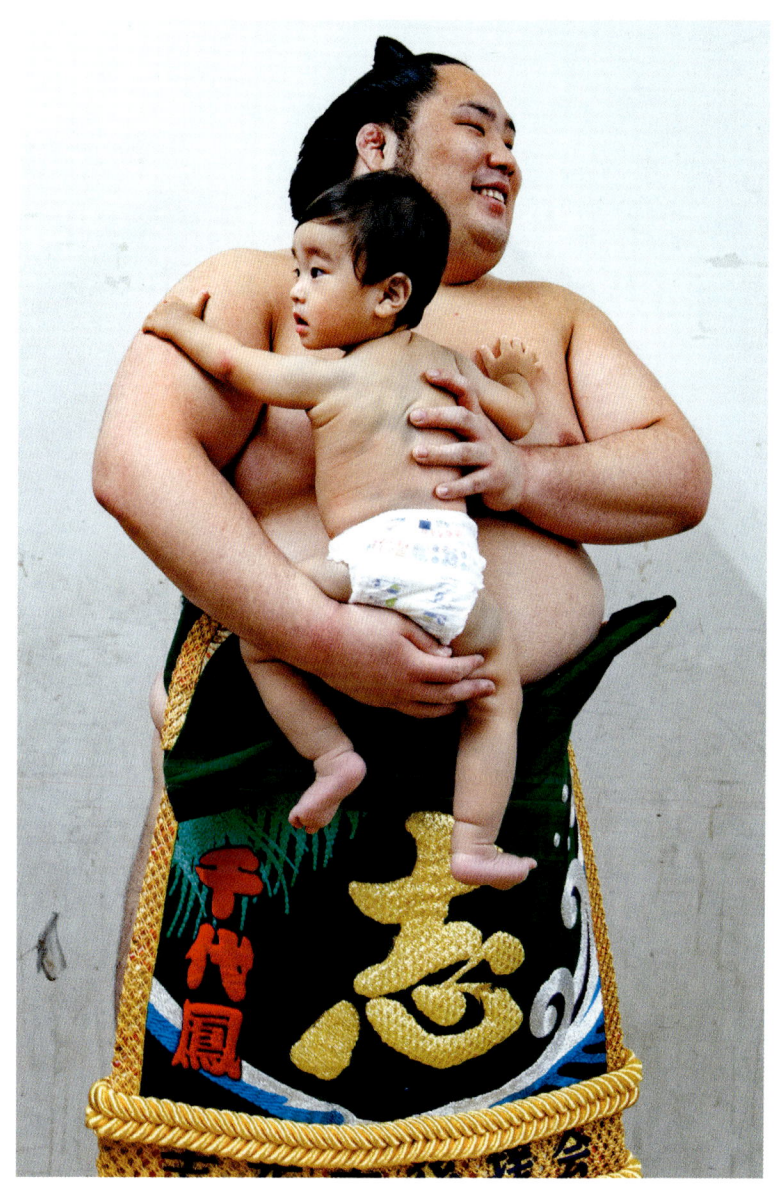

相撲　95

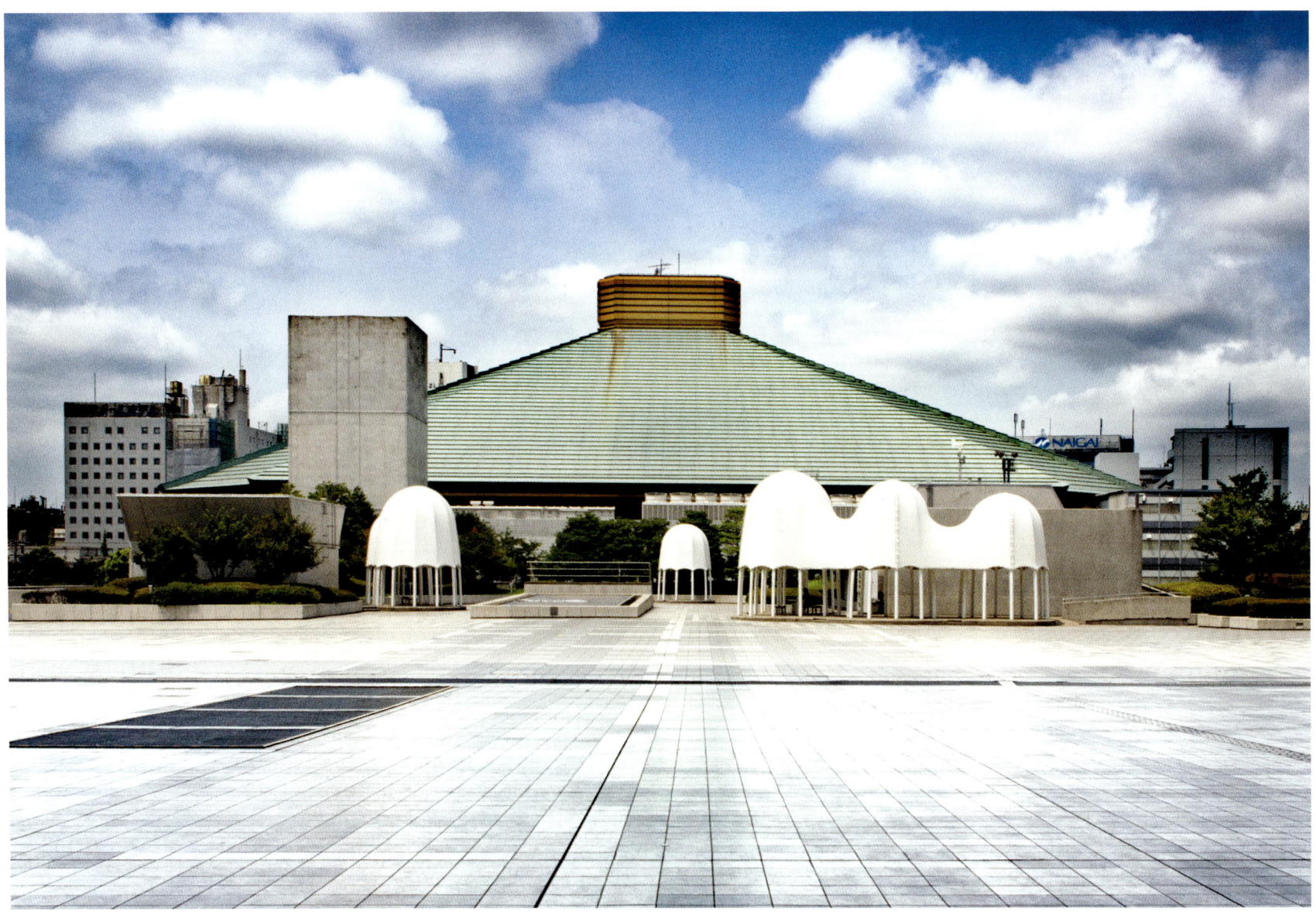

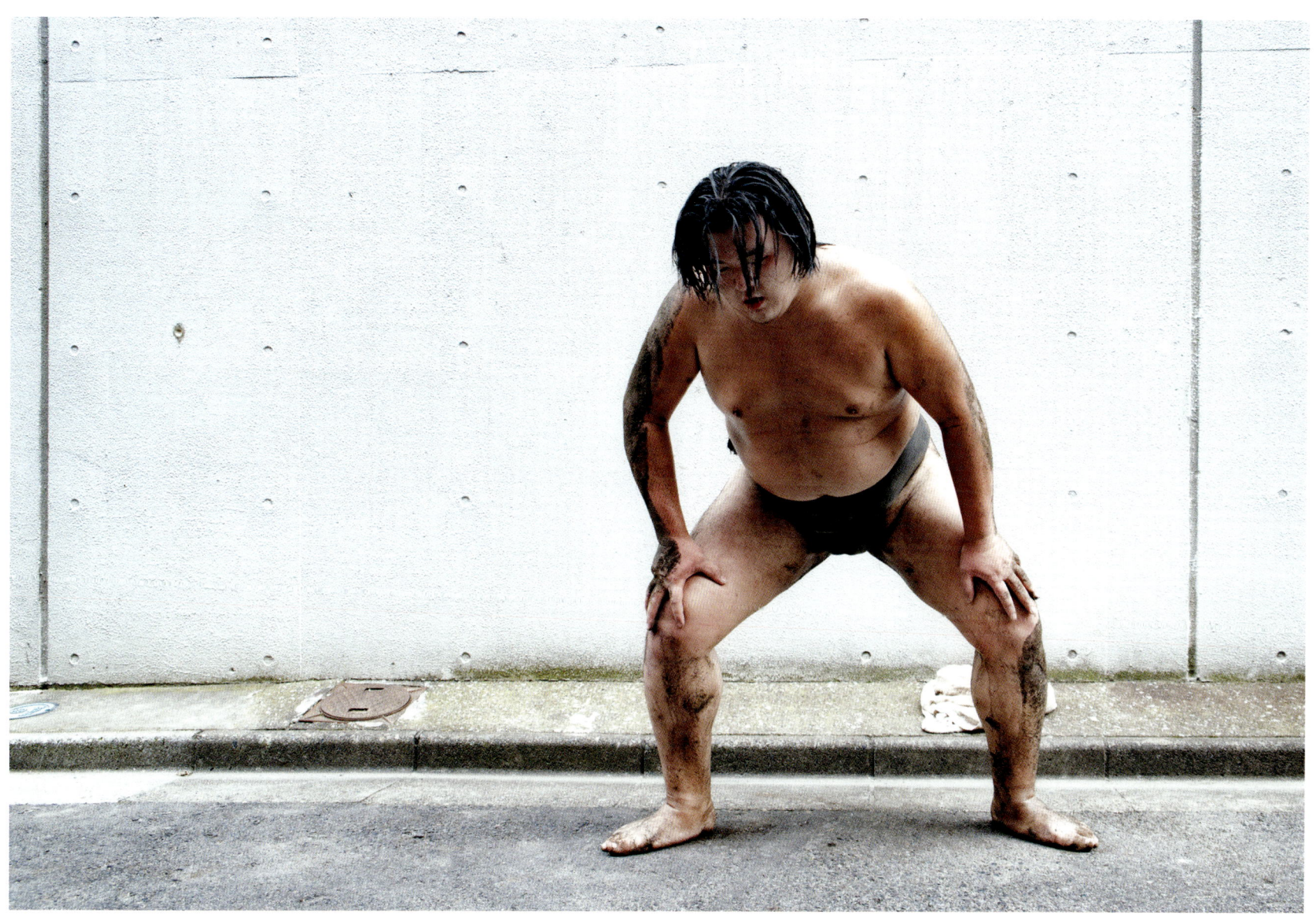

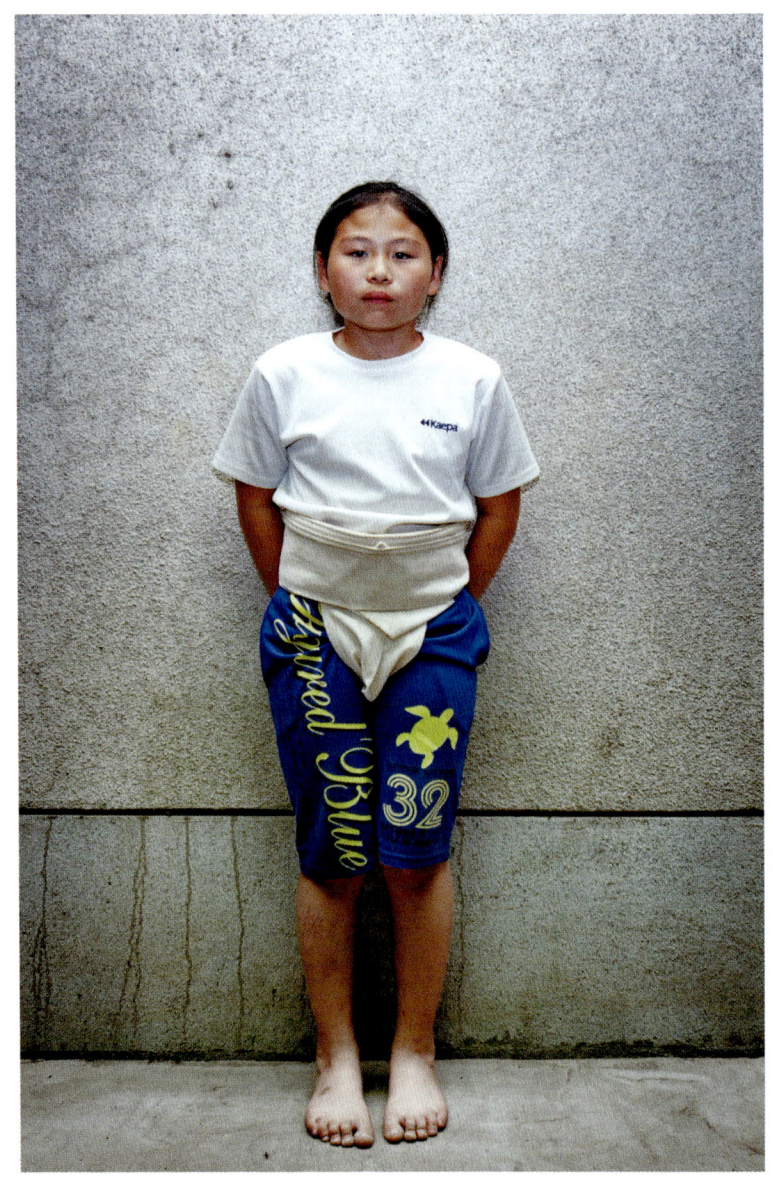

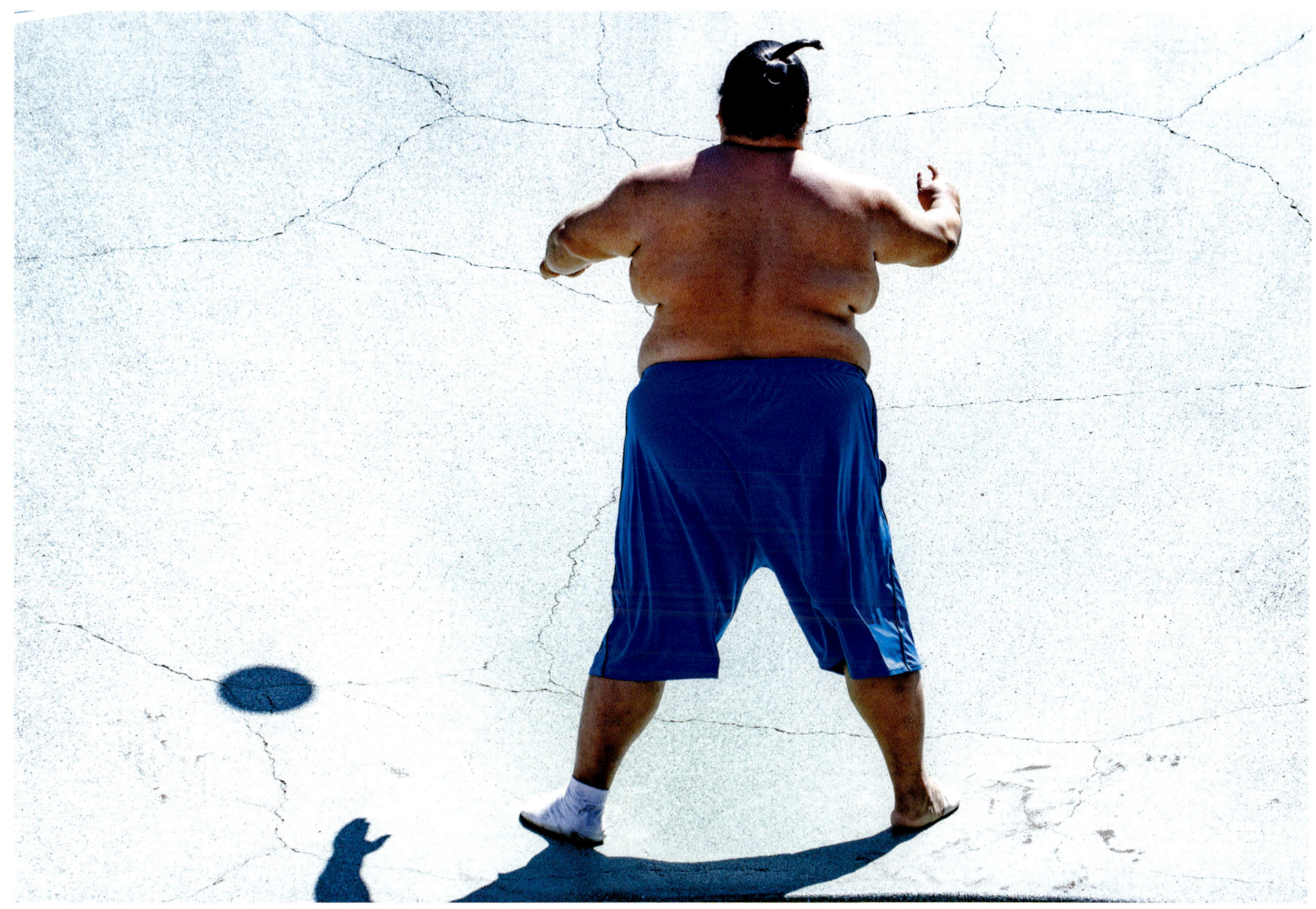

相撲 99

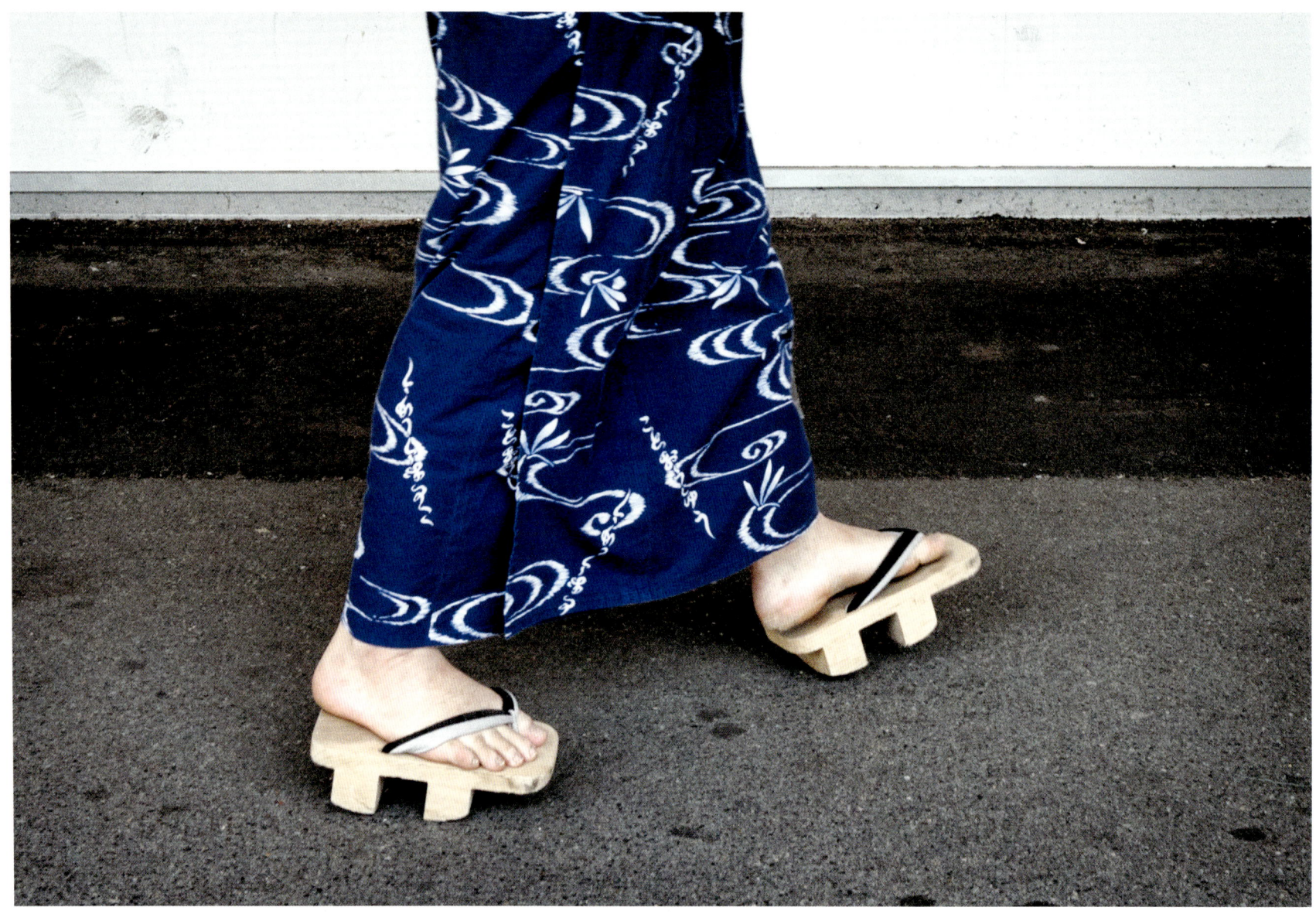

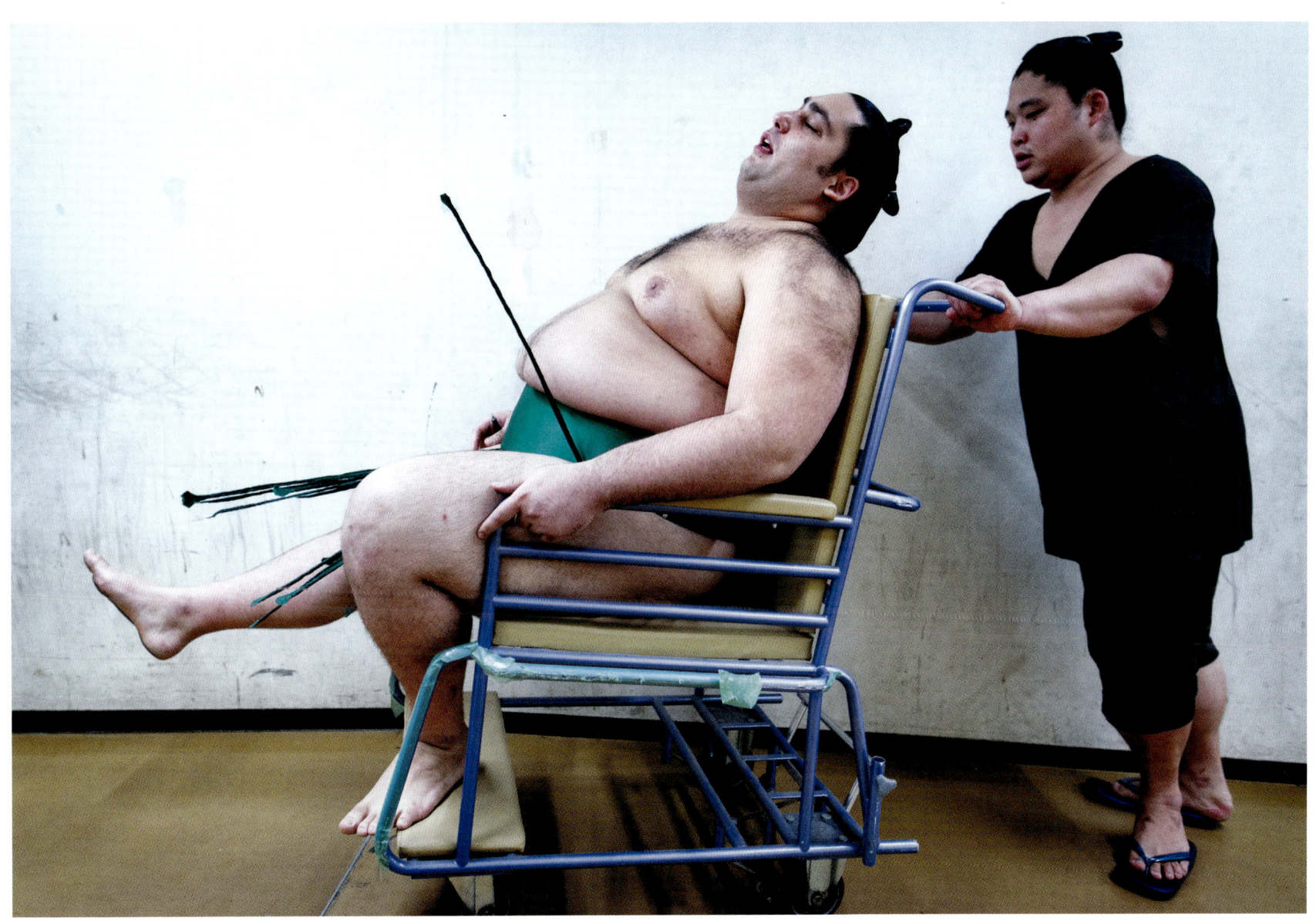

相撲 101

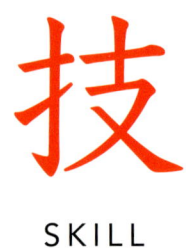

SKILL

IN ALL TRAINING SESSIONS WRESTLERS PERFORM *SANBAN-GEIKO* IN ORDER TO INCREASE THEIR ENDURANCE AND HONE TECHNICAL SKILLS WHILE THE *OYAKATA* LOOKS ON.

親方が見守る中、三番稽古中は力士たちが持久力と技を磨き上げるために何度もぶつかり合う。

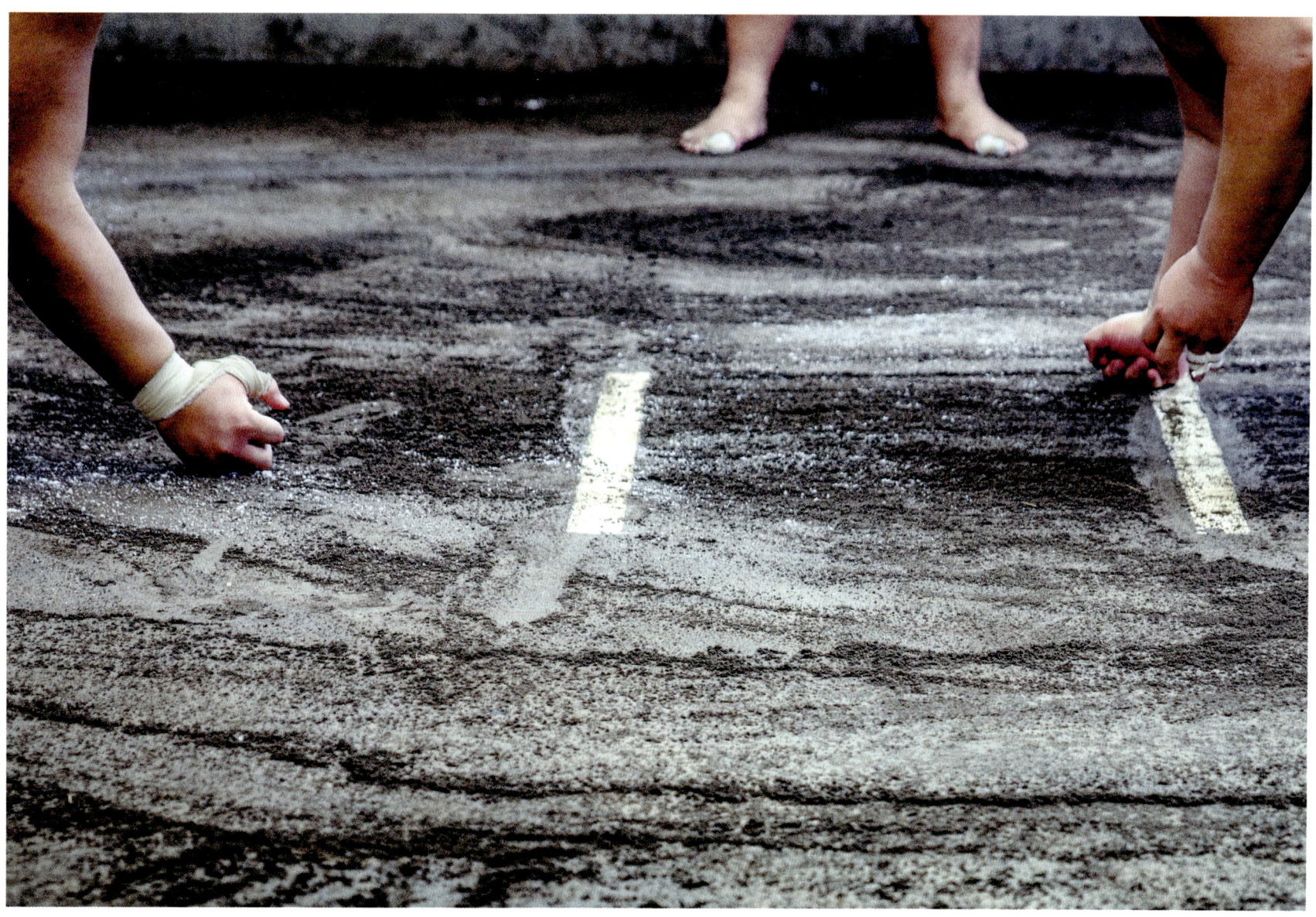

相撲 103

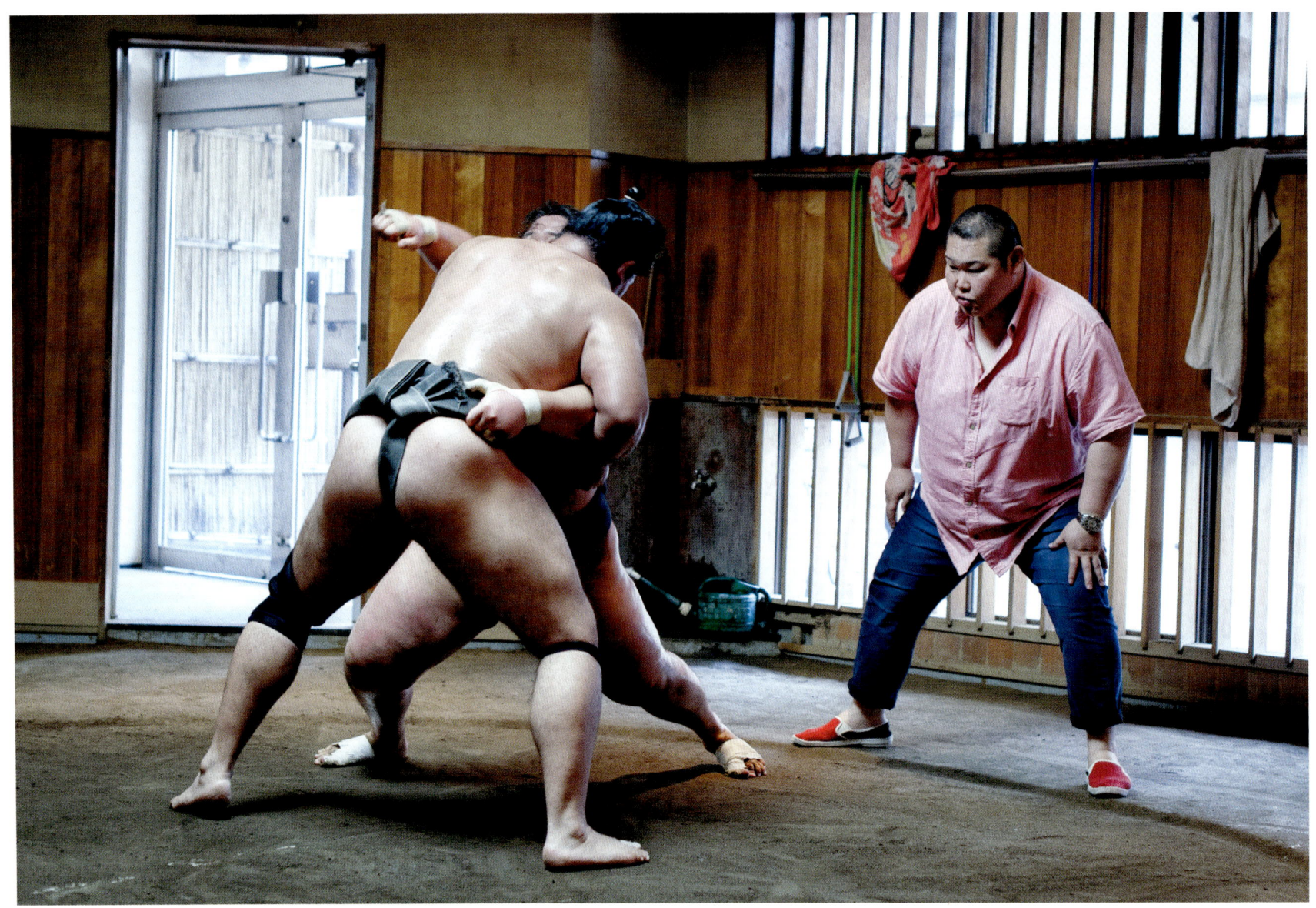

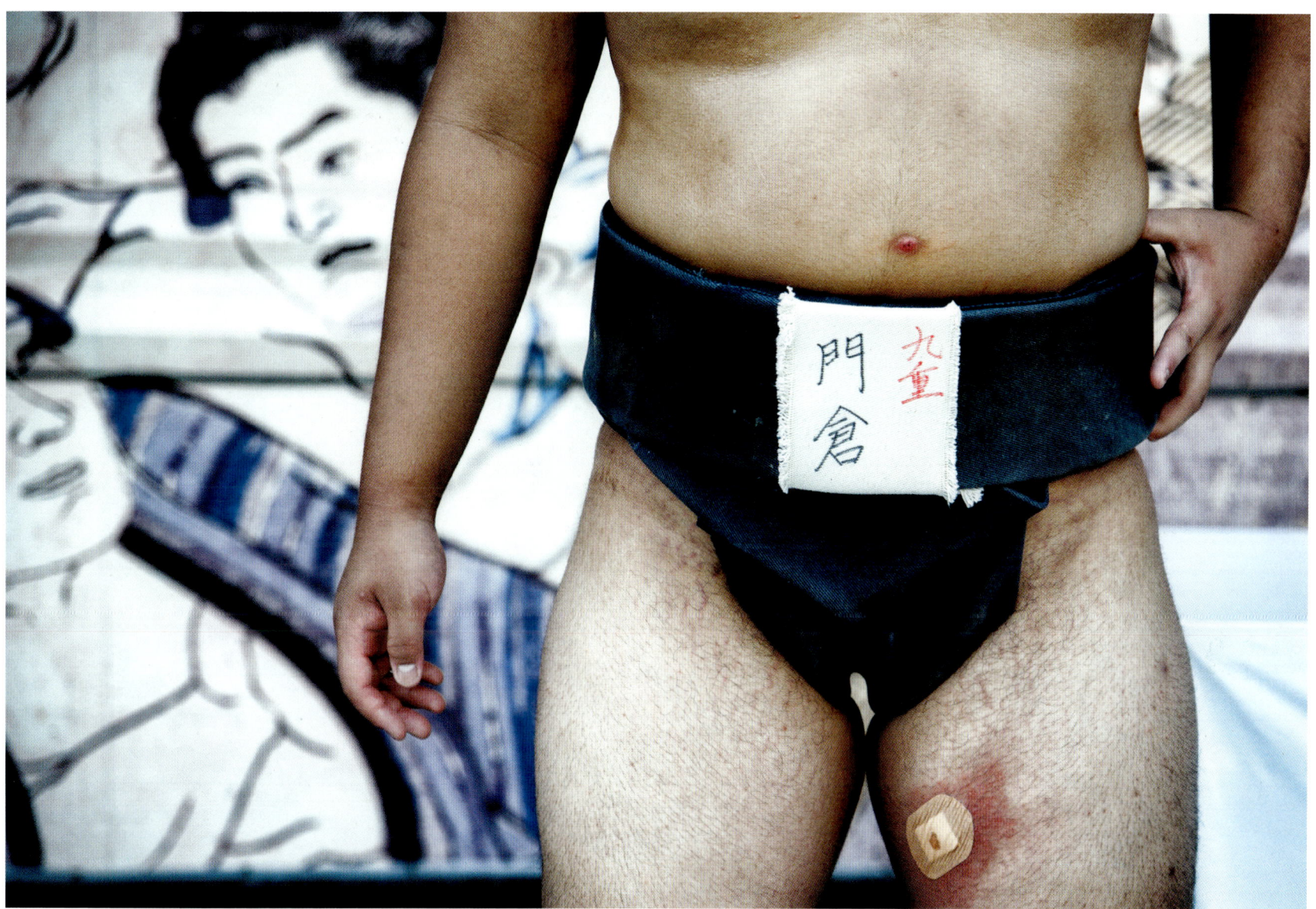

相撲 105

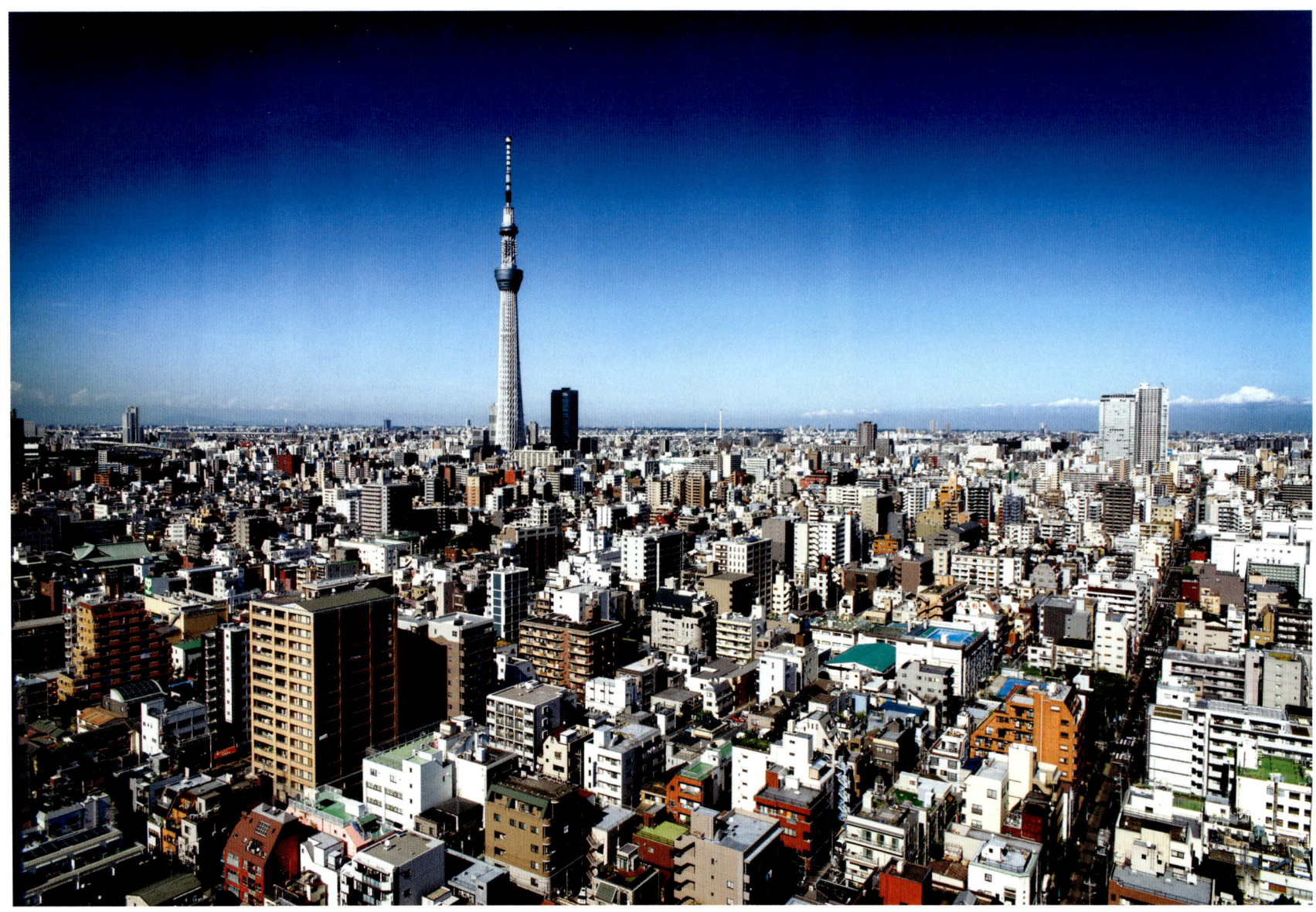

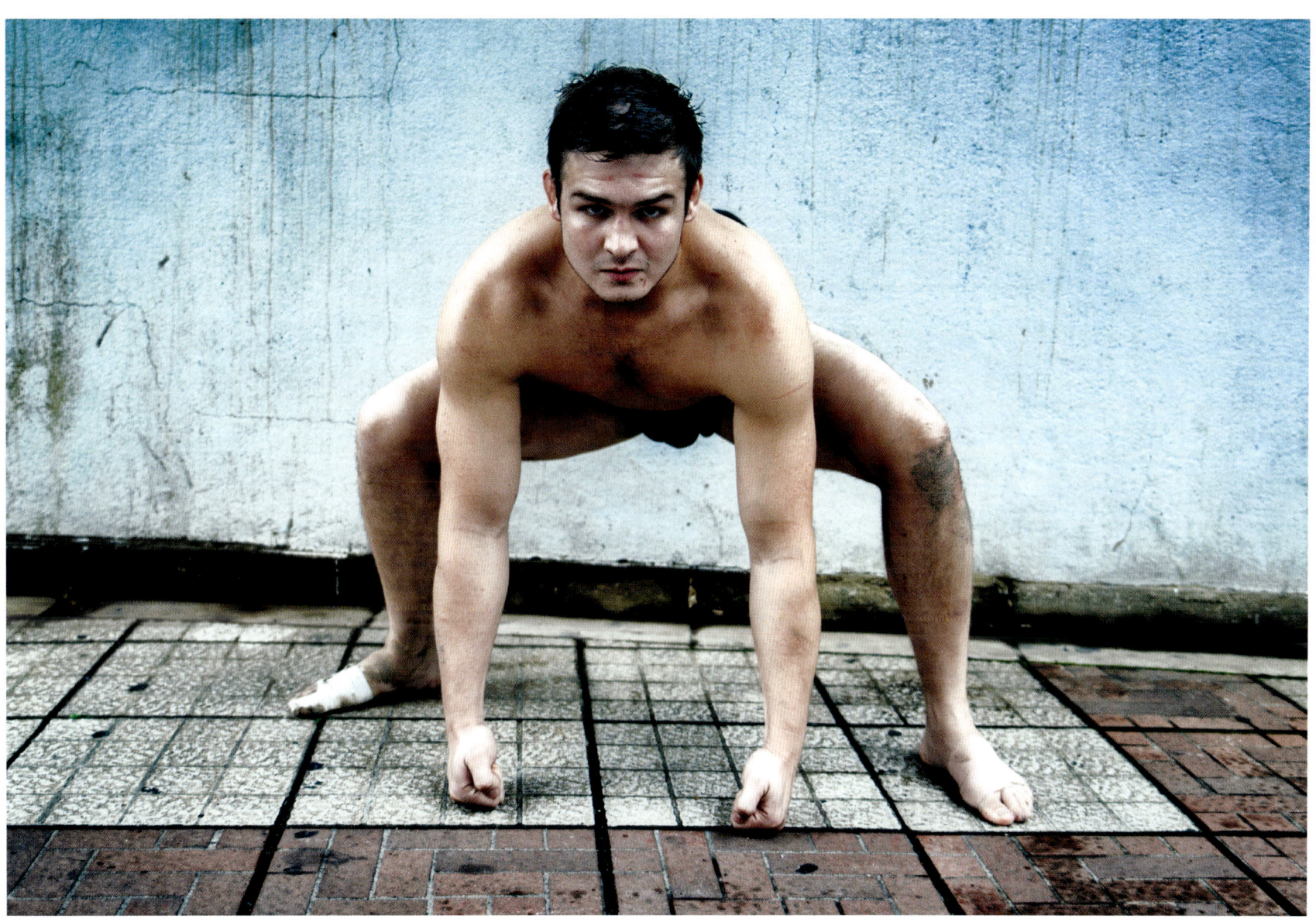

相撲 107

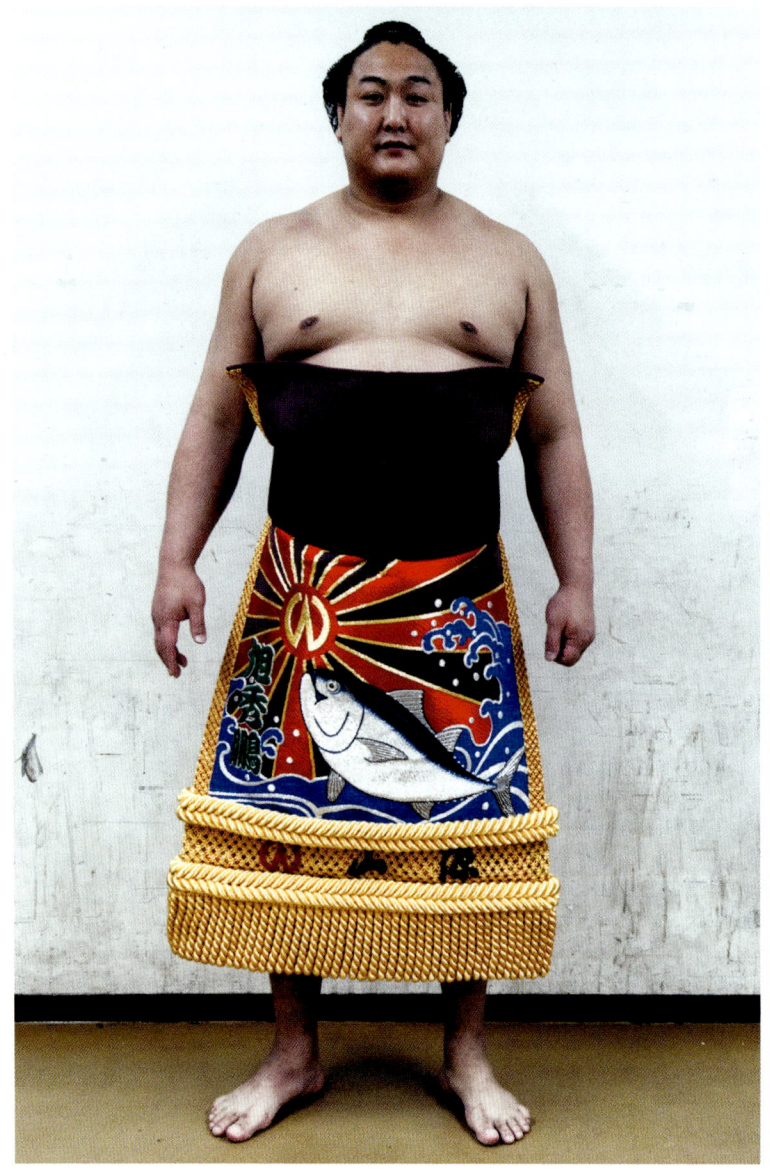

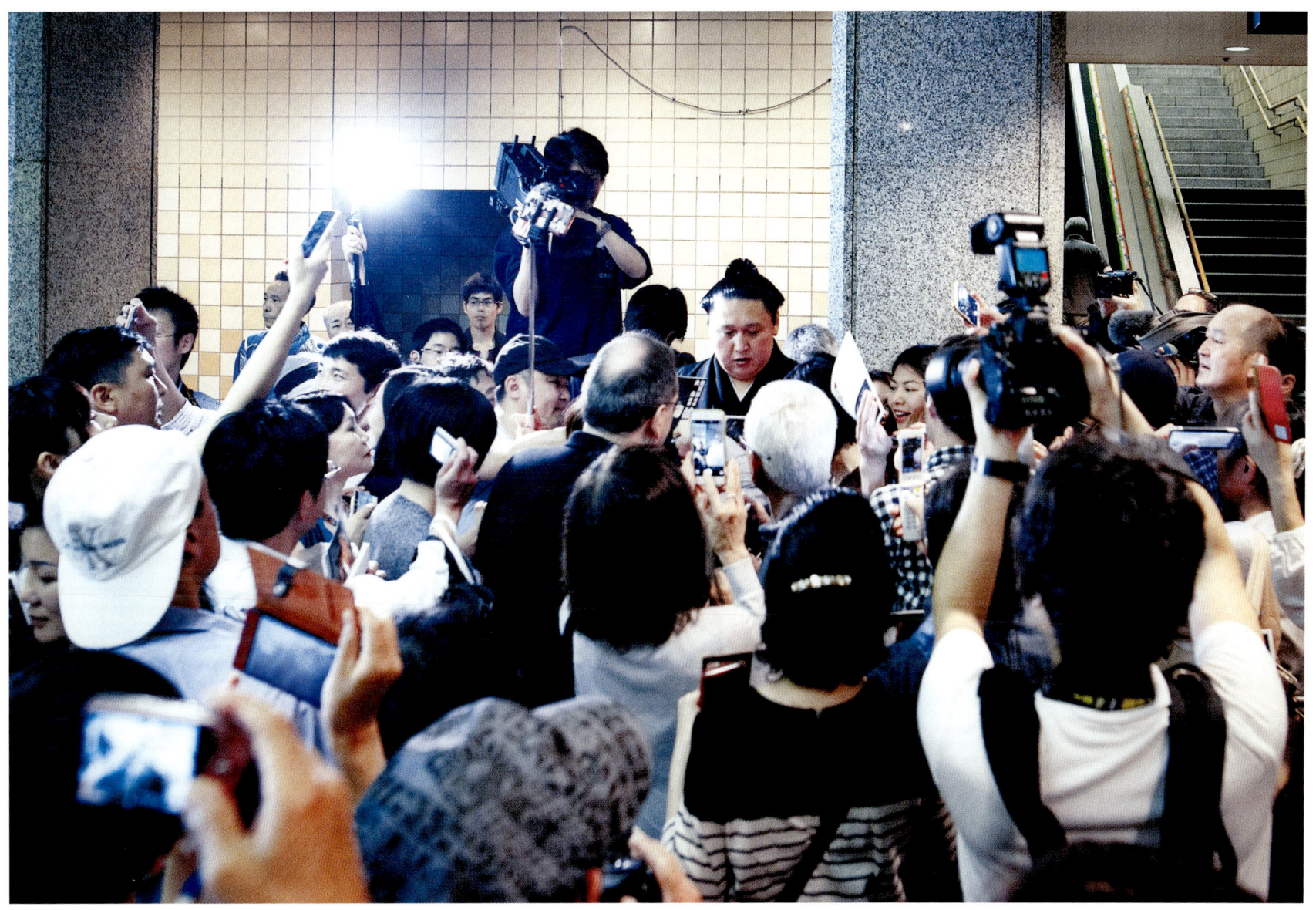

相撲 109

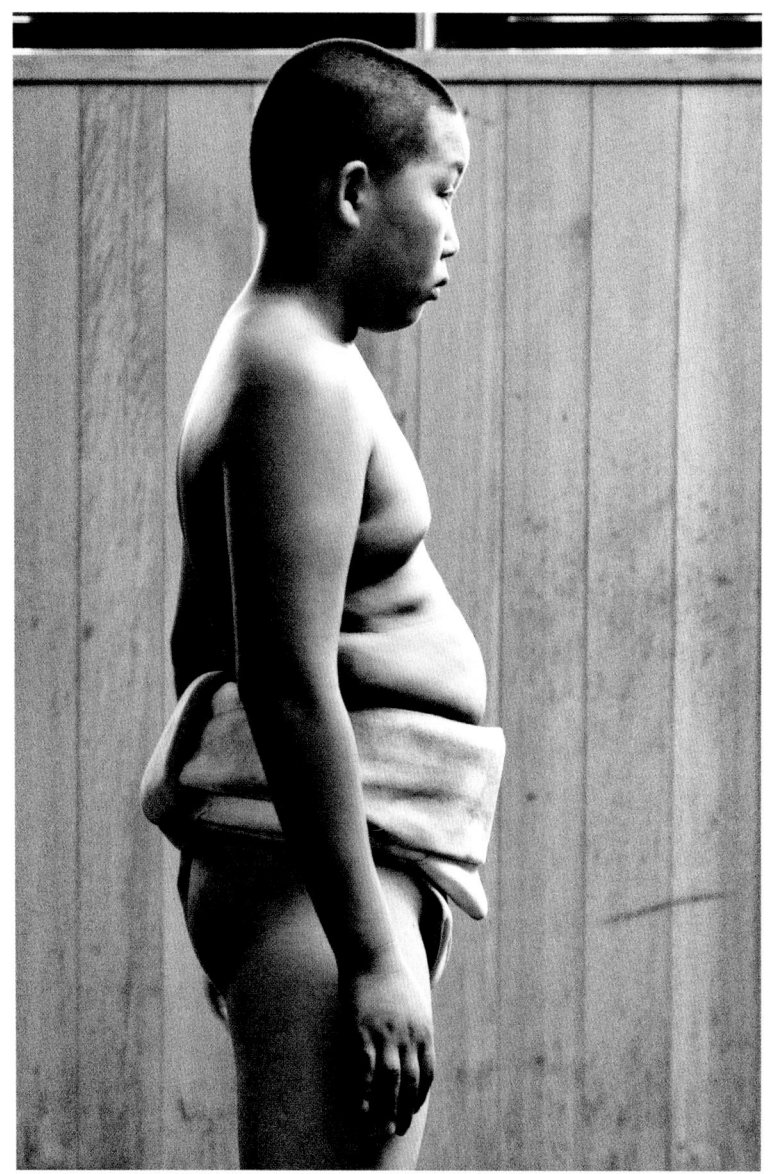

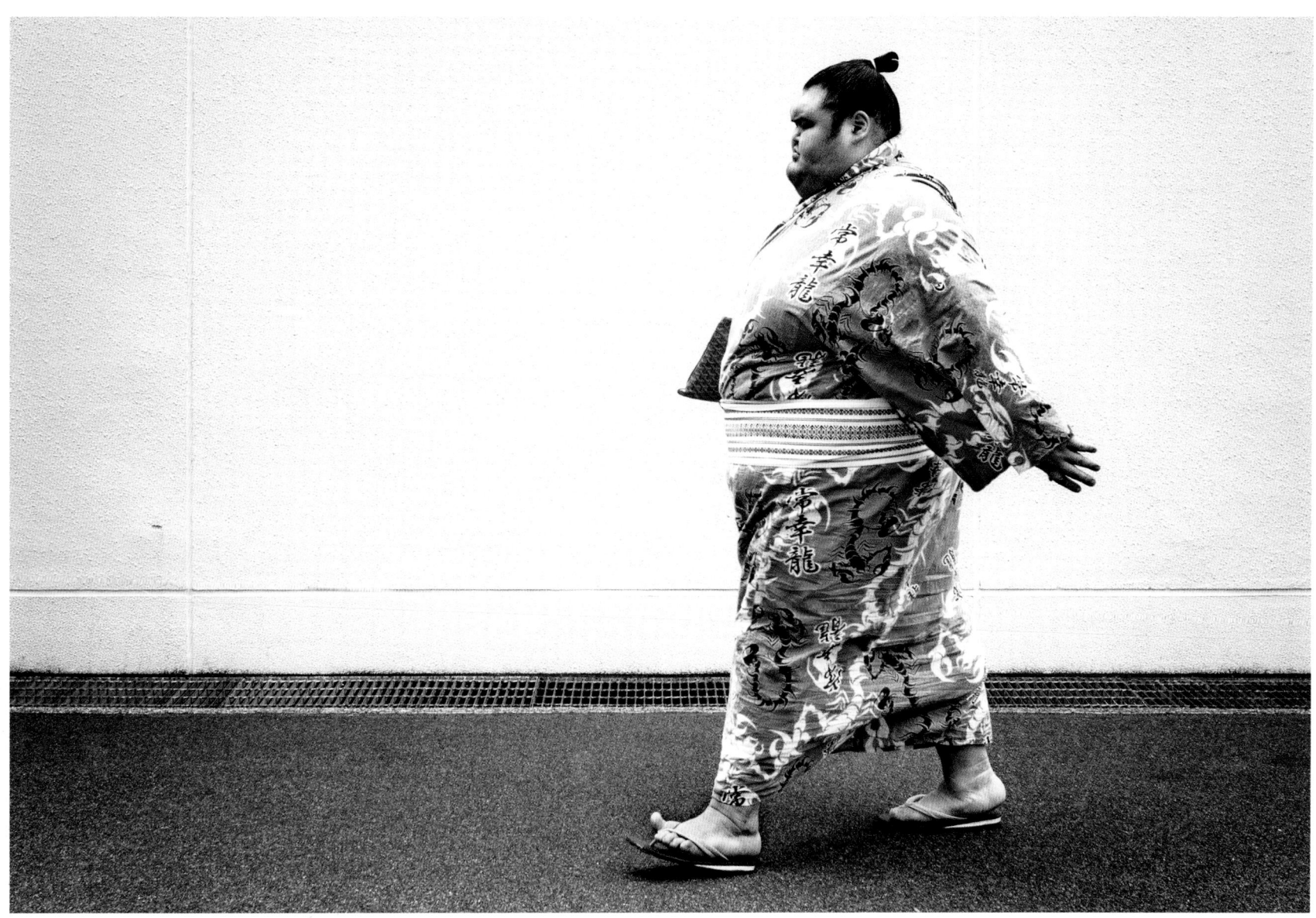

APPENDIX
付録

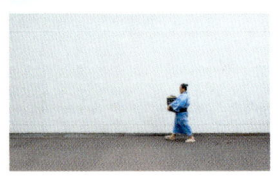

Page 2
A *rikishi* walks inside the grounds of the Kokugikan Stadium.

国技館の敷地内を歩く力士。

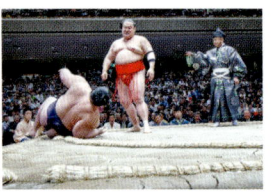

Page 4
A *rikishi* stares down at his opponent after manoeuvring him to the ground. It is not customary to express emotions at the end of a bout. A *rikishi* may be fined or banned if he does so, since it is considered undignified.

見事な手さばきで対戦相手を地面へ倒した後に見下ろす力士。取組の後に感情を表す事は慣習的ではない。それは威厳がないとみなされるため、罰金を科されたり、禁止されることもある。

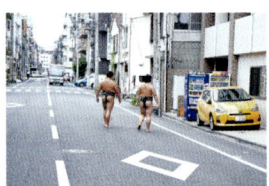

Page 7
It is not out of the ordinary to see *rikishi* walking in the vicinity of their *beya* sporting *mawashi* post workout.

力士が稽古後に廻しを締めた姿で相撲部屋近くを歩いているのを見ることは珍しい事ではない。

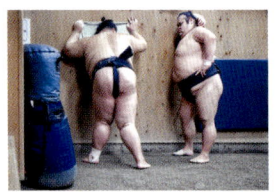

Page 8
Two *rikishi* casually converse after a workout at Kise beya.

木瀬部屋で稽古後に会話をする2人の力士。

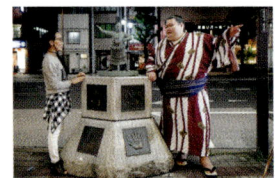

Page 11
Ōrora Satoshi – the heaviest *rikishi* of all time – converses with a fellow Russian on the streets of Tokyo.

東京の路上で同郷のロシア人と会話する史上最重量の力士、大露羅敏。

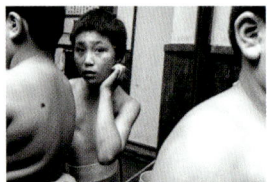

Page 13
A young boy may have the ambition to turn professional, yet, he will not know until over decade later if his height and weight will suffice.

この少年はプロになるという志を持つかもしれない。しかし、身長と体重が十分な要件を満たすかどうかを知るのは10年以上も先のことである。

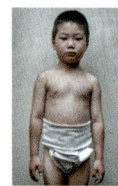

Page 14
A trainee at the Tachikawa training school in Tokyo. Boys commence training in sumo from as young as five.

東京の立川練成館相撲道場の生徒。男子は5歳の時から相撲の稽古を始める。

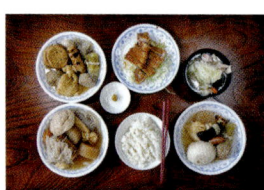

Page 15
Chanko Nabe prepared for breakfast. It is estimated that the average *rikishi* consumes around 8,000 calories per day.

朝食のちゃんこ鍋の消費。力士は平均して1日に約8000カロリーを消費すると推定される。

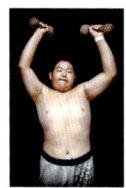

Page 16
For an aspiring wrestler to be accepted to a commercial sumo *beya*, he must show he has the right attitude and determination from a very young age.

相撲部屋に入るためには若い年齢から然るべき態度と強い志を持っていることを示さなければならない。

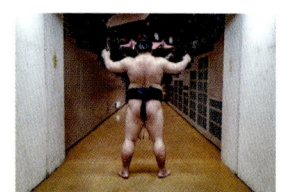

Page 17
A *rikishi* prepares to enter the auditorium for a bout at the prestigious Kokugikan Stadium.

名誉ある国技館で取組の準備をする力士。

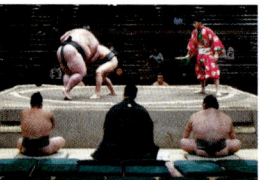

Page 18
Unlike boxing, sumo has no weight divisions, so a giant can pair up against a much smaller opponent. In such an event the smaller wrestler would normally try to knock the heavier wrestler off balance.

ボクシングと異なり、相撲には体重の区分がないため、大柄な力士と小柄な力士が組み合うことがある。このような場合、小柄な力士が大柄な力士のバランスを崩すように仕掛けるのが一般的である。

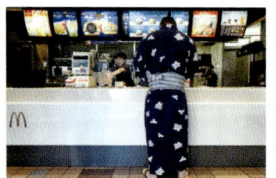

Page 19
Rikishi can be spotted in the Ryogoku district's numerous eateries day and night.

両国では昼夜を問わず、数多くの飲食店で力士の姿を見ることができる。

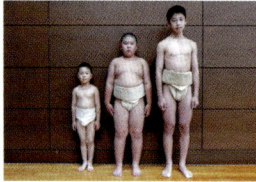

Page 20
Aspiring professional wrestlers pose obediently at Akiruno sports centre in Tokyo. Training is tough even at an early age. If a child does not possess a fighting spirit, he will be discouraged from pursuing a career in sumo.

東京のあきる野スポーツセンターでプロを夢見る力士たち。幼い歳でもトレーニングは大変である。子どもが闘志を持ち合わせていない場合、相撲界でのキャリアを積むことは勧められない。

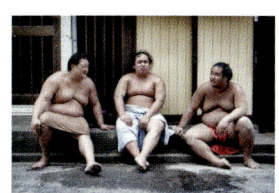

Page 21

Rikishi sit patiently outside their *beya* on a hot summer's day as they await their breakfast after finishing training.

暑い夏の日、部屋の外で辛抱強く座って朝食を待つ力士たち。

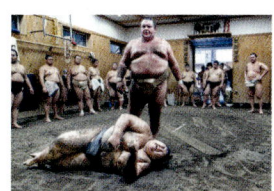

Page 29

A *rikishi* collapses with exhaustion during a *butsukari-geiko* session with Georgian wrestler Gagamaru Masaru at the Kise *beya*.

木瀬部屋で、ジョージア出身の力士臥牙丸勝とのぶつかり稽古中に疲れきって倒れる力士。

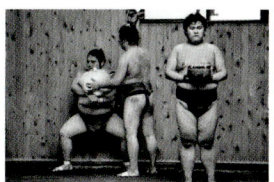

Page 23

New recruits have to endure a life of discipline, obedience and hardships in order to progress and gain the acceptance of their seniors.

新弟子たちは先輩力士からの信頼を獲得するために、規律・従順さと共に困難に耐えなくてはならない。

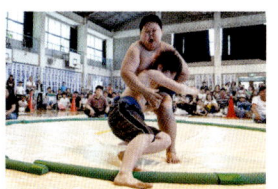

Page 30

A *rikishi* loses a bout after stepping outside the circle in an event at Zama school organised by the Japan Sumo Association. Children are categorized by age and not by weight, so obviously some have a major advantage.

座間の学校で開催された日本相撲協会のイベントで、土俵の外へ押し出され負けた力士。子どもたちは体重ではなく、年齢で分類されるので、圧倒的に有利な子たちがいるのは明らかである。

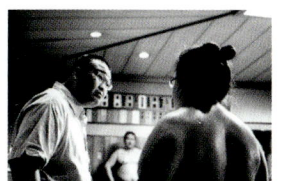

Page 24

Furiwake *Oyakata* disciplines his lower ranking wrestler for not showing enough aggression in training.

トレーニングにおいて攻撃性に欠ける低い階級の力士を指導する振分親方。

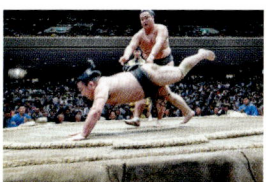

Page 31

A *rikishi* loses a bout after his hand touches the ground. It can be dangerous to sit close to the *dohyō* as wrestlers frequently fall onto spectators.

地面に手が触れて負けた力士。力士はよく観客席に落ちるので土俵の近くに座るのは危険である。

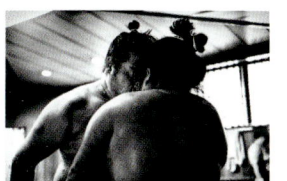

Page 25

A lower ranking wrestler endures a hazing session *kawaigari* – he is head butted and intimidated and must prove worthy of his spot in the *beya*.

「可愛がり」に耐える番付の低い力士。頭を突き合わせて威圧される。部屋の中で彼の居場所があることを証明しなければならない。

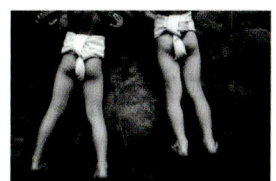

Page 33

Child wrestlers wind down after training with push-ups. They are given a taste of the discipline required to be professional early on in their careers.

腕立て伏せで練習を終わりにする子ども力士。相撲人生において、プロになるためには若い時期からの規律性を求められる。

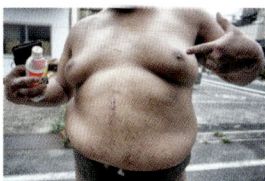

Page 26

A *rikishi* points to the scratches sustained during training.

トレーニング中についた傷。

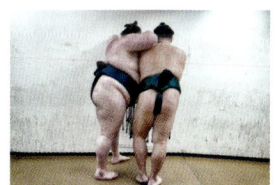

Page 34

Rikishi have a chatter while awaiting their turn to enter the auditorium at the Kokugikan Stadium.

国技館で会場に入る順番待ちの間に話をする力士たち。

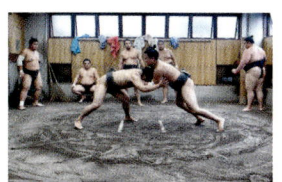

Page 27

A routine early morning training session at Hakkaku *beya* in Ryogoku.

両国の八角部屋での毎朝の早朝トレーニング。

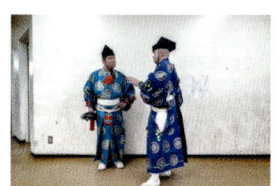

Page 35

Two *gyoji* converse in the tunnel of the Kokugikan before the action begins. *Gyoji* enter the profession in their teens and remain in it until they retire. Their families usually have a strong association with sumo.

国技館の通路で会話する行司の二人。行司は10代で入門し、定年まで現役で活躍する。行司の家系の多くは相撲との縁が深い。

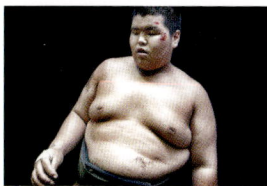

Page 28

A *rikishi* sports abrasions after being thrown face first on the hard, sandy flooring in training.

硬い砂の床に顔から投げられて傷ついた力士。

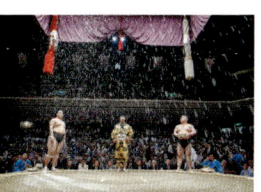

Page 36

Rikishi throw salt in the *dohyō* as a religious gesture to purify the ring before a bout.

試合の前、土俵を清めるために塩を撒く力士。

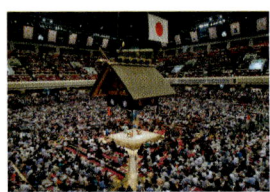

Page 37
The *tsuriyane* (suspended roof) over the *dohyō* at the Kokugikan Stadium resembles a shinto shrine. The tassels in the four corners symbolize the seasons of the year.

国技館の土俵の上のつり屋根は、四季を象徴しており、神社のそれと酷似している。

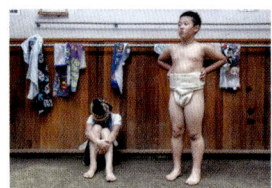

Page 45
A child covers her face while coming to terms with a rough training session at Tachikawa training school.

立川練成館相撲道場での過酷な稽古に、顔を覆いながら耐える生徒。

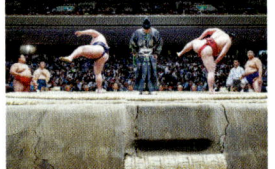

Page 38
Wrestlers perform *shikiri-naoshi* before the bout commences.

取組が始まる前に仕切りなおしをする力士。

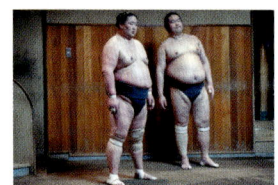

Page 46
Two *rikishi* look on while their peers train.

仲間の稽古を見つめる二人の力士。

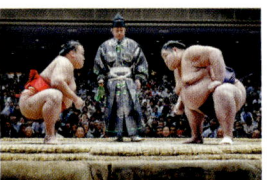

Page 39
Wrestlers psyche themselves up, plan their attack and attempt to intimidate their opponent before they clash. Once ready, they crouch, breathe in a synchronised manner and clash as soon as all four hands touch the ground.

取組開始前に気負い立ち、ぶつかり合う前に相手を威圧する力士。この間にどう相手を倒すかを考え決定する。準備ができると、しゃがみ、両者の呼吸を合わせ、双方の両手が地面についた瞬間にぶつかっていく。

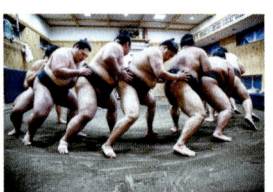

Page 47
Rikishi at the Kise *beya* go through a final drill to wrap up training.

木瀬部屋での稽古終了間際の力士たち。

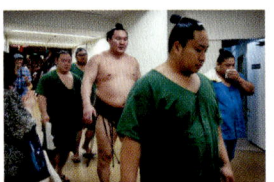

Page 40
Yokozuna Hakuhō Shō returns to the dressing room with his entourage after a routine victory.

お決まりの勝利の後に付け人とともに横綱白鵬翔が支度部屋に戻っていく。

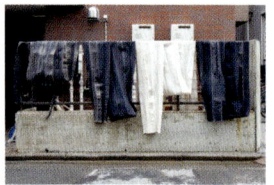

Page 48
Several *mawashi* are hung out to dry after a training session. The white colour is worn by *sekitori* and the black by *toriteki rikishi*.

稽古後に廻しが干されている。白は関取、黒は取的によって締められる。

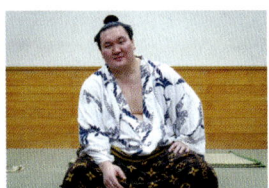

Page 41
A portrait of Mongolian *Yokozuna* Hakuhō Shō, the greatest sumo wrestler of all time.

大相撲史上最高の力士であるモンゴルの横綱白鵬翔の肖像画です。

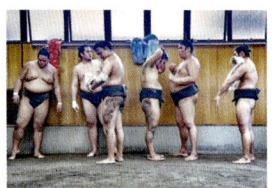

Page 49
Wrestlers wipe off sand and sweat at the conclusion of a training session at Hakkaku *beya*.

八角部屋でのトレーニング後に砂と汗を拭う力士。

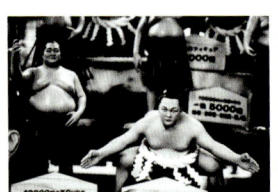

Page 43
A statuette of Hakuhō Shō on sale alongside those of other respected wrestlers at Kokugikan Stadium.

史上最高力士の一人である白鵬の像。国技館の店内で歴代の力士たちと共に鎮座している。

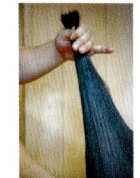

Page 50
A *tokoyama* attends to a *rikishi's* hair. *Rikishi* are expected to have their hair oiled and tied in a *chonmage*.

床山がびん付け油を使って力士のちょんまげを結い上げる。

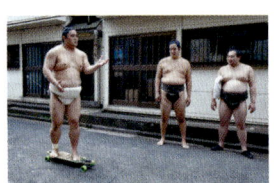

Page 44
Okinoumi Ayumi entertains his fellow wrestlers outside Hakkaku *beya* in Ryogoku. Even though sumo wrestlers take their careers very seriously, outside of work they are often playful and relatively approachable.

両国の八角部屋の外で仲間の力士と遊ぶ隠岐の海歩。相撲力士たちは仕事となると真剣で真面目だが、仕事の時以外は遊び心があり親しみやすい。

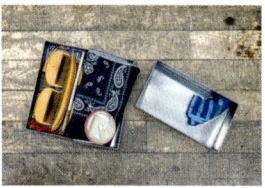

Page 51
The equipment used by a *tokoyama* to style the hair of a sumo wrestler. The awl is used to give some bulk to the hair when making a *oicho-mage*.

床山が力士の髪を結う際に使う道具。髷棒は大銀杏髷のかさ増しのために使われる。道具入れの中には激しい使用にも充分に耐え得る特別な木の素材で作られた櫛も入っている。

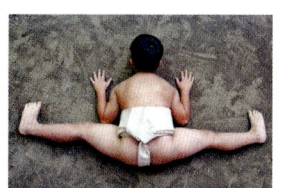
Page 53
Tremendous athleticism is required to perform *matawari*, a stretch that is practiced in virtually every training session.

稽古中ほぼ毎回練習される股割りは、多大な運動能力を必要とする。

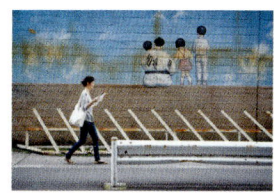
Page 60
In Ryogoku it is common to see artworks, posters and statues of *rikishi*, as well as spotting them in person around the district.

両国では、界隈で力士たちを見かけるだけではなく、力士に関する芸術作品や、ポスター、彫像がよく目につく。

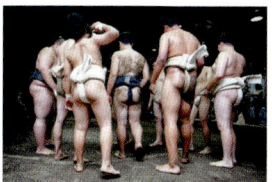
Page 54
Child wrestlers take it in turns to grapple in the *dohyō* of Tachikawa stable.

立川練成館相撲道場の土俵で交代で相撲をとる子ども力士たち。

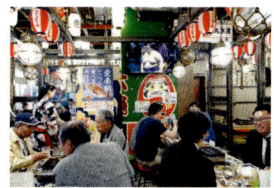
Page 61
Sumo wrestling is deeply engrained in the culture of Japan and is a part of everyday life. Wrestlers are frequently seen on television, in print media, as sculptures and in advertising.

相撲は日本の文化に深く浸透しており、日常生活の一部となっている。力士は芸術作品、テレビ、印刷物、広告などに頻繁に登場する。

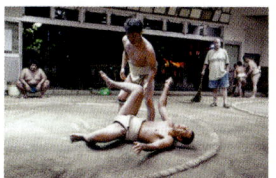
Page 55
Training drills at the Tachikawa training school tend to push young fighters to their limits of mental and physical endurance.

立川練成館相撲道場の稽古は、若い力士を精神的、肉体的に限界まで追い込む。

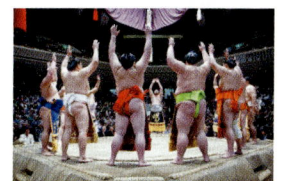
Page 63
High ranking *rikishi* in the *Jūryō* and *Makuuchi* divisions perform a ring entering ceremony called *dohyō-iri*. Wrestlers traditionally raise their hands to show they are not carrying any weapons.

十両や幕内の上位力士は土俵入りをする。土俵入りの際、力士は両手を上げて武器を持っていないことを示すのが習わしだ。

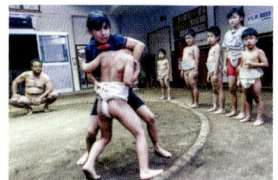
Page 56
A trainer and his pupils look on in admiration as a wrestler skilfully displaces her opponent out of the *dohyō*.

力士が巧みに相手を土俵の外に追い出すのを、指導者と弟子たちが感嘆のまなざしで見ている。

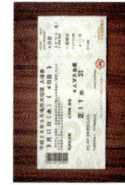
Page 64
A ticket to enter a Grand Sumo tournament at the Kokugikan Stadium in Tokyo. Prices range from 2,300 yen to 13,400 yen per person.

東京の国技館における大相撲のチケット。価格は一人2,300円～13,400円となっている

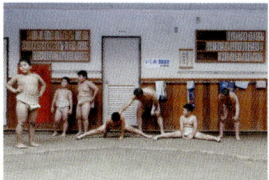
Page 57
A group of aspiring boys take their training very seriously. They need to show their worth in order to gain promotion to the professional sumo ranks.

志の高い少年たちが真剣に稽古に取り組んでいる。相撲のプロに昇進するためには、自分の実力を示す必要があるのだ。

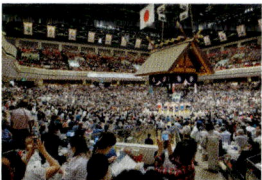
Page 65
The VIP seat (pertaining to the ticket above) at the Kokugikan Stadium. VIP spectators generally sit in boxes of four and feast on bento and alcohol.

国技館の升席(左のチケット参照)からの眺望。升席は、観客4名分の座布団、試合中には弁当と酒が振舞われる。

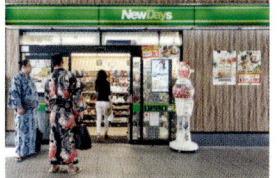
Page 58
Toriteki wrestlers in no hurry to return to their *beya* after competing in a tournament.

取的は取組後に相撲部屋まで急がずに戻っていく。

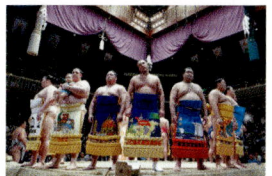
Page 66
Wrestlers wearing *keshō-mawashi* during a ring entering ceremony. Foreign wrestlers often sport their national flag; Japanese wrestlers tend to wear emblems from their sponsors embroidered on their garments.

土俵入りの際、力士は化粧廻しをつけて土俵に上がる。外国人力士は国旗をつけることが多いが、日本人力士はスポンサーのロゴやデザインを刺繍したものをつけることが多い。

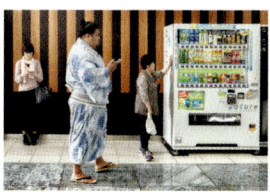
Page 59
Rikishi, who are easily recognized by their size, topknot and apparel, can be spotted walking around Ryogoku where they live and train.

まげや体格から簡単に認識される力士。彼らが生活をし、稽古を重ねる両国周辺を歩いているところを見ることができる。

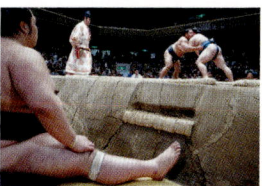
Page 67
A *rikishi* is expected to wait for his turn on the floor by the *dohyō* before the commencement of the prior bout.

取組前に土俵脇の地面で順番を待つ力士。

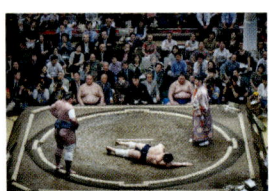

Page 68
Injuries occur in every tournament. *Rikishi* do not attempt to injure their opponents but they do grapple aggressively.

あらゆる取組で怪我が起こる。力士は対戦相手を傷つけようと意図するわけではないが、つかみ合いは激しく行われる。

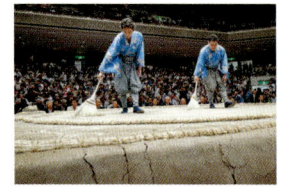

Page 76
The *dohyō* is swept between bouts so that the markings left at the end of each bout can help judge who won. The *dohyō* is 0.66m high and 6.7m wide, and the straw ring embedded in the clay is 4.55m in diameter.

残された足跡で勝者を判断できるように、土俵は取組ごとに掃き上げられる。土俵は高さ6,6M、直径6,7M、土に埋め込まれた俵の輪の直径は4,55Mである。

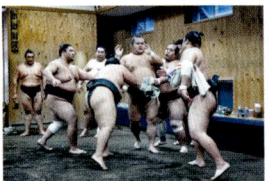

Page 69
A highly charged training session at Kise *beya* in Ryogoku, Tokyo.

両国の木瀬部屋での熱い稽古。

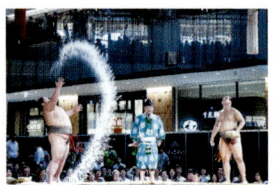

Page 77
Salt is thrown in the air at a Tokyo Regional Tournament in Kitte Shopping Mall. Sumo wrestlers throw salt in the *dohyō* as a religious gesture, to purify the ring before a bout.

大相撲KITTE場所で撒かれた塩。力士は取組前に土俵を清めるために塩を撒く。

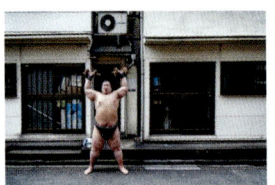

Page 70
In Ryogoku it is not uncommon to see *rikishi* training outside when the weather permits. *Beya* can be overcrowded – a lack of space is a common problem in Tokyo due to a high population and expensive property prices.

両国では天気が良い時、部屋の外で稽古をしている力士の姿を見ることは珍しくない。相撲部屋は、他の都内での問題と同じように、人口の多さと不動産の高価格のため、部屋が足りなく過密状態になる事もある。

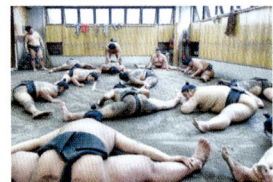

Page 78
Matawari is performed at the end of a training session at Hakkaku *beya*.

八角部屋の稽古の終わりに行われる股割り。

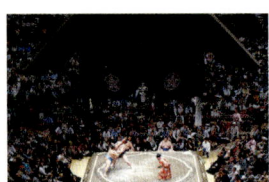

Page 71
It is permissible to thrust at the throat, but choking or strangling is forbidden.

喉を突く事は認められているが、首を締めたり、窒息させることは禁じられている。

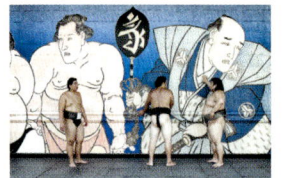

Page 79
Rikishi wind down after a stretching session is performed in front of an audience within the gates of Kokugikan Stadium.

国技館の門の中にて、観客の前でストレッチをし終わる力士たち。

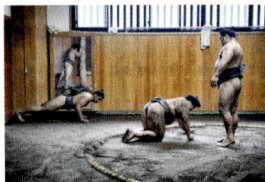

Page 73
A *rikishi* struggles to his feet during a *butsukari-geiko* session. Wrestlers regularly push each other to their limits of physical endurance in training sessions in order to become formidable warriors.

ぶつかり稽古で奮闘する力士。稽古中、力士達は互いに強靭な戦士を目指し、体力の限界まで互いに刺激し合う。

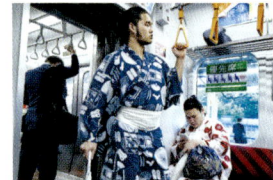

Page 80
Lower ranked *rikishi* return to their *beya* by train after competing in a tournament.

取組後に番付でランクの低い力士は電車で相撲部屋に戻る。

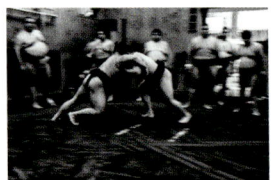

Page 74
Rikishi look on as two of their stablemates charge at each other.

相撲部屋仲間の2人が掴みあうのを見つめる力士たち。

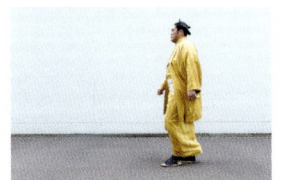

Page 81
A highly ranked *rikishi* is permitted to wear a swanky silk kimono.

番付でランクの高い力士はお洒落な絹の着物を着ることが許されている。

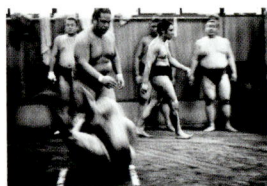

Page 75
Towards the end of a typical training session *butsakari-geiko* is performed. A senior *rikishi* continuously charges a smaller wrestler across the *dohyō* until he has exhausted all his energy.

稽古の終盤までぶつかり稽古が行われる。体格の小さな力士が土俵の向こう側にいる先輩力士まで当たり続け、体力が続く限り繰り返される。

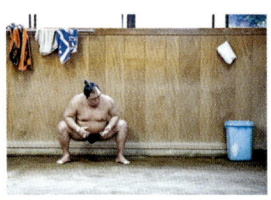

Page 83
A *rikishi* at Fujishima *beya* performs *shiko* during training in order to strengthen his stance.

構えを強くするために四股を踏む藤島部屋の力士。

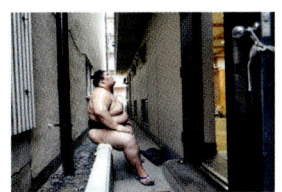

Page 84
A wrestler takes a breather after a gruelling training session at Kise *beya*.

木瀬部屋での過酷な稽古の後に一息つく力士。

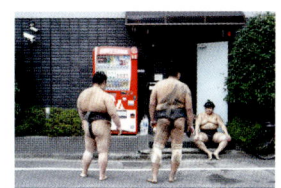

Page 91
Rikishi at Fujishima *beya* take in some sunshine and drink fluids from the vending machine while awaiting breakfast.

藤島部屋にて。朝食までの間、日光浴をしながら水分補給をする力士。

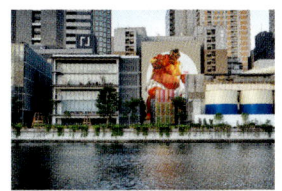

Page 85
A mural in Tennoz Isle, Tokyo, painted by German artist Case Maclaim depicts E. Honda (a video game character). Painting a sumo wrestler is an obvious choice since foreigners often associate Japan with the sport.

東京、天王洲アイルの壁画。ドイツ人アーティストCase MaclaimによってビデオゲームのキャラクターであるE.ホンダが描かれている。外国人はよく日本と相撲を関連付けるので、相撲力士を描く事は明白である。

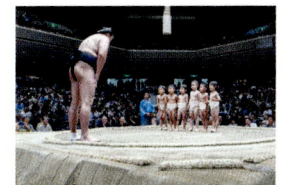

Page 93
Fans fill the Kokugikan Stadium to capacity in order to honour Kyokutenhō during his *danpatsu-shiki*. The next generation looks up in awe at one of the all time favourites.

旭天鵬を称えて、断髪式には国技館は多くのファンで埋め尽くされた。次世代の子ども達が史上最高の力士の一人として畏敬の念で彼を見上げている。

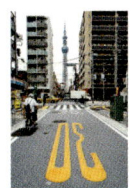

Page 86
The Ryogoku district in Tokyo is also known as 'Sumo Town'. It's a laid back, traditional area where the majority of sumo stables are based as well as Kokugikan Stadium, the headquarters of the Japan Sumo Association.

東京の墨田区に位置する両国周辺は「相撲タウン」とも呼ばれている。多くの相撲部屋があるゆったりとした伝統ある地域で、日本相撲協会の本部である国技館があり、相撲博物館もある。

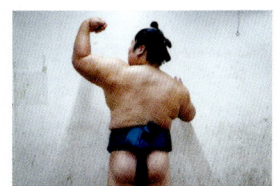

Page 94
A quick pose in the tunnel of the Kokugikan. Given the levels of fat, it may surprise many how immensely strong and athletic *rikishi* are.

国技館の通路でポーズをとる力士。体脂肪を考えると、力士がどれだけ非常に強いアスリートであるかという事に驚く人は多いだろう。

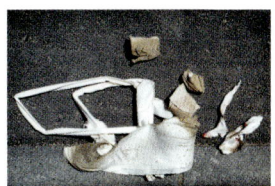

Page 87
Due to the *dohyō* being laced with sand, wrestlers often apply bandages to their feet due to abrasions.

土俵は土で作られているため、力士は擦り傷のためによく足に包帯を巻いている。

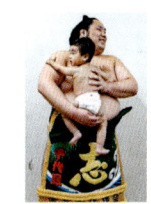

Page 95
Even though *rikishi* have a fierce demeanour when performing, they are seen by the public as gentle giants and may display an affectionate side.

取組中は激しく見える力士だが、一般人からは、彼らは大きくて優しい男性であり、愛情深いとさえ見なされている。

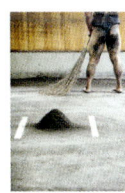

Page 88
Sand is gathered from the *dohyō* after training sessions so that blessings are made in order to ward off evil spirits.

稽古後に土俵の土が集められ、邪気を払う儀式が行われる。

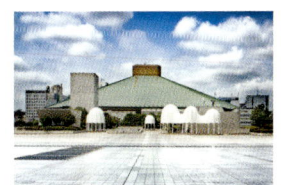

Page 96
The Kokugikan Sumo Stadium in Tokyo has a capacity of 12,000. Competitions are held during January, May and September. The premises also houses the Japan Sumo Association, a sumo school and a museum.

東京の国技館の収容人数は12,000人である。場所は1月、5月、9月の間に15日間行われる。敷地内には日本相撲協会、相撲学校、そして美術館もある。

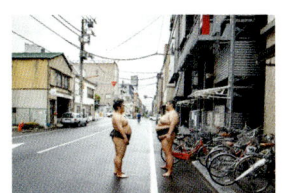

Page 89
Rikishi take a breather outside Kise *beya* in Ryogoku.

両国の木瀬部屋で一息つく力士たち。

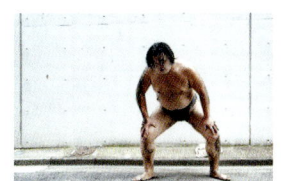

Page 97
An exhausted wrestler goes through the motions in the fresh breeze outside his *beya*.

部屋の外で疲れ切った様子の力士が新鮮な風を感じている。

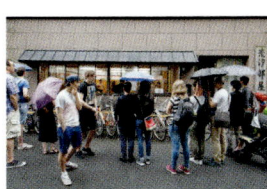

Page 90
Tourists peer through the windows at Arashio *beya*. Tourists are discouraged from visiting sumo stables on their own. They are advised to be accompanied by a Japanese person who is familiar with the customs.

東京・両国の荒汐部屋を窓越しに覗く観光客。個人で相撲部屋を訪問することは推奨されない。激しい稽古の邪魔にならないよう、習慣に詳しい日本人が同行することが求められる。

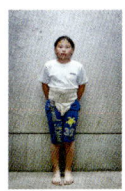

Page 98
Though women are welcome to train at the Tachikawa training school, they are not permitted to have careers in sumo, nor are they allowed to step into a professional *dohyō*.

女性は立川練成館相撲道場の稽古場には入れるが、相撲界で活躍することはできず、土俵にも上がることもできない。

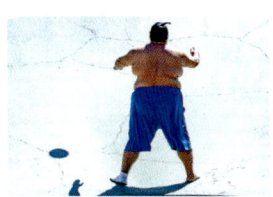

Page 99
Toyonoshima Daiki trains with a ball during a one-on-one session at a public garden while he recovers from injury. He attracts the attention of locals who attempt to interact with him during his breaks.

怪我の復帰中に両国の公立庭園でボール使い練習をする豊ノ島大樹。休憩中には交流を求めてやってくる地元の人々の興味を惹きつけている。

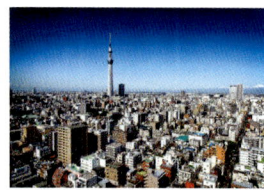

Page 106
Tokyo holds three of the six major sumo tournaments each year. Three other cities (Fukuoka, Osaka and Nagoya) hold one event each.

日本の首都である東京では、年間での主要な6場所のうち3場所が開催される。他の3都市（福岡・大阪・名古屋）は各1場所ずつの興行となる。

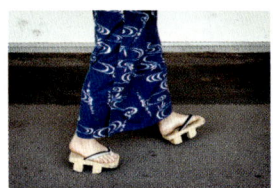

Page 100
Rikishi in the lowest two divisions (Jonokuchi and Jonidan) must wear *geta* wooden sandals with their *yukata* at all times outside of training.

階級の下2位（序ノ口・序二段）の力士は稽古外でも下駄と浴衣を着なければならない。

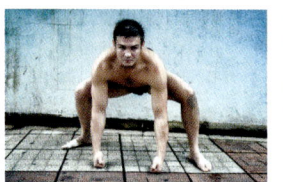

Page 107
Russian wrestler Batyr Altyev poses on the street after a training session at Michiniko *beya*.

陸奥部屋で稽古後に路上でポーズをとるロシア人力士バティールアティエフ。

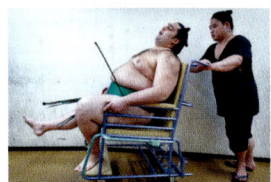

Page 101
Brazilian *rikishi* Kaisei Ichirō sits in a wheelchair in the tunnel of the Kokugikan. Sumo wrestlers commonly injure their knees and ankles due to the excess weight they carry as well as rough treatment in the *dohyō*.

国技館の通路で車椅子に座るブラジル人力士魁聖一郎。力士は土俵の上で激しく争うだけでなく、自らの重い体重のためによく膝や足首を負傷する。緊急時に備えて、車椅子は競技場の外で待機している。

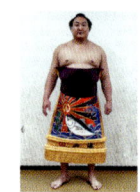

Page 108
A *sekitori* poses with his *keshō-mawashi* before entering the arena to perform a ring entering ceremony with his peers.

土俵入り前に化粧廻しをつけてポーズをとる関取。

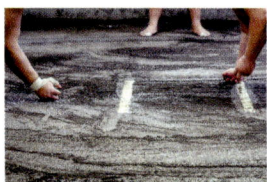

Page 103
In all training sessions wrestlers perform *sanban-geiko* in order to increase their endurance and hone their technical skills while the *Oyakata* looks on.

親方が見守る中、三番稽古中は力士たちが持久力と技を磨き上げるために何度もぶつかり合う。

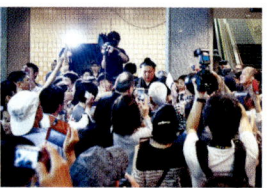

Page 109
Popular Mongolian wrestler Kyokutenhō is mobbed by fans and media during his *danpatsu-shiki* at the Kokugikan Stadium.

ファンやマスコミに囲まれる中、モンゴルの人気力士、旭天鵬の断髪式が国技館で行われた。

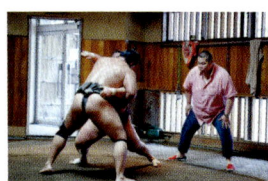

Page 104
Ushiomaru Motoyasu guides his *rikishi* through a tactical session at Azumazeki *beya*.

潮丸元康が東関部屋で力士を指導する様子。

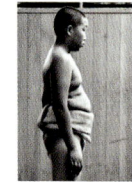

Page 110
A young wrestler who trains at a professional stable stares at his seniors during training. The road ahead is long . . .

先輩力士の背中を見つめ、プロへの階段をのぼっていく若い力士。この先の道のりは長い。

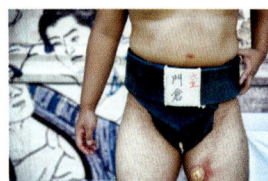

Page 105
A junior wrestler grasps his *mawashi*.

廻しを掴む若い力士。

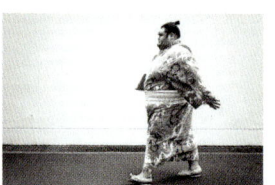

Page 111
A *rikishi* walks in the grounds of Kokugikan. *Rikishi* pack on so much weight and are prone to diabetes and hypertension. The average life expectancy of a *rikishi* is ten years less than the average for a Japanese male.

国技館の敷地内を散歩する力士。体重が重く、糖尿病や高血圧になりやすい。力士の平均寿命は60~65歳で、平均的な日本人男性より10年短い。

GLOSSARY 用語集

Beya: Often pronounced 'heya', a *beya* is a sumo stable where professional wrestlers train, eat and sleep.

部屋：よく「部屋」と呼ばれ、相撲部屋では力士が稽古をしたり、寝食をする場所のこと。

Butsukari-geiko: A wrestler is put through hell during one of the last phases of training. He is pushed to his physical and mental limits by a series of collisions and throws to complete exhaustion. This phase often lasts around ten minutes.

ぶつかり稽古：稽古の終盤、力士は地獄を味わう。連続したぶつかりで肉体的および精神的な限界に追いやられ、完全に消耗することとなる。これは約10分の間続く。

Chanko Nabe: Originally created by Kawasaki Chanko in 1937 in Ryogoku. *Chanko Nabe* is the staple dish of sumo wrestlers, usually consumed in vast quantities. The stew consists of practically anything found in the kitchen. Meat or fish and vegetables are always included.

ちゃんこ鍋：元々はちゃんこ川崎で1937年に両国で作られた。ちゃんこ鍋は相撲力士の定番料理で、通常膨大な量が消費される。この鍋は台所で見つかるものなら何でも入っていて、肉や魚、野菜は常に入っている。

Chonmage: A topknot similar to the samurai hairstyles of the Edo period. This haircut is retained until the hair-cutting ceremony marking the end of a wrestler's career.

ちょんまげ：江戸時代の侍の髪型に似た結い上げ。この髪型は引退時の断髪式まで保持される。

Danpatsu-shiki: An official retirement ceremony held for a top wrestler at the Kokugikan Stadium in which his topknot is finally cut off. A wrestler must have fought in the top two divisions in at least 30 tournaments to qualify for a ceremony at the Kokugikan.

断髪式：国技館ではトップの力士の正式な引退式が行われ、髷が切り落とされる。国技館で断髪式を行うには、少なくとも30場所以上関取を務めなければならない。

Dohyō: A ring in which sumo bouts are held.

土俵：相撲の取組対戦が行われる競技場のこと。

Geta: Sandals which are carved from solid wood. It is believed that wearing them makes a wrestler stronger and more stable.

下駄：硬い木から作られたサンダルのこと。下駄を履くことで力士はより強く安定すると信じられている。

Gyoji: A referee.

行司：審判

Jūryō: The second highest division, below *Makuuchi*. The number of wrestlers in this division is capped at 28.

十両：階級において二番目に高く、幕内の下。十両と幕内は1場所につき15日の取組があり、下位4階級は7日取組がある。

Kawaigari: The literal translation is 'to be affectionate', yet in practice, it is the brutal hazing of a wrestler in order to toughen him up and instil discipline. A wrestler is put through hell to the point of sensing he is on the verge of death. This type of extreme punishment has its critics.

かわいがり：文字通りの意味は「愛情を注ぎ可愛がる」だが、実際にはしごきであり、力士の心身的強化と規律を徐々に教え込む。文字通り死の危機を感じるまで地獄を味わうこととなる。この種の極端な罰には批判もある。

Keshō-mawashi: A ceremonial belt worn by wrestlers in the *Jūryō* and *Makuuchi* divisions which typically displays their sponsor's logo, although foreign wrestlers have been known to display their national flags. These garments cost thousands of dollars. They are usually gifted by a sponsor or one of the rikishi's support groups.

化粧廻し：通常スポンサーのロゴが多いが、外国人力士は国旗が刺繍されているものもある。数千万円にも及ぶ高価なものである。通常はスポンサーか、力士の後援会によって贈られる。

Makuuchi: The top division in sumo wrestling. The number of wrestlers in this division is capped at 42.

幕内：番付における上位。この地位における力士の定員は42人である。

Matawari: A groin stretch designed to loosen the body and help maintain flexibility.

股割り：身体をほぐし、柔軟性の維持を促すように考えられた股関節のストレッチ。

Mawashi: The heavy-duty loincloth that wrestlers wear in the *dohyō*. Black is worn by wrestlers in the lower divisions; wrestlers in the top two divisions wear a white *mawashi* during training and wear silk loin cloths in different colours when competing.

廻し：力士が土俵で締める極めて丈夫なふんどし。黒は幕下以下の力士によって締められ、十両以上の関取は稽古用の白い廻しと取組用は絹素材の様々な色の廻しを締める。

Nihon Sumo Kyokai: The Japan Sumo Association.

日本相撲協会：日本における相撲興行団体のこと。

Oicho-mage: A hairstyle reserved for the highest ranked wrestlers. It looks similar to a gingko leaf.

大銀杏：十両以上の力士が許される髪型で、髷が大きな銀杏の葉に似ている。

Oyakata: A sumo stable master. The literal translation is 'the way of the parent'.

親方：相撲部屋の主人。

Rikishi: A professional sumo wrestler.

力士：相撲取りのこと。

Sanban-geiko: A type of training where two wrestlers square up and fight a number of bouts together.

三番稽古：2人の力士が構えては掴み合いを何度も続けて行う稽古。

Sekitori: Wrestlers from the *Makuuchi* and *Jūryō* divisions. The wrestlers in these divisions are capped at 48 and 28 respectively. Wrestlers in these divisions compete fifteen times per tournament, while the four lower divisions compete seven times.

関取：幕内と十両の力士。この地位の定員は42人と28人以内とされる。この地位の力士たちは1場所に付き15日の取組で、幕下以下は7日の取組がある。

Shikiri-naoshi: A three or four minute period wrestlers are permitted to prepare for their bout. There have been calls to shorten this period since many of the new generation of fans complain that there is too much time in between bouts, but the Japan Sumo Association wishes to stick to tradition.

仕切り直し：力士が対戦前に3～4分間（時間は各段による）準備する事を許される。新世代はこの集中できる時間がはるかに短く、取組の間には長すぎると文句も出ているが、相撲協会は伝統を守り変化を好まない。

Shiko: A trademark squat specifically associated with sumo which strengthens the muscles and joints of the hips and legs in order to maintain a solid and low centre of gravity.

四股：相撲のトレードマークでもあるスクワットで、しっかりとした低い重心を維持するため股関節と足腰の筋肉を強化する。

GLOSSARY 用語集

Tokoyama: A hairdresser who belongs to a stable. They generally start as a teenager and progress gradually through the ranks. It takes about ten years before a hairdresser is permitted to sculpt a topknot.

床山：美容師のこと。各床山は部屋に属している。一般的に10代からキャリアが始まり、徐々に段階が上がる。髷を結う事を許されるまで、10年かかると言われている。

Toriteki: A trainee wrestler who is lowly ranked. A *toriteki* attends to higher ranking wrestlers in the stables, doing such tasks as wiping off sand from their bodies, serving them meals and cleaning the stables.

取的：階級地位の低い力士のこと。取的は、部屋内の上位の力士の世話をする事になっており、体についた砂を落としたり、食事の用意、部屋の掃除などの仕事をする。

Yokozuna: A sumo wrestler who has reached the sport's highest rank. Promotion to *Yokozuna* is attained after winning two consecutive championships and after the approval of the Japan Sumo Association's board of trustees who evaluate the level of a wrestler's dignity and physical strength before admission. The monthly salary of a Yokozuna is over 3,000,000 Yen.

横綱：番付における最高位の力士。横綱への昇進は、2回連続の優勝を獲得し、力士としての「尊厳」と「力量」のレベルを評価するJSA評議会からの承認後に達成される。横綱の月給は300万円以上である。

Yukata: A traditional Japanese garment.

浴衣：日本の伝統的な衣装

ACKNOWLEDGEMENTS

Firstly, I'd like to thank my connections in Japan: Fumiko Ito, my administrative lawyer for making this book possible, and Vandan Davaa, for helping me navigate the sumo industry. I'd also like to thank the Japan Sumo Association for their cooperation and Wakana Murai Fournier for her translations. A big thanks to Ryan Libre for mentoring me in photography and nurturing my growth. Thank you Francis Wilmer for your creativity in editing my text, and Jen Christie, Xiaoting Yu, Keina Kono and Matias Damián Batllosera for assisting me in the final phases of the book.

First published 2022 by Ammonite Press an imprint of Guild of Master Craftsman Publications Ltd, Castle Place, 166 High Street, Lewes, East Sussex, BN7 1XU, United Kingdom • Text and images © David Sharabani, 2022 • Copyright in the Work © GMC Publications Ltd, 2022 • ISBN 978 1 78145 463 3 • All rights reserved. • The rights of David Sharabani (Lord K2) to be identified as the author of this work have been asserted in accordance with the Copyright, Designs and Patents Act 1988, Sections 77 and 78. • No part of this publication may be reproduced, stored in a retrieval system or transmitted in any form or by any means without the prior permission of the publishers and copyright owner. • The publishers and author can accept no legal responsibility for any consequences arising from the application of information, advice or instructions given in this publication. • A catalogue record for this book is available from the British Library. • Publisher: Jonathan Bailey • Production Director: Jim Bulley • Design Manager: Robin Shields • Designer: Annie Monfort • Senior Project Editor: Tom Kitch • Colour reproduction by GMC Reprographics • Printed and bound in China

To place an order, contact: **GMC Publications Ltd**, Castle Place, 166 High Street, Lewes, East Sussex, BN7 1XU, United Kingdom
Tel: +44 (0)1273 488005

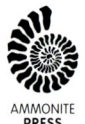

AMMONITE PRESS

www.ammonitepress.com